# The First Ladies Cook Book

## FAVORITE RECIPES OF ALL THE PRESIDENTS OF THE UNITED STATES

*HISTORICAL TEXT*  **MARGARET BROWN KLAPTHOR**
Curator, Division of Political History
Smithsonian Institution

*CONSULTING EDITOR*  **HELEN DUPREY BULLOCK**
Former Senior Editor and Historian
National Trust for Historic Preservation

*RESEARCH DIRECTOR*  **CELIA G. SEGAL**

*CULINARY EXPERT*  **DIONE LUCAS**

*HOME ECONOMIST*  **JANET C. GLENN**

*FOOD PHOTOGRAPHY*  **OTTO MAYA**

*SPECIAL OIL PORTRAITS*  **GEORGE GEYGAN**

1982 Edition
Revised by

## GMG PUBLISHING

25 West 43rd Street
New York, N.Y.10036

Published by

## PARENTS MAGAZINE ENTERPRISES

New York, New York

# CREDITS

| | |
|---|---|
| *Coordinating Editor* | Robert H. Doherty |
| *General Research* | Susan F. Park<br>Assistant to the Director<br>The Women's Archives<br>Radcliffe College |
| | John D. Knowlton<br>Division of Manuscripts<br>The Library of Congress |
| *Special Project Research* | Willa Beall<br>Kathryn Oestreich |
| *Copy Editing and Proofreading* | Hella Freud Bernays<br>Juliette L. Garito<br>William E. Meyers<br>Helene S. Zahler |
| *Typography and Layout* | Morton L. Garchik |
| *Photography Coordination* | Rick Martin |
| *Art and Production* | Nicholas Amorosi<br>Phyllis Fisher<br>Earl Miller |
| *Color Separation and Positives* | Cyril J. Myatt |
| *Cover* | George Geygan |

## 1982 EDITION

Printed in the United States of America by W.A. Krueger

# *Preface to the Historical Text*

THE STORY of America's First Ladies is, above all, a history of the manners, morals and morality of our country since its foundation, and the more we know about these women the more we know about ourselves as a people. This First Ladies Cook Book provides an opportunity to review some of America's strengths and weaknesses as they are mirrored in the social life of the White House. From this exploration of the past, we may find clues which will give us the strength and the inspiration to solve the problems which face our nation both now and in the future.

The 1976 Bicentennial celebration has caused many Americans to become more interested in the White House and its historical traditions. Aided by the imaginative efforts of recent First Ladies, the average citizen of this country now knows the White House better than it has ever been known before, and he appreciates the fact that this historic residence of the Chief Executive belongs to the people of the United States. Accordingly, the people have been visiting the mansion in increasing numbers. Since 1964 more than one million persons each year tour its rooms. The White House Guide Book, prepared and sold to inform the people about the house, was first published in 1962 and has sold well over 3 million copies.

This intense public interest gives the person who holds the position of First Lady a great influence in American social life. Her importance can be understood and appreciated by studying the social life of the succession of administrations. An attempt is made in this book to capture the essence of these administrations, and in doing so the hope has been to make the Presidents and First Ladies emerge as individual personalities, for it is not only the social activity, but the reaction of the President and his family to life in the White House which gives each administration its particular personal flavor.

By using contemporary accounts wherever they were available, the aim has been to convey some of the feelings and opinions surrounding each administration along with the impact each President and First Lady had on the American people. The selections were made with great caution, since all too often political opinions were found to influence the social judgment of the individual who left the contemporary account. Thus it became necessary to delve into the personality of each President and each First Lady to determine his or her influence on the social life of the particular administration.

From all these varied sources the White House emerges as a mirror of accepted social customs and, at the same time, an important creator of social innovations.

**Hayes' state china**

**Monroe's state china**

This book seeks to portray the stately hospitality of the Executive Mansion of the eighteenth century and to show how the backgrounds of President George Washington and his wife influenced them in establishing the protocol for the first administration, which set the pattern for those to follow. In contrast, the lavish social events of the Victorian era are presented, together with the conditions and personalities which called that period into being. Those social events are all illustrative of the times in which they took place just as the social activities of the White House today reflect our own times.

It is for this reason that the social history of so fundamental an institution as the White House can be an exacting record of the constantly changing pattern of social life in America.

M.B.K.

# Notes on Early American Cookery

To "THE COMPLEAT HOUSEWIFE" of the eighteenth and early nineteenth centuries, the art of cookery was compounded of more steps than the mastering of a vague and inexact recipe with such directions as "stir in some milk and put it to the fire until it is enough." It also meant a painstaking management of the fire, regulating the temperature by turning the Dutch oven so that she would not have a "sad cake" that sloped up sharply to one side that was barely done, while the other side was close to burning. It meant raising and lowering heavy pots and kettles over the fire with pothooks. It meant knowing which kind of wood gave a quick light fire, and which burned with a slow even heat and made the best bed of coals. It meant continual vigilance to avoid getting severely burned by an overturning kettle, or having long skirts and aprons take fire.

Both the mistress of a great house (especially in the South where so many of the early First Ladies lived) and the humblest frontier housewife had to master all of these problems and many more. The training of servants required of the mistress practical knowledge and skill. Few servants could read or write, and despite their vagaries cook books were a help in preparing very special dishes such as "Great Cakes" for the holidays, or some special fancy pudding, such as a "Solomon's Temple in Flummery." To teach the servant, the mistress had to be capable herself of making the dish.

Certain ingredients including sugar were expensive luxuries; to make preserves and jams over the open hearth meant lavish use of sugar, as they were made on a pound-to-pound basis. To prevent burning, scorching, or waste, the mistress of the household either made these luxuries herself or closely supervised the process. Martha Washington was a notable housekeeper and not only made quantities of preserves and pickles from the orchards and vegetable gardens of Mount Vernon but preserved red rose leaves and candied violets from the flower gardens. She also taught her grandchild, Nellie Custis Lewis, all the domestic arts, including the art of cookery and fine needlework.

It was no coincidence that the first cook book published in America was printed in hospitable Williamsburg, Virginia, and bore the charming title "The Compleat HOUSEWIFE: or, accomplish'd Gentlewoman's Companion: being a Collection of upwards of several Hundred of the most approved Receipts. . . . by *E. Smith* Collected from the fifth Edition, *Williamsburg*, printed and sold by *William Parks*, 1742." It is certain that it was well known to the Virginia dynasty of First Ladies, who also compiled volumes of their own favorites in handwritten form for the young ladies of their own families.

Early cook books were for the professed cook, one who already

**Eisenhower's state china**

understood the art. A literate beginner would search the books in vain for routine household recipes for cooking eggs, ordinary vegetables, and most breads. They contained only the unusual and the special. Such cook books provide little clue to how the daily food was prepared.

In searching out the answers, there is a strong relationship here to the techniques used by the folklorist in tracing ballads and their variants to a verbal tradition preserved by those who learned the ballads from ancestors who in turn had learned them from their own ancestors.

As a white-collar historian and black-pot cook, I was often puzzled by the original early recipes used for my *Williamsburg Art of Cookery*. There had to be a study of quantities to reduce them to the amount ordinarily consumed by today's family. Certain ingredients were very different in the period represented by the First Ladies whose cookery involved open-hearth cookery.

To name but a few:

Eggs were much smaller, so that a good pound cake involved weighing the eggs rather than counting them, as a dozen eggs could vary greatly in size. Sugar was very coarse and had to be pounded and sifted from the loaf or cone. Butter, especially in the winter months, was extremely briny and had to be washed repeatedly to free it of salt, and even then it might be somewhat rancid. Flour was inclined to be very heavy. To get an equivalent texture with the modern product almost a third more is needed.

Truman's state china

Gelatin was made from calves' feet, or from a product called isinglass, taken from the swim bladders of fishes. These products were tasty enough in meat dishes or in court bouillon, but in the elaborate molded desserts they gave a meaty or fishy flavor to the pudding. In addition, since these elaborate "made dishes" were designed to please the eye sometimes more than the palate, they often smacked strongly of the "spinage" used to make them a lively green, or the beet juice whose flavor could be as obvious as its color.

The quantity of spice seems excessive for modern taste. But this may have been owing to the fact that spice was needed to cover certain strong flavors in other ingredients. Meat was frequently tough, and prolonged cooking, pounding, and marinating were needed for many cuts. By modern standards an unusual quantity of water was used in soups and vegetables, but the reason becomes apparent when one cooks in black pots over open fires—evaporation is so much greater.

Brewer's yeast or other liquid strains of yeast were common as leavening for breads and many kinds of cakes. Others were leavened simply with eggs, or with soda and sour milk until the fairly late invention of baking powder.

After adjusting the recipes from Presidential cook books to all of the variants in the ingredients, and in the complex techniques of open-hearth and beehive oven cookery, there still remains the problem of determining probable menus through the records of guests and diarists who described some of the exceptional dishes which quite literally covered the Presidential tables but who left tantalizing gaps in their records of the more ordinary dishes. For example, there are Joshua Brookes' cryptic jottings, describing a dinner on February 4, 1799: "Dinner with G. Washington. Leg boil pork, top head of table, goose bot. of table, roast beef, round cold boiled beef, mutton chops, hommony, cabbage, potatoes, pickles, fried tripe, onions etc. Table-cloth wiped, mince pies, tarts, cheese, cloth off, port, madeira, two kinds of nuts, apples, raisins. Three Servants."

For the "etc." and its rival the "&c, &c" of early diarists, it is necessary to know the vegetables and fruit available in the market at the season, the combinations of foods customarily served together, and also the tastes of the First Family from their letters, their garden records, and their purchases of supplies at home and abroad.

Thomas Jefferson was one of the greatest gourmets to occupy the Executive Mansion. He was also a gentleman farmer and an ardent gardener. While enduring "the splendid misery" of the Presidency from 1801 to 1808, he prepared a very detailed chart which reveals his own taste: "A Statement of the Vegetable Market of Washington, during a period of 8. years, wherein the earliest and latest of each article within the whole 8. years is noted." The market products listed included lettuces, parsley, spinach, sprouts, corn salad, radishes, sorrel, asparagus, broccoli, cucumbers, cabbage, strawberries, peas, turnips, Irish potatoes, snaps, artichokes, carrots, salsify, raspberries, squashes, Windsor beans, beets, currants, parsnips, watermelons, corn, tomatoes, melons, mushrooms, lima beans, grapes, endive, celery, eggplant, cauliflower, and cresses.

**Truman's state china**

Until almost the end of the nineteenth century the Washington markets also afforded a supply of fowl and wild game of every kind, and quantities of choice fish and seafood. Until the remodeling of the White House during the Fillmore administration, when an iron cookstove was installed, most of this food was prepared over an open fireplace. The old cook who presided over the kitchens when the radical innovation occurred was at such a total loss to operate the draughts and other complications of the newfangled gadget that he was helpless to cope with it. The President himself had to make a trip to the Patent Office and master the problems of operating the vast stove before an uneasy peace was restored.

Despite the roles that many of the Presidents undertook in the management of the household, the very great burden of maintaining a happy domestic routine and coping with official entertaining fell chiefly upon the First Ladies. With few exceptions they and their Presidents had one problem in common from the time when the capital of the nation was still in Philadelphia. This was the servant problem.

Samuel Fraunces, a famous New York innkeeper whose inn still stands on Broad Street, was the first steward retained by President Washington to preside over a staff of 15. Washington wrote him that he was to pay particular attention to the cookery, "seeing that everything pertaining to it is conducted in a handsome style, but without waste or extravagance . . ." The President agreed that Fraunces was "an excellent cook, knowing how to provide genteel dinners, and giving aid in dressing them, prepared the dessert, made the cake etc.," but Fraunces was dismissed for a period because Washington found that his steward had as genteel a taste in food and fine wines as the President himself and that he was supporting a very lavish establishment below stairs.

Abigail Adams in a hot August of 1789 wrote from Philadelphia to her sister in London of the same problem, which she had as wife of the Vice President:

"I have been fully employed in entertaining company, in the first place all the Senators who had ladies and families, then the remaining Senators and this week we have begun with the House, and tho we have a room in which we dine 24 persons at a time, I shall not get through them all with the public Ministers for a month to come. . . . The weather so warm that we can give only one dinner a week. I cannot find a cook in the whole city but what will get drunk."

When the capital was moved from Philadelphia to Washington, Mrs. Adams was First Lady. The Executive Mansion was unfinished. as indeed was the city itself. But she faced the problems she met there with the same courage and determination that the mansion's occupants have shown throughout its history—from the day when the big iron cookstove replaced the open fireplace, to the era of electronic cooking, electric frozen food saws, thermostats, and automatic timers. Today's art of cookery has come a long way from the day of the open hearth and the salamander, and the problems to be coped with in managing the domestic affairs of the White House are greater than ever before. They require of the First Lady that she be now, as much as ever, "the compleat housewife."

H. D. B.

**John Quincy Adams' state china**

# Contents

# *Acknowledgments*

The publisher wishes to thank the following individuals and organizations for their help in the preparation of this book. Where assistance was given for a specific President the name of the President appears in parentheses following the individual's name. Where no parentheses appear, the individual is thanked for his help with more than one President. Grateful acknowledgement is made to staff members of each administration for their help in preparing this book.

Mrs. Margery Lee Adams, Dover, Massachusetts (John Quincy Adams)

Miss E. Florence Addison, Assistant to Director, The Society for the Preservation of New England Antiquities, Inc. (John Quincy Adams)

Mrs. Harold D. Augenstein, The Harding Memorial Association (Warren G. Harding)

James A. Bear, Jr., Curator, Thomas Jefferson Memorial Foundation, Inc. (Thomas Jefferson)

Mrs. Agnes Farrar Black, Santa Barbara, California (William Henry Harrison)

Gervis Brady, Director, The Stark County (Ohio) Historical Society (William McKinley)

Mrs. Helen E. Braithwaite, Administrator, Decatur House, Washington, D.C. (Martin Van Buren)

Mrs. Elizabeth Harrison Buckner, Cincinnati, Ohio (William Henry Harrison)

Lyman Henry Butterfield, Editor-in-Chief, Adams Papers, Massachusetts Historical Society (John Quincy Adams)

Huntington Cairns, Chairman, Publications Fund, National Gallery of Art

Mrs. LeRoy Campbell, Curator, Roger Morris-Jumel Mansion, New York, New York

Mrs. Julia B. Carroll, The National Archives

Mrs. John Coolidge, Farmington, Connecticut (Calvin Coolidge)

James Cooper, Executive Secretary, Lake County (Ohio) Historical Society (James A. Garfield)

Mrs. Walter N. Curry, Curator, The Stark County (Ohio) Historical Society (William McKinley)

Miss Virginia Daiker, Reference Librarian, Library of Congress

Benjamin H. Davis, Superintendent, Roosevelt-Vanderbilt National Historic Sites (Franklin D. Roosevelt)

Mrs. Ada Denman, Marion, Ohio (Warren G. Harding)

Mrs. J. W. Finger, New York, New York

Sanford L. Fox, Chief, Social Entertainments Office, The White House

Malcolm Freiberg, Editor of Publications, Massachusetts Historical Society (Franklin Pierce)

J. R. Fuchs, Acting Director, Harry S. Truman Library (Harry S. Truman)

Robert R. Garvey, Jr., Executive Director, National Trust for Historic Preservation

Richard Hagen, Lincoln Memorial, Springfield, Illinois (Abraham Lincoln)

Mrs. Charles A. Hamke, Curator, Grouseland, Vincennes, Indiana (William Henry Harrison)

Mr. and Mrs. Alan Hanau, New York

Mrs. C. B. Harrison, Columbus, Ohio (Warren G. Harding)

Mrs. William Henry Harrison IV, Independence, Missouri (William Henry Harrison)

Laurence Gouverneur Hoes, President, The James Monroe Memorial Foundation

George Frederick Howe, Washington, D.C. (Chester A. Arthur)

Mrs. Susan King, Administrator, The Woodrow Wilson House, Washington, D.C. (Woodrow Wilson)

Mrs. Jessica Kraft, Museum Curator, Sagamore Hill National Historic Site (Theodore Roosevelt)

Mrs. Ida Lansden, Home Service Representative, Washing-ton Gaslight Company, Washington, D.C.

Steve S. Lawrence, Director, Ladies' Hermitage Association (Andrew Jackson)

Miss Martha Lindsey, Corresponding Secretary, Ladies' Hermitage Association (Andrew Jackson)

Miss Eleanor Lowenstein, The Corner Book Shop, New York, New York

Mrs. Helen H. Lyman, Head, Reference Department, Lockwood Memorial Library, State University of New York at Buffalo (Millard Fillmore)

Michael T. McNeill, Curator of Manuscripts, Buffalo and Erie County (New York) Historical Society (Millard Fillmore)

Watt P. Marchman, Director, The Rutherford B. Hayes Library (Rutherford B. Hayes)

Paul D. Mitchel, Secretary, The Harding Memorial Association (Warren G. Harding)

Dr. Roy Franklin Nichols, Philadelphia, Pennsylvania (Franklin Pierce)

Mrs. Gordon Parker, Curator, Wheatland, Lancaster, Pennsylvania (James Buchanan)

Miss Mary Pierce, Hillsborough, New Hampshire (Franklin Pierce)

Dr. C. Percy Powell, Historian, Manuscript Division, Library of Congress

Miss Louise Harrison Reynolds, Burlington, Vermont (William Henry Harrison)

Rodale Press, Allentown, Pennsylvania, for permission to reprint the Warren G. Harding recipes on page 180 from *To a President's Taste* by Lee Ping Quan, 1939.

Marvin D. Schwartz, Curator, Department of Decorative Arts, The Brooklyn Museum, Brooklyn, New York

Fred Shelley, Head, Presidential Papers, Library of Congress

Oscar A. Silverman, Director of Libraries, State University of New York at Buffalo (Millard Fillmore)

John Y. Simon, Executive Director, The Ulysses S. Grant Association (Ulysses S. Grant)

Robert E. Stocking, Curator of Manuscripts, University of Virginia Library (Thomas Jefferson)

Charles P. Taft, Cincinnati, Ohio (William H. Taft)

Wayne C. Temple, Director of Lincolniana, Lincoln University (Abraham Lincoln)

John A. Townsley, Management Assistant, Sagamore Hill National Historic Site (Theodore Roosevelt)

Mrs. J. Alfred Tyler, Sherwood Forest, Virginia (John Tyler)

Mrs. Gordon B. M. Walker, Chairman, Van Cortlandt Museum Committee, The National Society of Colonial Dames in the State of New York (Millard Fillmore)

Charles C. Wall, Resident Director, Mount Vernon, Mount Vernon, Virginia (George Washington)

Miss Beryl Walter, Tea Council of the U.S.A., Inc.

Mrs. Alene Lowe White, Librarian, The Western Reserve Historical Society (William McKinley)

R. N. Williams II, Director, The Historical Society of Pennsylvania (George Washington)

Mrs. Elisabeth Woodburn, Booknoll Farm, Hopewell, New Jersey

Mrs. R. Woodworth, Curator, President Benjamin Harrison Memorial Home, Indianapolis, Indiana (Benjamin Harrison)

x

# Notes to Special Illustrations and Photographs

## *Notes to Old Recipes*

# Guide to Recipes

Page numbers shown in italicized type refer to illustrations of the food.

xiii

# Notes to Research

THE PRESENT-DAY RESEACHER'S task of compiling recipes for a book subtitled *Favorite Recipes of All the Presidents of the United States* would have been relatively simple had the early First Ladies foreseen the interest future generations would show in their husbands' food preferences. Undoubtedly they would have carefully recorded for posterity even the smallest detail having to do with the eating habits of the Presidential household. Unfortunately, this is not the case. Nor were newspapers of those times, unlike our contemporary papers, of much help. They showed scant interest in recording such mundane matters as the eating habits of Presidents. Occasionally when such interest was shown it was to make political capital of an epicurean Presidential taste. Such an instance was the criticism levelled at Martin Van Buren for his fondness for lavishly prepared foods. The opposition made much of President Van Buren's aristocratic tastes in defeating him for reelection.

**Benjamin Harrison's state china**

There are however some bright spots in this obscure picture. There is a wonderful manuscript cook book written by Mrs. John Custis, mother-in-law of Martha Washington by her first husband, and given by Martha Washington to her granddaughter, Eleanor Parke Custis. Some of the recipes now associated with Martha Washington are in this manuscript book and we have reproduced on page 22 two typical pages from that notebook. While there is no similar hand-written account for the Adams family, there is in the Smithsonian Institution a printed book, *The House-keepers Pocket-Book,* which belonged to the Adams family (facsimilies appear on page 29). It is not unreasonable to assume that at least some of the recipes were favorites of John Adams and John Quincy Adams.

When we come to Thomas Jefferson we find that his taste in foods was as sophisticated as was his political philosophy. He gave expression to the latter in the great documents of the American Revolution and to the former in notes of recipes collected during his stay in France and those used at Monticello. Moving on, we come to that great early American hostess—Dolley Madison. Of course we do not know whether she had posterity in mind, but she did leave the future researcher some of her culinary interests in a series of neatly handwritten notes containing recipes and home remedies she favored. For James Monroe there are documents in the James Monroe Memorial Foundation archives known as the Monroe recipes. These have been copied by several transcribers, one being Rose Gouverneur, great-granddaughter of James Monroe, and may be presumed to represent some of his favorite dishes.

Generally, the present-day researcher has had to ferret out the information in the correspondence of Presidential friends, relatives, and visitors to the White House. This research has also included finding living descendants of the Presidents and First Ladies with the hope that perhaps in some attic trunk a long-forgotten letter would be found containing a clue or a reference to an actual recipe. Often when a reference to a preferred dish was found, no recipe was available. The researcher then had to find a recipe for this dish popular during the time of the particular President and hope that some future disclosure would confirm that the recipe was actually the President's favorite. An example is Abraham Lincoln, who was apparently completely indifferent to the type of food he ate, but it is known that he had some preference for fricasseed chicken. Of course no actual recipe for this particular fricasseed chicken is available. However, store records show that on December 31, 1846, Mrs. Lincoln bought a copy of Miss Leslie's *Directions for Cookery*. There is a recipe for fricasseed chicken in this cook book, and this is the one used in our book. Other instances of ascribed recipes are contained in the Notes to Old Recipes appearing on page xii.

When the twentieth century is reached the researcher's task becomes easier but more varied. Abundant public records are now available. There is also the opportunity for personal interviews with those White House staff members concerned with food matters. But most important is the satisfaction and the reward of being able to communicate directly with the present and former First Ladies about their husbands' food preferences. We therefore gratefully extend thanks to Mrs. Bess Truman, Mrs. Mamie Eisenhower, Mrs. Jacqueline Kennedy, Mrs. Lady Bird Johnson, Mrs. Pat Nixon, Mrs. Betty Ford, Mrs. Rosalynn Carter, and Mrs. Nancy Reagan, for making available to us recipes they consider among their husbands' favorites.

Whenever actual recipes were found these have been given in their original form. If it was necessary to extensively modify recipes, the original recipe is shown in italicized type and the modification is printed in the regular type of the book. The early original recipes rarely contained exact ingredients, so in the actual testing of the recipes the home economist had to establish a proportion of the ingredients to be used.

The reader will find some inconsistencies in titles to recipes, in spelling, and in the designation of weights and measures, but to have used a consistent style would have required tampering with the original recipes and thus have rendered the authenticity of the modified recipes questionable.

Occasionally some license was taken in the garnishing of the recipe, or in doubling or tripling the recipe, in order to make the photography more attractive. Whenever such a procedure was followed, mention of such modification is made in the text.

In the Acknowledgments appearing on page x, due credit is given to archivists, curators, and descendants and relatives of Presidents and First Ladies for supplying recipes, documents, pictures, and other help without which this book could not have been published.

C. G. S.

**Lincoln's state china**

George Washington

Martha Dandridge Custis Washington

# George WASHINGTON

WHEN GEORGE WASHINGTON and his "agreeable consort for life," Martha, assumed the position of President of the United States and First Lady they had no example to follow in regulating the official social life of the new Republic. There was no country then existing in the world which had a democratic form of government whose social protocol they could use as a pattern. They had as a guide only the court forms and etiquette inherited from their mother country. Theirs was the difficult task to harmonize aristocratic exclusiveness with republican simplicity. They must never forget that as the titular heads of a republic they still had to command the respect of the European monarchies who were eagerly waiting the opportunity to despise any poor or crude attempts of the new nation to establish itself with dignity, insolvent and inexperienced though it was. Fortunately the new President was equal to the challenge.

He had been born and raised in the social world of eighteenth-century Virginia where hospitality was a fine art. Entertaining guests was one of the daily duties of the plantation owners of tidewater Virginia. Both George Washington and his wife had their backgrounds among people who gave welcome to everyone—from the casual caller who came to spend the day, to the poor relation whose visit stretched through a lifetime; the traveler who was unknown almost as often as the one who was introduced; and the continual crowd of neighbors and relatives who came by horse, coach, or boat to the balls, house parties, and other great gatherings of the social season.

Martha Washington was trained in childhood by her mother to know about such things as how to handle servants and how to entertain and feed numbers of guests, in addition to learning the arts of dancing, playing cards, and doing needlework. She was taught these things rather than more cultural and learned studies because these were things she would have to know as mistress of a Virginia plantation.

After his marriage, George Washington acquired ample experience at playing the host at his Mount Vernon estate. His diaries are full of references to the daily comings and goings of his gregarious neighbors. When he left Mount Vernon at the outbreak of the Revolutionary War, his position as Commander-in-Chief of the military forces continued to make social demands.

Martha did not like to be alone and life was dull in her husband's absences so she joined the General at his winter encampments with the Continental Army. Washington's expense account is an impressive record of Martha's journeys to and from the camps where accommodations were crude and makeshift. She was with him at Cambridge, Morristown, Valley Forge, and Newburgh. In later years she could reminisce that she had heard the opening and closing guns of every campaign. Table expenses for these years are recorded in Washington's account book at about $1,000 a month. Even at Valley Forge when the fortunes of the army were at their lowest ebb Martha wrote that the General "had a log cabin built to dine in which has made our quarters much more tolerable than at first."

Interesting evidence of entertaining at Washington's headquarters may be found in a letter he wrote from West Point in August, 1779, to Doctor John Cochran, Surgeon-General of the Northern Department of the Army, in which he says, "I have asked Mrs. Cochran and Mrs. Livingston to dine with me tomorrow; but am I not in honor bound to apprise them of their fare?" Then he continues, "Since our arrival at this happy spot, we have had a ham, sometimes a shoulder of bacon, to grace the head of the table; a piece of roast beef adorns the foot, and a dish of beans, or greens, almost imperceptable, decorates the centre. When the cook has a mind to cut a figure, which I presume will be the case tomorrow, we have two beef-steak pies, or dishes of crabs, in addition, one each side of the centre dish, dividing the space and reducing the distance between dish and fish to about six feet, which, without them would be nearly twelve feet apart. Of late he has had the surprising sagacity to discover that apples will make pies; and it is a question if, in the violence of his efforts, we do not get one of apples, instead of having both of beef-steaks. If the ladies can put up with such entertainment and will submit to partake of it on plates once tin but now iron, I shall be happy to see them. . . ."

With the end of the Revolutionary War and the return of General and Mrs. Washington to Mount Vernon, their lives and their home threatened to be completely swamped with the steady flow of guests. The General himself called Mount Vernon "a well resorted tavern." He and his wife were forced into the role of the nation's hosts but even in their unofficial capacity as private citizens they accepted the duties with graciousness.

They soon found out that their immediate

**Mount Vernon, west front**

**Mount Vernon, east front**

family was only a small part of those who sat down to dinner in midafternoon. On occasion as many as ten or fifteen extra guests, invited or uninvited, were at the table. Many of these guests were welcome and only a few actually imposed, but in the aggregate they accounted for many beeves, sheep, roasting pigs, and a considerable part of the 8 tons of pork sent to the smokehouse in a given year. In addition we must consider the quantities of flour, vegetables, milk, butter, fish from the river, and game from the marshes. Claret, Madeira, and spirits disappeared in large volume. The cost of candles was not a small item as many of the guests stayed overnight. Quarters for their servants and horses were an additional burden. And all of the cost of this hospitality came from the hosts' own pockets. It was indeed well that Washington considered this hospitality an important part of his duty to his country and that Martha had learned from him "never to oppose her private wishes to the public will." With Martha "the General" always came first; her whole life was devoted to things which benefited her husband.

For his own protection Washington finally evolved a system of entertaining these endless guests. He turned many of them over to members of his household for part of their entertainment. Certain hours of each day he reserved for care of his estate and his voluminous correspondence. He had a set bedtime at nine o'clock unless the visitor proved of special interest. He made the best of his difficult role as national host and he took pride in maintaining a home, an estate, and a table which would impress visitors.

So it was that when George and Martha Washington accepted their obligation as President and First Lady to be the official host and hostess of the nation they came to the job well fitted for it both by training and experience.

Even before the inauguration it became evident that there must be some regulation of the pressing demands for social activity on the new President and his household. The rule was established that anyone wishing to pay his respects to the Chief Executive must call at a specified hour on one or two designated days of the week. The President himself would make no return visits and his social life outside his home was to be confined to occasional visits to the theater or to public receptions and balls. These rules were established in the interest of simplifying the task of being President. As Washington himself said, "Had I not adopted it (meaning a system of protocol) I would

**Beefsteak and kidney pie**

have been unable to have attended to *any* sort of business."

At the President's insistence his wife also placed restrictions on her daily life. All her private visiting had to be done with discretion and she must not go to public places. In her own words she found herself "more like a state prisoner than anything else," and adds "As I cannot do as I like, I am obstinate and stay home a great deal."

Two weeks after her arrival in New York to join the newly inaugurated President she wrote back to Mount Vernon to her niece, Fanny Washington, "I have not had one half hour to myself since the day of my arrival. . . . My hair is set and dressed every day and I have put on white muslin habits for the summer."

Despite her love of her own home and the reluctance with which she left it to become First Lady, Martha wrote that she had learned from experience that "the greater part of our happiness or misery depends upon our dispositions and not our circumstances." She was immediately loved and revered in her new position and played a major role in the social success of the administra-

*The Washington Family* by Edward Savage

tion. By her pleasing smile and her genuine warmth toward others, Martha made friends feel welcome and put strangers at ease, thus continuing in the home of the Chief Executive the gracious hospitality for which the Washingtons' home at Mount Vernon had already become famous.

Abigail Adams, the reserved New Englander, wife of the Vice President, wrote enthusiastically, "No lady can be more deservedly beloved and esteemed than she is and we have lived in habits of intimacy and Friendship."

When the Washingtons set up housekeeping in New York, it was with fourteen white servants and seven slaves from Virginia. Their dinners were frequent, large, and elaborate; powdered lackeys were conspicuous in the halls. The big social events of the season were the Christmas Eve party, the New Year's Day reception, and Washington's birthday celebrations. In addition the First Lady

was at home on Friday of each week and those who presented themselves in full dress were admitted to the Republican Court.

Martha received all of her guests seated. They passed by her, bowed or curtsied respectfully, and found seats in the drawing room. The President then circled around the room greeting the guests. Finally refreshments were served and a more relaxed social atmosphere prevailed while the guests mingled and chatted with one another.

Official dinners were Tuesdays and Thursdays at four o'clock. Martha presided at the table, elegantly gowned in satins and silks with her hair fashionably dressed and covered with the familiar mobcap.

The Washington account books reveal that food was consumed in amazing quantities; orders for claret and champagne were placed 26 dozen at a time. To Washington official hospitality of the Executive Mansion was an important part of his position as Chief Executive and he never neglected it however exacting the schedule became.

A description of a dinner at the Philadelphia Mansion at 190 High Street gives an idea of the elaborate menus of that period. Senator William Maclay of Pennsylvania reports, "It was a great dinner, the best of its kind I ever was at. . . . First the soup, fish roasted and boiled, meats, sammon, fowl, etc. This was the dinner. The middle of the table was garnished the usual way with small images, flowers (artificial), etc. The dessert was, first apple-pies, puddings, etc.; then iced creams, jellies, etc.; then watermelons, musk melons, apples, peaches, nuts. . . .

"It was the most solemn dinner ever I sat at. Not a health drank; scarce a word said until the cloth was taken away."

With the popularity of breakfasts as a form of entertaining in the political life of today, we find it interesting that the Washingtons also did a bit of official entertaining at breakfast. A travelling Britisher named Henry Wansey leaves a description of breakfast at the Executive Mansion in Philadelphia: "Mrs. Washington, in person, made the coffee and tea. On the table were plates of sliced tongue, dry toast, bread and butter, but no broiled fish as is the general custom. Miss Custis, a pleasing young lady nearing sixteen sat next to her grandmother. . . . There was but little appearance of form; one servant only attended who had no livery." According to Mr. Wansey a silver urn for hot water was the only item of luxury on the table.

Several firsthand descriptions have survived of the President's levee on Tuesday afternoons in Philadelphia. The reception was held at three o'clock in the dining room from which all chairs had been removed. On entering, the visitor saw the tall "figure of the President" often clad in black silk velvet, his hair in full dress; powdered and gathered behind in a large silk bag, yellow gloves on his hands, holding a cocked hat with a black cockade in it, its edges adorned with a black feather. He wore knee and shoe buckles and a long sword. He stood always in front of the fireplace with his face towards the door of entrance. The visitor was conducted to the President and his name distinctly announced. Washington received his visitor with a dignified bow avoiding to shake hands—even with best friends. At quarter past three the door was closed and a circle was formed around the room. The President then began on the right, spoke to the visitor, and exchanged a few words. After making the complete circle he resumed his place by the fireplace; visitors approached in turn, bowed, and departed. By four o'clock the ceremony was over. This extreme formality marked all the official functions of our first presidential administration, even though it was a subject of criticism against President Washington by his opposition during his second term.

In 1797 the Washingtons said farewell to Philadelphia and to public life and set out with light hearts for their beloved home on the Potomac. Once again Mount Vernon became the Mecca for visiting strangers. In July of that same

**Mount Vernon, west parlor**

year Washington commented in a message to a friend, "I am alone at present and shall be glad to see you this evening. Unless someone pops in unexpectedly Mrs. Washington and myself will do what I believe has not been done within the last twenty years by us—that is to sit down to dinner by ourselves."

This one night of relief was by no means typical of the days that followed. The steady parade of visitors continued, so much so that Washington invited his nephew, Lawrence Lewis, to live with them to assist with "the many visitors . . . I require some person . . . to ease me of the trouble of entertaining company, particularly of nights . . . in taking these duties, which hospitality obliges one to bestow on company, it would render me a very acceptable service."

Charming accounts of the Washingtons in retirement are left us by a few of their many visitors. A young Englishman named Joshua Brooks describes his visit in 1799: "Washington became pleasant, free and sociable at the table. The meal was bountiful. Besides the leg of pork on the platter at the head of the table where Martha sat,

**Washington's china banquet service**

## To Make Cheescakes

Take 6 quarts of stroakings or new milke & runett
it with runnett as for an ordinary cheese, & put
it with a strayner & hang it up in a tin or else presse
it in a strayner & hang it up in a tin or else presse
it with 2 pound weight, & break it to very small with
y'r hands or run it thorough a sive then put to it
for 8 eggs well beaten, 3 quarters of a pound of currans, halfe a pound of sugar, a nabmegg grated, rose
rans, halfe a pound of sugar, a nabmegg grated, rose
cloves & mace beaten 2 or 3 spoonfulls of rosewater
a little salt, y'n take a quart of cream, & when it boyle
thicken it with grated bread & boyle it very well as
thick as for an hasty pudding, then take it from the
fire & stir therein halfe a pound of fresh butter then
let it stand till it be allmoste cold & y'n mingle it with
y'r cream & when y'r coffins are filled y'r coffins nevr
your curd very well, then fill y'r coffins a quarter
they are ready to set into y'r oven scrape them some
sugar & sprinkle or some rosewater with a feather
if you have good store of currans in them you may put
in whole pound, & a little sack if you please. Soe take

## To Make Cheescake another way

Take 2 pound of fine flower, & rub into it halfe a pound
of fresh butter, y'n make some new milke blood warme, put
to it, & melt y'r bread in 6  or 8 eggs, & bake it, let it be 2 or 3 day
old, y'n put a little milke creame, in a gallon of cream, mix
with, when it is come seperate y'r curd from y'r whey with a
skimming dish, y'n tosse it betwixt 2 in a thin strayner till all
whey be dreyned away, y'n slyce in 3 or y'r rosemary & card
put in some cream, & rub it 'tis till it come thorough a sive
y'n will come, season it with white sugar, cinnamon & mace
beaten, currans, a little sack or rosewater, y'n thin quantity of
curd you must put 8 or 10 eggs beaten, & bake them in puff paste

## To Make rise floure

Take a pound of rise & cree it in milke with a little
whole mace, then season it with cinnamon cloves sugar
& a little sack, & a little rose water, & halfe a pound of
rasons & halfe a pound of currans, 3 or 4 eggs & a little
butter, y'n lay it in puff paste in a dish & when it
is baked scrape or some sugar.

## How to make a custard meat

Take 2 quarts of cream & put to it whole mace nutmeg
& cinamon slyced, y'n boyle it with a bay leafe, y'n break
16 eggs except 8 whites & beat them well together
with a little sack when y'r cream is taken of y'e fire
sweeten it well with sugar & keepe it stirring
& when it is halfe cold put in y'r eggs, beat some bran
of almons with y'r sand of y'r rowting pinn with a
little rose water, strow it on y'e y'n fill it into y'e coffins.

## To Make A Custard

Take a quart of sweet creame & strayne therein 2 whites
of eggs & 8 yoalks well beaten but them in a dish with
a grated nutmegg & a little salt & halfe a pound of sugar
stir them well together & soe bake it, you may also
but in some rose water if you please.

## To make an Almond Caudle

Take blanch y'r almonds & grinde them with a little ale or
boyle ale very fine, then strayne it with white sugar, cinnamon & mace
& boyle it with whole mace cinnamon & sugar.

Mount Vernon, the banquet hall

Mount Vernon, the library

and the roast goose in front of Lear at the foot, there were two kinds of beef as well as mutton chops. With the dessert of tarts and cheese, large wine glasses were brought for the port and Madeira. Three servants liveried in white with trimmings of crimson and lace waited on the table."

Another visitor of this period records the table conversation as "talk of many things: build-ing improvements in the United States, bridges in particular, New England roads, mutual acquaint-ances, progress of public buildings in the Federal city—the weather, conditions of crops, etc." This leaves us with the thought that social customs and menus may change with the times and the admin-istrations, but table conversation remains pretty much the same through the ages.

# *Favorite Recipes*

### *Beefsteak and Kidney Pie*

| | |
|---|---|
| 4 small veal or baby beef kidneys | 1 cup sliced mushrooms |
| 1½ pounds rump or round steak (to be cut into 1-inch pieces) | suet or bacon drippings flour, for dredging and thickening |
| 1 cup claret or other dry red wine | 1 pint hot water salt |
| 2 onions (1 sliced, 1 diced) | 1 teaspoon coarse black pepper |
| 2 bay leaves | 1 teaspoon marjoram |
| ½ cup chopped parsley | pastry of puff-paste, |
| ½ cup chopped celery (including tender leafy tops) | pie crust, or bis-cuit dough (to cover casserole) |

Separate the kidneys with a sharp knife, dis-carding all gristly portions and fat. Sprinkle with salt. Cover with claret, add bay leaves, sliced onion, pepper. Let it marinate 2 hours.

Pound the steak with flour, and cut into 1-inch pieces. Brown suet or heat bacon drippings in iron skillet. Then add diced onion and cook until clear; remove onion from skillet.

Over medium heat, brown steak well. Next drain the kidneys, reserving the marinade; dredge with flour, and brown, stirring carefully. Add 1 pint or less of hot water, stir well, add chopped celery and parsley, and marjoram.

Mix all well, and transfer to the casserole from which you intend to serve the pie. Strain into it the marinade. Cover with a tight lid, and bake at 325°F for about 1 hour.

Remove from oven. Brown the mushrooms in bacon drippings, and if they need thickening, thicken with flour mixed in cold water and stirred carefully to avoid lumps. Add the mushrooms to the casserole mixture. Cover with a crust of puff-paste, pie crust, or biscuit dough, and return to 400°F oven, and bake until brown, about 20 to 30 minutes. Serve at once.

◄ **Manuscript cook book by Frances Parke Custis**

## Trifle

*Put slices of Savoy cake or Naples biscuit at the bottom of a deep dish; wet it with white wine, and fill the dish nearly to the top with rich boiled custard; season half a pint of cream with white wine and sugar; whip to a froth—as it rises, take it lightly off, and lay it on the custard; pile it up high and tastily—decorate it with preserves of any kind, cut so thin as not to bear the froth down by its weight.*

| | |
|---|---|
| sponge cake, Naples biscuit, or jelly roll, cut into slices | 1 tablespoon sugar rich custard (see below) |
| ½ cup white wine, sherry, or brandy | candied fruits and angelica for decoration |
| 1 pint whipping cream | |

Mount Vernon, the common parlor

Line the bottom and sides of a deep dish with slices of sponge cake, Naples biscuit, or jelly roll. Wet them with ⅓ cup wine, and fill the dish nearly to the top with rich boiled custard (see below).

Season ½ pint of heavy cream with 1 tablespoon wine and 1 tablespoon sugar; whip to a froth and lay it on the custard. Cover and decorate with the remaining ½ pint whipped cream, preserves of any kind (jelly rolls were used in the picture shown) candied fruits, and angelica.

**Trifle**

## Rich Custard

| | |
|---|---|
| 1 quart milk, scalded | 6 eggs, whole |
| ½ cup cold milk | ¼ teaspoon vanilla or almond extract |
| ½ cup sugar | |
| pinch salt | |

Scald 1 quart milk; add ½ cup sugar, and a pinch of salt. Beat 6 whole eggs and add cold milk to them. Stir, and gradually add to the hot milk mixture. Cook in top of double boiler until custard coats the spoon. When cold, add the flavoring.

## Chess Cakes

| | |
|---|---|
| 1 cup butter | ¼ teaspoon salt |
| 1 cup sugar | pastry for 1 9-inch |
| 6 egg yolks, beaten | pie or 12 tarts |
| ⅓ cup dry white wine | (made in muffin |
| 1 tablespoon lemon juice and grated rind of 1 lemon | tins or fluted patty pans) |

Cream butter and beat into it slowly ½ cup sugar, reserving the rest of the sugar. Beat egg yolks with salt until light and lemon colored, then slowly beat in the remaining ½ cup sugar; with a whisk fold in the lemon juice and grated lemon rind. Combine with the creamed mixture, stirring in the wine.

Pour into pie shell or tart shells, and bake at 350°F for 50 to 60 minutes until set.

Abigail Smith Adams

John Adams

# John ADAMS

THE ADMINISTRATION of President Washington was followed by that of his friend, John Adams, his close associate and his Vice President.

John Adams came of a New England background and had grown up in a more austere social climate than that of George Washington, yet he was in complete sympathy with the social protocol established during the Washington administration.

Both John Adams and his wife, Abigail, had enjoyed an opportunity to observe and learn European social forms at first hand.

In 1779 Adams was sent to Europe as a representative of his newly established country and five years later he was joined there by his wife and their daughter, Abigail.

In Paris the Adams set up housekeeping in Auteuil in the elegant mansion of the Count de Rouault. The house was enormous and quite inadequately furnished. Abigail had to order three dozen spoons and forks to be made of silver, a tea set, and china for the table. In this setting they lived pleasantly, entertaining their fellow Ameri-

cans, other members of the diplomatic set, and the few Frenchmen who entered into their quiet circle. The family especially enjoyed the theater, the ballet, and concerts. Housekeeping, however, was not without its problems. Abigail found the ducks, geese, and turkeys "very indifferent" and very expensive; even stuffed with truffles they were poor fare. Fish was also expensive; she paid three gold louis for a turbot and ten livres for an eel. By contrast, the capons and chickens were the best in the world. It was a continual financial struggle for the Adams, who were dependent on the meager pay provided by Congress.

In February of 1785 Adams was appointed the first American ambassador to the Court of St. James. Abigail's presentation at Court was part of the official agenda. For the occasion she had her dressmaker make a gown that was "elegant, but plain as I could possibly appear, with decency." The result does not sound very plain. The gown was of "white lutestring, covered and trimmed with white crepe, festooned with lilac ribbon and mock point lace over a hoop of enormous extent." With it she wore ruffled cuffs, a dress cap with lace lappets, two white plumes and a lace handkerchief, pearl pins, earrings, and necklace. In writing of the ceremony, Abigail said that she "found the court like the rest of mankind, mere men and women, and not of the most personable kind neither." She felt that she and her daughter, Nabby, made a very adequate appearance, but she was not especially impressed or pleased with the royal ceremony which was so contrary to all her democratic sentiments.

In England the Adams lived a pleasant, social life. They were delighted with the country and felt more at home there than they ever had in France. However, in comparison, many things were lacking in England that they had enjoyed in France. The theater was heavy and lacked "Pari-

**Adams' china gravy boat**

sian ease and grace." English manners were bad. Abigail disliked the social gatherings where the women were segregated from the men. And English cookery could not compare with French. John complained repeatedly about their half-cooked vegetables and raw meat, which seemed to be all that English cooks knew how to prepare, and he contrasted them unfavorably to the inspired sauces and superb dishes of the French. The class system under which the British existed, with its emphasis on inherited titles was especially distasteful to John and Abigail. Even with all these drawbacks they still preferred England.

Their house on Grosvenor Square was soon headquarters for all the American colony in Lon-

don, but their meager salary kept official entertaining to a bare minimum. Finally they resolved that, money or no money, they must have a dinner for the foreign ministers. As luck would have it a New England sea captain arrived with a giant cod from New England waters together with a hundred-pound turtle from the West Indies. John was delighted that such a classic New England dish as cod would be available for the foreign ministers and he was pleased to report the dinner a social success.

Homesick for his native land and convinced that his contribution to the diplomatic relationship of the United States and Great Britain was no longer necessary, Adams asked for and received orders to return to America in 1788.

He arrived in the midst of the turmoil which accompanied the ratification of the new Constitution and was soon actively engaged in public office, this time as Vice President of the United States during Washington's administration.

In New York the Adams had a house on Richmond Hill. The house was large, spacious, and pleasant. Richmond Hill was country then and the house had a charming view over the Hudson River and the surrounding countryside. They were hardly settled when the stream of visitors started. The social life in which the Vice President and his wife became involved soon proved to be quite heavy. Abigail received a great number of visitors and returned dozens of calls. She and the Vice President were usually in attendance when the President and the First Lady held their weekly levees. In addition they personally entertained all the members of Congress and their families, as well as the "public ministers." Here, too, they were seriously handicapped by their small salary. That summer when John returned to Boston for a short visit he was commissioned by Abigail to bring back cheese, butter, "some of the russet apples," pears, bacon, tongue, several dozen hams, and thirty or forty dozen eggs, as well as six barrels of cider. They found the food in New York to be not only expensive, but also of poor quality.

Their next move was to Philadelphia when the seat of government moved there in 1790. There they lived at Bush Hill, a handsome house about two miles from the city. They were not even settled before hosts of visitors began to arrive. Every day between eleven and three they came to pay their respects to the Vice President and his lady. Evenings were crowded with social affairs, state dinners, and the theater. The only relief from the

**Beggar's pudding**  **Baked salmon**  **Oyster rolls**  **A pompetone**

incessant rounds of entertainments were the few summer months the Adams reserved for themselves at their home in Quincy, Massachusetts. The return to Philadelphia each fall marked the beginning of a new round of social activity.

The Vice President and his wife had a "public evening" at home each week when they received "those strangers" who came to Philadelphia either on "business or curiosity." They also allotted Wednesday evening for company to dinner—generally as many as sixteen or eighteen persons. Abi-

gail stayed in Massachusetts for the winters after 1792 because of ill health and, much as John missed her, it was the first time since his election that he was able to live within his income. His social life as a bachelor was quiet and more to his liking than the demands made upon him when he was in residence with a hostess.

In 1797 when John Adams was elected President of the United States Abigail was in Quincy and she was not in Philadelphia with him at the time of his inauguration.

It was quite evident that the new President would have to live austerely. Everything had doubled or tripled in price in the past eight years and as a consequence Adams thought "all levees and drawing rooms and dinners must be laid aside," to which he added, "I am glad of it." Furnishing the Presidential Mansion was another problem. He had to provide glasses, kitchen utensils, crockery, chairs, settees, secretaries, china, glass and firewood, etc. The house was nearly empty and a shambles when the Washingtons left it, taking their personal belongings with them. The public furniture was in deplorable condition— "There is no chair fit to sit in." The servants had made the house a scene of "drunkeness and disorder" between the time the Washingtons left and the Adams moved in. To add to the disarray, a cheese "as big as a chariot wheel," weighing 110 pounds, arrived as a gift from the state of Rhode Island. Maybe they could "live on it when money ran out." Adams was deeply discouraged about finances. "I expect to be obliged to resign in six months because I can't live. I had rather live on potatoes and beef and pork, fresh or salt, of my own growth." Through it all, domestic tribulations and presidential problems, John fretted for his wife: "You must come," his letters reiterate time and time again, "I can do nothing without you." Without Abigail, John was always only half a man; with her by his side he could face and solve every problem.

Abigail arrived in Philadelphia on May 9, 1797, and a few days later held her first reception— "thirty-two ladies and near as many gentlemen." She then turned her attention to her husband's health and to running the large and complicated household. She usually rose at 5 A.M. and until 8 she enjoyed the privacy of the early morning hours to read, write letters, pray, and compose herself for the activities of the day. At 8 she had breakfast with the family and until 11 o'clock she attended to household tasks. Menus were planned, food ordered, instructions given to Briesler, the major-domo, and to the cook—all details being dispatched with efficiency. At 11 she dressed for the day, then received company from noon until dinner. Dinner was an elaborate meal with wine and dessert. Afterwards she "rode out" until 7, visiting, shopping, or taking the air in the countryside. She often had thirty or forty guests to dinner— the whole Senate on one occasion and the House in rotation, members of the Cabinet, foreign ministers, and visiting dignitaries.

Washington had established the precedent of a presidential party on the Fourth of July for Members of Congress, the gentlemen of the city, the governor, and the officers and men of the militia companies. Long tables were spread in the yard to hold the overflow from the house, and Abigail was informed that over two hundred pounds of cake and two quarter-casks of wine were consumed annually, besides the rum that went into the wine. She dreaded the occasion, but her weeks of planning bore fruit and she got through the day with "more ease" than she expected.

One interlude which afforded some relief from the atmosphere of crises over foreign affairs was the appearance at the President's mansion of the kings of three Indian nations. After paying their respects to the President they were presented to Abigail—nine tall, brown savages in full regalia. They sat in silence facing her for a few minutes and then one arose and declared that "he had been to visit his father (meaning the President) and he thought his duty but in part fulfilled until he had visited also his mother and he prayed the Great Spirit to keep and preserve them." That said, all nine rose and shook hands solemnly and then had wine and cake.

The President created a controversy when he declined to attend a handsome ball and festivities in honor of George Washington's birthday held by prominent citizens of Philadelphia. He and Abigail had always thought this celebration was dangerously regal in implication, but in past years had reconciled themselves with the thought that the celebration honored the office of the President, rather than the man. When Adams became President and received an invitation to the festivities he felt it was an insult to the office, that the President of the United States should never be asked to attend the birthday celebration of a private citizen "however good, however great" the individual.

Unfortunately, his refusal was attributed to jealousy and to pettiness, despite the real motives.

In the summer of 1797 the Adams left fever-ridden Philadelphia for the peace and comfort of their New England home. Abigail wrote ahead asking to have "some coffee burnt and ground, some bread and cake made" for their arrival. If there seemed to be plans for a local reception committee to welcome their arrival she felt she must also have wine and punch to refresh them. The wine could be drawn from the casks in the cellar and the punch made by the gallon of Jamaica rum and brandy.

The New Year's Day reception, held without Abigail's presence, included government officials, Congressmen and Senators, and the officers of the Army. Thirty gallons of punch and wine were consumed and cake in proportion. Lord Nelson's victory at the Nile was the subject of conversation.

Abigail arrived in Philadelphia in November of 1799 and was immediately involved in the social life of the capital. When she received a shipment of codfish, she invited a company of New Englanders to enjoy it. Because the President missed his white potatoes and cider, Abigail ordered twenty bushels of potatoes and six barrels of cider to carry him through the winter.

Abigail found social life more crowded than ever and her explanation was that the ladies thought Adams would be defeated for reelection and that "it will be the last opportunity they will have to show their personal respect." All these visits had to be returned and she continues, ". . . what with dining company always twice a week, frequently three times, I find my time altogether occupied."

Abigail followed fashions closely—cambric muslin, embroidered with gold and silver, velvet cloaks, and fur-trimmed bonnets of black, purple, red, or green. But the First Lady deplored the immodesty of the Empire styles just coming into vogue. She wrote her sister that some of the young ladies were exposing the greater part of their breasts and wore no stays or bodice with dresses so clinging "as perfectly to show the whole form."

This was the winter that Gilbert Stuart painted his portrait of Abigail.

Now that she was almost ready to leave the city she suddenly found she was attached to it and wished that the scheduled move to Washington might have waited until the end of the administration. She left for Quincy on May 19, leaving the President the chore of moving his household as well as the government to the new seat of government.

The campaign for the election of 1800 was an especially bitter one, with both Republicans and Federalists hurling abuse at the President. Abigail felt especially resentful that a man who had devoted his life to "the best interest of his country" should have to suffer such treatment and sad reward for his services.

That fall President Adams left his comfortable home in Quincy for the crude new capital arising out of the wilderness. When he arrived in Washington, he found the new Executive Mansion

**Cook book owned by the John Adams family**

42    *The House-keeper's*    Fish.

will make it very rich. Serve it hot, and garnish with fried Oysters or Smelts, and Lemon sliced, with Horse-radish and fried Bread.

LOBSTERS, *to butter*. Break the Shells, take out the Meat, and put them into a Sauce-pan with a little seasoned Gravy, a Nutmeg, a little Vinegar, and drawn Butter; fill the Shells, and set the rest in Plates.

2] Or, *to do them sweet*. Season them with Sack, Sugar, Mace, and Lemon-juice, and garnish it with sliced Lemon.

OYSTERS, *to fry*. You must make a Batter of Milk, Eggs and Flour; then take your Oysters and wash them, and wipe them dry, and dip them in the Batter; then roll them in some Crumbs of Bread and a little Mace beat fine, and fry them in very hot Batter or Lard.

2] Or, Beat four Eggs with Salt, put a little Nutmeg grated, and a Spoonful of grated Bread, then make it as thick as Batter for Pancakes with fine Flour; drop the Oysters in, and fry them brown in clarified Beef-suet. They are to lie round any Dish of Fish; Ox-palates boiled tender, blanched and cut in Pieces, then fried in such Butter as is proper to garnish Hashes or Fricasfees.

COD, *to broil*. Take a large Cod, and cut the thick Part into Pieces an Inch thick, then flour it well, and put it on your Gridiron over a slow Fire; make your Sauce with a Glass of white Wine, an Anchovy, some whole Pepper, or a little Horse-radish, a little Gravy, a Spoonful of the Kitchen Sauce, or pickled Walnut Liquor, with some Shrimps or Oysters, or pickled Mushrooms; boil it together, and thicken it with Butter rolled in Flour, with some of the Liver of the Fish that has been parboiled, and must be bruised in it. Garnish with Lemon sliced, and Horse-radish scraped.

COD, *to stew*. Take your Cod and lay it in thin Slices at the Bottom of a Dish, with a Pint of Gravy, and half a Pint of white Wine, some Oysters and their Liquor, some Salt and Pepper, and a little Nutmeg; and let it stew till it
is

Fish.    *Pocket-Book.*    43

is almost enough, then thicken it with a Piece of Butter rolled in Flour; let it stew a little longer; serve it hot, and garnish with Lemon sliced.

WHITINGS, *broiled*. Wash your Whitings with Water and Salt, and dry them well, and flour them; then rub your Gridiron well with Chalk, and make it hot; then lay them on; and, when they are enough, serve them with Oyster or Shrimp Sauce. Garnish them with Lemon sliced. *Note*, The Chalk will keep the Fish from sticking.

FISH, *to spitchcock*. Clean Eels well with Salt, skin them, slit them down the Back, or do them whole; then serve them up. Season them with Pepper, Nutmeg and Salt, a few sweet Herbs shred fine, and grated white Bread; then broil them over Coal. Serve them with Anchovy Sauce; so do them for great Dishes of Fish.

SALMON, *to bake whole*. Draw your Salmon at the Gills, wash it and dry it, lard it with a fat Eel; then take a Pint of Oysters, shred some sweet Herbs, some grated Bread, four or five buttered Eggs, with some Pepper, Salt, Cloves, and Nutmeg; mix these together, and put them in the Belly at the Gills, then lay it in an earthen Pan, borne up with Pieces of Wood in the Bottom of the Dish; put in a Pint of Claret, baste your Salmon well with Butter before you put it in the Oven. When it is done, make your Sauce of the Liquor that is under the Salmon, some Shrimps, some pickled Mushrooms, and two Anchovies, some Butter rolled in Flour; boil these together, and garnish with fried Oysters, fried Bread, and Lemon sliced; serve it hot. A Cod baked in this Manner is very good.

TROUT, *to stew*. Take a large Trout and wash it, put it in a Pan with Gravy and white Wine, then take two Eggs buttered, some Salt, Pepper and Nutmeg, some Lemon-peel, a little Thyme, and some grated Bread; mix them all together, and put it in the Belly of the Trout, then let it stew a Quarter of an Hour; then put in a Piece of Butter in the Sauce; serve it hot, and garnish with Lemon sliced.
*TENCH,*

an impressive building. He moved in with his major-domo and made himself as comfortable as possible. That first night he wrote to Abigail, his letter concluding with the touching prayer immortalized in stone in the State Dining Room of the White House: "I pray Heaven to bestow the best of blessings on this house and all that shall hereafter inhabit it. May none but wise and honest men ever rule under this roof."

It was not until November 1800 that Mrs. Adams arrived to join her husband in Washington.

Abigail Adams wrote her first letter from Washington on November 13 and on November 15 the Commissioners of the District of Columbia hurriedly contracted with a workman named James Clarke to do some of the things which were still undone on the already occupied house. The most important of these, the "necessary" and the back stairs, were to be finished in a fortnight. Other work, mostly interior doors and the big window on the east end of the house, were to be completed within the next fortnight. The main staircase in the house was not yet in place and was not to be built until some years later.

To Mrs. Adams, accustomed to the comforts of urban life in New York and Philadelphia, and familiar with the luxuries in the capital cities of Europe, life on the frontier was something to be endured while having to present a stiff upper lip to the public. Only to her own family could she unburden herself, and it is in Mrs. Adams' letter written to her daughter, Abigail Adams Smith, in 1800 that she pictures her new home with all its complications. In a letter dated November 21, she says that the house is on a "grand and superb scale" but that it has its drawbacks. It "required about thirty servants to attend and keep the apartments in proper order and perform the ordinary business of the house and stables. . . . The lighting the apartments from the kitchen to parlors and chambers is a tax indeed; and the fires we are obliged to keep to secure us from daily agues is another very cheering comfort. To assist us in this great castle and render less attendance necessary, bells are wholly wanting, not one single one being hung through the whole house and promises are all you can obtain. This is so great an inconvenience that I know not what to do or how to do . . . if they will put me up some bells and let me have wood enough to keep fires, I design to be pleased. I could content myself almost anywhere three months; but surrounded with forests, can you believe that wood is not to be had, because

people cannot be found to cut and cart it! . . . We have indeed, come into a new country.

"You must keep all this to yourself and when asked how I like it, say that I write you the situation is beautiful which is true. The house is made habitable but there is not a single apartment finished and all withinside except plastering has been done since Briesler came. . . . Six chambers are made comfortable; two are occupied by the President and Mr. Shaw, two lower rooms, one for a common parlor and one for a levee-room. Upstairs there is the oval room which is designed for the drawing room and has the crimson furniture in it. It is a very handsome room now; but when completed it will be beautiful. . . . It is a beautiful spot, capable of every improvement and the more I view it, the more I am delighted in it."

One senses Abigail's frustration and her feeling of being in alien surroundings. "If the twelve years in which this place has been considered as the future seat of government had been improved as they would have been in New England, very many of the present inconveniences would have been removed."

But the social life of the infant Republic was not to be delayed by lack of the niceties of civilization. Before the end of November the members of the entire Congress, all 138 of them, made a formal visit to the President, riding in state in hackney coaches rented from Baltimore, and preceded by the Sergeant at Arms, with the mace, on horseback.

The first full-scale social reception was the New Year's Reception of 1801. John Adams' elegance made up for the inadequacies of his menage, as he received the guests in full dress, wearing a black velvet suit, silk stockings, silver knee and shoe buckles, white waistcoat and gloves, with his hair powdered and pulled back in a queue.

On February 7 Mrs. Adams commented in a letter that, "Today the Judges and many others with the heads of Departments and Ladies dine with me for the last time."

The second week of February 1801 Abigail left Washington for the Adams home in Quincy, happy in the knowledge that John would join her in less than a month with public duties behind them.

Their declining years were spent in the family home in Quincy where they lived in comfort surrounded by their family and friends, and, as always, their greatest joy was their contentment in being together.

# Favorite Recipes

### Baked Salmon

| | |
|---|---|
| salmon | 1 tablespoon chopped |
| skinned eel | parsley |
| 1 pint oysters | 1 teaspoon thyme |
| 2 tablespoons oyster | dash of pepper |
| liquid (reserved) | 1 teaspoon salt |
| 4 cups bread crumbs | dash of cloves |
| 3 tablespoons melted | dash of nutmeg |
| butter | pint of claret |
| 3 eggs, beaten whole | |

Clean the salmon; wash and dry it. Lard it with a skinned eel. Combine a pint of oysters (reserving out the liquor), 4 cups bread crumbs, 3 tablespoons melted butter, 3 whole eggs, beaten, chopped parsley, thyme, pepper and salt, cloves, nutmeg, and 1 tablespoon oyster liquor. Fill the salmon with stuffing. Baste well with butter. Lay salmon on a rack in a roasting pan, pour over it a pint of claret, and cover salmon with buttered paper. Bake in a preheated oven (550°F) for 10 minutes; then reduce the heat to 425°F, and bake 20 to 35 minutes longer. Allow 10 minutes per pound for the first 4 pounds, and 5 minutes for each additional pound.

Baste several times. Ten minutes before the baking is done, uncover and bake until done.

### Sauce

| | |
|---|---|
| drippings from the | pickled mushrooms |
| salmon | 2 anchovies |
| some shrimps | butter, rolled in flour |

Boil ingredients together for sauce.

### Garnish

| | |
|---|---|
| fried oysters | lemon wedges |
| toast slices | watercress |

### A Pompetone

| | |
|---|---|
| 2 pounds of veal | 2 squabs, boned and |
| ½ pound beef suet | sliced thin |
| 2 eggs, well beaten | 1 sweetbread |
| 1 tablespoon chopped | small can asparagus |
| parsley | tips |
| ¼ cup chopped onion | ¼ pound mushrooms |
| ¼ teaspoon thyme | 3 hard cooked egg |
| 2 teaspoons salt | yolks, sliced |
| ¼ teaspoon pepper | 2 slices tongue, cut in |
| 6 thin slices bacon | slivers |

Take 2 pounds of veal, mince it small with

**Baked salmon**

½ pound suet. Beat in 2 well beaten eggs to bind it. Season it with the chopped parsley, chopped onion, thyme, salt and pepper. Line a large pie plate with half the meat; fill it by laying in the slices of bacon, the sliced squab, 1 cooked sliced sweetbread, asparagus tips, cooked mushrooms, sliced yolks of 3 hard cooked eggs. Over the top of all this spread the remaining minced veal. Bake in a moderate oven (350°F) for about 1 hour, until nicely browned. Serve in the pie plate, ungarnished.

### Oyster Rolls

| | |
|---|---|
| 6 French rolls | 3 or 4 peppercorns |
| 1 pint oysters (reserve | 2 tablespoons butter |
| the liquor) | parsley sprigs for |
| dash of mace and | garnish |
| nutmeg | |

Take 6 French rolls, scrape or grate the outside, then cut a piece out of the top, and scoop out all the crumbs.

Drain the oysters, saving the liquor. Wash oysters in water and salt. Add mace and nutmeg to strained oyster liquor, also a few peppercorns, and place in saucepan over low heat. Add oysters and the 2 tablespoons butter. Stew them until the

**Oyster rolls**

mash the bread. Add ginger, nutmeg, salt, rose water, sugar, and currants. Mix all these well together.

Lay the mixture in a pan that has been well buttered on the sides. Flatten well with a spoon, then lay some pieces of butter on top. Bake it in a gentle oven (325°F) for about ½ an hour. Serve hot. If you prefer, you can turn it out of the pan when it is cold, and it will eat like fine cheese cake.

In either case, serve with heavily whipped cream, arranged in dabs with a cherry on top of each dab.

edges of the oysters curl. Pour them into the rolls, and set them in a hot oven (375°F to 400°F) till they are hot enough. Garnish with sprigs of parsley.

### Beggar's Pudding

| | |
|---|---|
| 20 slices stale bread | 1 cup sugar |
| 1 teaspoon powdered ginger | ½ cup currants |
| ½ teaspoon grated nutmeg | pieces of butter |
| ¼ teaspoon salt | 1 pint heavy cream, whipped |
| 2 teaspoons rose water | candied cherries, for garnish |

Over the slices of stale bread, pour hot water until they are well soaked. Press out the water, and

**Beggar's pudding**

Thomas Jefferson

Martha Wayles Skelton Jefferson

# Thomas JEFFERSON

WHEN THOMAS JEFFERSON moved into the White House in 1801 he had been a widower for nineteen years, yet the country soon found that it was blessed with a President who was as capable of regulating the social life of the capital city as he was of managing the destiny of the country. His background as a member of one of the old Virginia families had made him a social being from the day of his birth. His natural talents had been given opportunity to develop during the long public life which began with the writing of the Declaration of Independence in 1776 and was crowned with his election to the Presidency. In those twenty-five years Thomas Jefferson had been in continuous public service, as Governor of Virginia, Member of Congress, Minister to France, Secretary of State during the first administration of George Washington, and then Vice President under President John Adams.

After Jefferson's inauguration he continued to live at Mrs. Conrad's boarding house, C Street and New Jersey Avenue, from March 4 until March 19. It probably took that long to bring up from Mon-

ticello the furniture, servants, decorative accessories, and scientific collections which he brought to Washington to surround himself in the President's house. He also installed in the house some of the ingenious gadgets by which he delighted to simplify his existence. One of these was a "machine to hang clothes on" which was a kind of revolving clothes tree built in the wardrobe so that its rotation brought a day's clothing out of the depths for easy access.

Thomas Jefferson brought from Monticello servants familiar with his mode of life, his open hospitality, and his generosity. To his steward he turned over the management of the household and the purchasing of provisions.

The rooms in the house soon took on an intimate, friendly atmosphere. Jefferson wanted to have about him, within easy reach, the things that interested him, his collections, his hobbies, and the strange fossils that waited to be studied or classified. Experiments in horticulture stood about in glass-covered saucers. Notebooks, diaries, and memoranda were always at hand for notes and reference. Musical instruments, books, letters to his family and friends at home and abroad claimed his free time.

It was while Jefferson was Minister to France that he acquired the habit of conducting official business while acting as dinner host. He had been immediately attracted to the French people and from the first enjoyed many of their social customs. He brought back to this country along with his French furniture and an enthusiasm for their arts the best of the Old World's style of living, which he incorporated gracefully into his Virginia heritage.

Despite his fondness for French cookery Jefferson retained his liking for sweet potatoes, turnip greens, baked shad, Virginia ham, green peas, crab, and many other native delicacies. He was so fond of his Virginia sweet corn that he raised it in his Paris garden. His kitchen garden at Monticello contained a variety of vegetables including his favorite peas, of which he was familiar with more than thirty varieties. He also liked salads and often attributed his long life to the many vegetables and greens included in his diet and his preference for wine instead of liquor.

Jefferson was the greatest connoisseur of wines to live in the White House, and regarded fine wines as one of the necessities of life.

Soon after he moved in he abolished the weekly levee and issued a declaration that each

**Wyeth's English plum pudding      Hard sauce      Boeuf à la mode      Wine jelly**

year he would hold only two large receptions—one on New Year's Day and the other on the Fourth of July to which all were welcome. Naturally the ladies were disturbed at the curtailment of their official social activities and they made an effort to get the President to receive at a levee but the President made it plain that he would not change his mind. This was due at least in part to the fact that much of the time there was no official hostess in residence at the White House.

Whenever he needed a hostess, he could call upon Dolley Madison, the wife of his Secretary of State. She presided at his table and helped to take care of his guests, especially the "female friends" who were being entertained at dinner at the White House.

However Mr. Jefferson might choose to limit the formality of his entertaining, there was never any limit to his hospitality. His table was filled almost every day. Dinner at half-past three or four had the intimacy of a family dinner with the guests often sitting and talking until night. It was said that often fifty dollars was spent for a single day's marketing. Whether or not this statement is true, many guests at the White House have left a record of Mr. Jefferson's generous hospitality.

A typical dinner invitation of the Jefferson administration was worded:

"Th. Jefferson requests the favor of Mr. and Mrs. Smith to dine with him on Tuesday next (26th) at half after three, and any friends who may be with them.

"April 25: 1803
"The favor of an answer is asked."

One of the first descriptions of a dinner at the White House during the Jefferson administration gives us perhaps the secret of his success as a host. Mrs. Samuel Harrison Smith (of the invitation), who was the wife of the publisher of the *National Intelligencer*, noted, "Mr. Smith and I dined at the President's; he has company every day, but his table is seldom laid for more than 12. . . . This prevents all form and makes the conversation general and unreserved."

Mrs. Smith also gives her interpretation of the President's preference for a round table:

"One circumstance, though minute in itself, had certainly a great influence on the conversational powers of Mr. Jefferson's guests. Instead of being arranged in straight parallel lines, where they could not see the countenance of those who sat at the same table, they circled a round or oval

**Monticello, west front**

table where all could see the others' faces and feel the animating influence of looks as well as words.

"Let any dinner-giver try the experiment, and he will certainly be convinced of the truth of this fact. A small, well-assorted company, seated around a circular table, will insure more social enjoyment than any of the appliances of wealth and splendor without these concomitants."

Another of Jefferson's unique "conveniences" contributed to the hospitality of his dinner table. In the wall of the dining room he had installed a set of circular shelves. Upon touching a spring these shelves would turn into the room loaded with food placed on them by the servants on the other side of the wall. By the same process the empty dishes could be removed from the room. When the talk was to be especially confidential, beside each guest was placed a dumbwaiter, containing everything necessary for the progress of the dinner from beginning to end so that attendance of servants was unnecessary.

To Jefferson the food served at his dinner table and the company with which he enjoyed it was the practice of the highest art of living and one of the marks of the civilized man. To run his household Jefferson had as chief steward and purveyor of the household, Etienne Lemaire, who had served his apprenticeship with some of the best families abroad. He also had a French chef and a well-trained staff of 14 servants. Every detail of gracious living merited Mr. Jefferson's personal attention. He kept track personally of the dates for various fresh vegetables including broccoli, mushrooms, endive, and artichokes. After his stay in France he regularly imported for his table Parmesan cheese, capers, pistachio nuts, and anchovies. His most important imports were wines on which he spent over two thousand dollars a year. Among his records is a recipe for ice cream and one of his guests has left us a description of a dessert which was "ice-cream brought to the table in the form of small balls enclosed in cases of warm pastry."

Senator Cutler, of Massachusetts, recorded a dinner at the White House, February 6, 1802.

"Dined at the President's—Rice soup, round of beef, turkey, mutton, ham, loin of veal, cutlets of mutton or veal, fried eggs, fried beef, a pie called macaroni, which appeared to be a rich crust filled with scallion of onions or shallots, which I took it to be, tasted very strong, and not very agreeable. Mr. Lewis told me there were none in it; it was an Italian dish, and what appeared like onions were made of flour and butter, with a particularly strong liquor mixed with them. Ice cream very good, crust wholly dried, crumbled into thin flakes; a dish somewhat like a pudding—inside white as milk or curd, very porous and light covered with cream sauce—very fine. Many other jim-cracks, a great variety of fruit, plenty of wine and good."

Affairs of state, agriculture, science, and manufactures were discussed by the President and his guests in the long afternoons spent around the table. The same Senator Cutler tells of presenting the President with a "specimen of wadding for Ladies cloaks and of bed ticks" from a Massachusetts factory to be handed around the table and discussed by the guests.

It was on the occasion of one of President Jefferson's dinner parties that he was guilty of what appeared as a great offense to the diplomatic circle when he took the arm of Mrs. Madison to escort her into dinner and left Mrs. Merry, the wife of the British Ambassador, with no escort.

Sir Augustus Foster, the secretary of the British Legation, understood exactly what President Jefferson was doing. "Mr. Jefferson," he wrote "knew too well what he was about—he had lived in too good society at Paris, where he was employed as Minister from the United States previously to the French revolution . . . not to set a value on the decencies and proprieties of life, but he was playing a game for retaining the highest office in a state where manners are not a prevailing feature in the great mass of society, being, except in the large towns rather despised as a mark of effeminacy by the majority, who seem to glory in being only thought men of bold, strong minds and good sound judgment."

The President had done it deliberately, in fact, and he then proceeded to call his Cabinet together and issued a statement on social equality, "When brought together in society, all are perfectly equal, whether foreign or domestic in or out of office" and emphasized that title and grade of diplomat gave no preference in the New World.

During the winter of 1802, the President's two daughters were in Washington with their father. It seems to have been an especially gay social season. Senator Cutler speaks of Martha Jefferson Randolph and her younger sister, Maria Jefferson Eppes, being at a large dinner in that year, adding, "They appeared well-accomplished women, very delicate and tolerably handsome."

Another guest describes the New Year's Day reception of that year. He writes that the Secretaries of the Navy, State, Treasury and other departments, and the foreign ministers, with their wives, were in attendance:

"Arriving late, I met a whole troop of ladies and their attendant gallants coming down the outside stairs and going to their carriages. On passing the great hall and entering the north drawing room, I found still a large party there. The President was standing near the middle of the room to salute and converse with visitors. The male part of

**Martha Jefferson Randolph**

them walked about or made groups for conversation while the ladies received the bows and adorations of the gentlemen. Among the ladies were the President's two daughters, Mrs. Randolph and Mrs. Eppes, to whom I paid my obeisance; then to Mrs. Madison and her sister Miss Payne; then to Miss Gallatin and Miss Nicholson besides a number of others. Beaux growing scarce or inattentive towards the last, I had to officiate myself and to escort several of the fair creatures in succession to their carriages. Several belles from Virginia and elsewhere were brought out on this gala day and it was allowed on all hands that the company made a brilliant appearance."

With only two public receptions each year they became memorable events. At the Fourth of July celebration Jefferson shook hands with all his guests, thereby establishing a precedent which continues to our own day. Refreshments were served to all comers and the "excellent band attached to the Marine Corps" played martial music.

One of Jefferson's Fourth of July receptions is recorded by the same Mrs. Smith: "About twelve O'clock yesterday, the citizens of Washington and Geo. Town waited upon the President to make their devours. . . . We found about twenty persons present in a room where sat Mr. Jefferson surrounded by five Cherokee chiefs. After a conversation of a few minutes, he invited his company into the usual dining room, where four side-boards were covered with refreshments, such as cakes of various kinds, wine, punch, etc. Every citizen was invited to partake, as his taste dictated . . . and the invitation was most cheerfully accepted and the consequent duties discharged with alacrity. The company soon increased to near a hundred including all the public officers and most of the respectable citizens and strangers of distinction. . . . Mr. Jefferson mingled promiscuously with the citizens and far from designating any particular friends for consultation, conversed for a short time with everyone that came in his way."

At one of the Fourth of July receptions, a gift was presented to Jefferson by a delegation from Pennsylvania; it was a "mammoth cheese" weighing over twelve hundred pounds and bore a banner with the inscription "The greatest cheese in America for the greatest man in America." It had taken six horses to haul the wagon which brought the cheese. Jefferson was so adamant about not accepting presents that in his personal account book he noted "To the bearer of the cheese $200."

Year after year these midsummer receptions

swelled until it was necessary to erect temporary tents and booths on the White House grounds to take care of the huge crowd. Bareheaded, Jefferson stood on the White House steps and shook hands with all who attended. The European diplomats

Monticello, the tea room

murmured that the President paid more attention to the "aborigines from the West" than to his foreign dignitaries.

The Fourth of July reception for the year 1803 was especially gay as the country on that day celebrated the acquisition of the Louisiana territory. The scene was colorful and impressive with banners and bands, speeches and cheers in honor of the nation, the President, and the new territory.

The next step was to send an expedition to explore the new land, and President Jefferson got Congress to provide funds to staff the expedition while he delegated Dolley Madison to head a drive among the ladies whose stated purpose was to provide "everything which could possibly be needed on such a perilous journey." Dolley was successful in this as she always was and collected handsomely for the cause.

In 1809 Jefferson left office, riding on a wave of popularity. He chose to play the role of a private citizen at the inauguration of President Madison, riding on horseback to the Capitol and accompanying the crowd to the reception at the Madisons' house following the ceremony. It was only at the earnest request of the people that he returned to the White House to be presented with a written testimonial of their high regard of his virtues as a philosopher, philanthropist, patriot, statesman, and as a man.

During the remaining seventeen years of his life, Jefferson ventured only a few miles from his haven at Monticello. Here he met incessant demands on his hospitality as people from far and near came to sit at his table. Surrounded by his family, in his last years he faced financial disaster with philosophical serenity. Jefferson died at Monticello on the Fourth of July 1826, the fiftieth anniversary of the Declaration of Independence.

# *Favorite Recipes*

## *Boeuf à la Mode*

*Take a fleshy piece; (pièce de tranche) beat it & lard it & season it with the ingredients below mentioned: salt, pepper, laurel leaf & green lemons; put all in a pot together & shut it perfectly close; cook it by a slow fire & when the juice is well out, put in a glass of wine; let it boil and when it is pretty near dry, serve it up with lemon juice.*

| | |
|---|---|
| 4 pounds top round | ¼ teaspoon pepper |
| 4 onions (1 chopped fine; 3 cut fine) | ⅜ teaspoon grated nutmeg |
| 3 carrots, peeled and sliced | suet for larding |
| | 12 bacon strips |
| 1 tablespoon chopped parsley | ⅓ cup brandy |
| ½ teaspoon salt | ⅓ cup white wine |

### *Vegetables*

| | |
|---|---|
| celery stalks | 1 package frozen peas |
| carrots, cut long | 1 package frozen cut string beans |
| small white onions | |
| sweet potatoes | mushrooms, fluted |

Cut off most of the fat from the 4-pound top round. Make a mixture, in which suet or bacon strips are to be rolled, the mixture to consist of: 1 finely chopped onion, 1 tablespoon chopped parsley; ½ teaspoon salt, ¼ teaspoon pepper, ⅛ teaspoon grated nutmeg, ¼ teaspoon thyme. Now roll the suet or 4 strips of lean bacon and the fat from the meat in the above mixture, and lard the meat with them.

Put 4 slices of bacon into the bottom of a Dutch oven; lay the beef on it, and lay on the roast 4 more bacon strips. Put into the pot the finely cut onions and the sliced carrots. Add salt and pepper, ¼ teaspoon grated nutmeg, a pinch of thyme, brandy, and white wine.

Place the Dutch oven on a low fire and let it boil gently for 3 hours, taking care from time to time that the meat does not stick to the bottom.

Strain the gravy through a fine sieve, skim off the grease, and serve hot in a gravy boat.

Garnish the boeuf à la mode with the boiled or sautéed vegetables, arranged in contrasting colors.

**Boeuf à la mode**

## Stuffed Boned Capon

| | |
|---|---|
| 2 6- to 7-pound capons | unsweetened |
| 2 pounds of lean | chestnut puree |
| ground veal | 1 can artichoke |
| ½ pound boiled ham | bottoms (about 8) |
| or tongue | 1 cup dry white wine |
| 2 ounces of blanched | 1 cup strong chicken |
| pistachio nuts | stock |
| 6 egg whites | 1 teaspoon red currant |
| 2 cups light cream | jelly |
| 4 teaspoons salt | 1 teaspoon tomato |
| ½ teaspoon nutmeg | paste |
| ¼ teaspoon cayenne | 1 teaspoon meat |
| pepper | glaze |
| 1 level teaspoon | 1 teaspoon potato |
| freshly ground | flour |
| white pepper | 1 large truffle |
| ½ cup apple brandy | watercress for |
| 6 ounces salt butter | garnish |
| 1 1-pound can | |

With a cleaver, remove the tips of legs from the capons. Turn the capons on the breast side, and with a sharp knife cut right down the center of the backs, and carefully remove all the meat from the carcass, starting from the oyster.

On a board, flatten out the birds, skin side down. Sprinkle well with apple brandy, season with salt and pepper. Roll the birds up tightly, and allow to stand while making the stuffing.

For the stuffing, put the lean ground veal in a mixer bowl, add the egg whites, and beat well. Slowly add the light cream, then 2 ounces of chestnut puree, 3 teaspoons salt, cayenne pepper, and 3 tablespoons apple brandy which have been heated and flamed. Beat well.

Unroll the capons, and spread this mixture on top. Sprinkle each capon all over the top with blanched pistachio nuts. Cut ham or tongue in strips as thick as your little finger, and place on top of the stuffing, about 1 inch apart. On top, lay 1 or 2 pieces of truffle. Fold over, and sew together with white thread.

Reshape the birds and tie with butcher's string. Place on a rack and brush with melted butter. Preheat oven to 350°F, and roast at this temperature for 1½ hours to 2 hours, basting every 20 minutes. Each time you baste, add a little stock, about 2 to 3 teaspoons, and white wine, and brush with melted butter.

When the capons have been in the oven for 40 minutes, turn them over on the breasts, and let them roast that way for another ½ hour. Then turn them back again, breast side up, and finish

**Stuffed boned capon**

roasting that way. While the capons are roasting, use the capon livers to make the following gravy:

In a small heavy pan, heat 1 teaspoon salt butter. When it colors, add the capon livers. Quickly brown them on both sides without stirring. Heat the rest of the apple brandy and pour over the livers. Remove the livers from the pan, and stir in 1 tablespoon butter, 1 teaspoon tomato paste, 1 teaspoon meat glaze, 1 teaspoon potato flour, and 1 teaspoon red currant jelly. Stir all this over low heat until it is smooth. Add the rest of the wine and the chicken stock, and all the juice and drippings from the roasting pan and any apple brandy that might be left. Stir continuously, until it comes to boil. Then put back the liver, and simmer gently for 20 minutes with one truffle cut in half.

Take 8 artichoke bottoms, and heat them

gently for a few minutes in a little butter, salt, and pepper. Put the rest of the chestnut puree in a saucepan and season it with salt and pepper. Beat with wooden spoon until smooth and hot. Put into a large star tube, and pipe a large rosette on the top of each artichoke bottom.

*To serve*

Carefully slice one of the capons, and arrange the slices overlapping on the side, on a hot platter. Place the uncarved capon alongside. Take two skewers, and on each place 2 pieces of liver and ½ a truffle; stick the skewers into the breast of the uncarved capon. Decorate the drumsticks with paper frills. Around the edge of the platter arrange the artichoke bottoms, and garnish with watercress.

Pour a little gravy over the platter, and serve the rest separately in a gravy boat.

## Chartreuse (Vegetable Mold)

*At Monticello the vegetables, all roots, no cabbage, were cut in slices & arranged in a fanciful way, alternating carrots with white vegetables, in a straight-sided vessel. It turned out in a beautiful form and made a very pretty dish for a ceremonious dinner. The inside was fitted up with forced meat balls.*

| | |
|---|---|
| 1 can asparagus tips | 1 cup cooked strained |
| 1 bunch tender young | peas |
| carrots | 2 eggs whole |
| 1 pint young Brussels | 3 egg whites |
| sprouts | ⅓ cup sour cream |
| 3 cups cooked strained | salt and pepper |
| spinach | butter |
| 1 cup cooked strained | |
| carrots | |

Boil asparagus tips in salted water until tender. Boil peeled carrots in salted water until tender, and cut into thin round slices. Boil Brussels sprouts in salt water until tender, and cut in half. Drain, and allow vegetables to cool.

Take 1 2-pound pyrex bread loaf oblong dish, and butter it thoroughly. Line the dish alternately with thin-sliced cold carrots, cold asparagus tips, and cold Brussels sprouts.

Now fill the lined dish with a mixture of strained spinach, strained carrots, strained peas, mixed with 2 whole eggs plus the egg whites, ⅓ cup sour cream, salt, and pepper. Cover with a piece of buttered paper. Stand in pan with a little water in it, and put in a 350°F oven for 1 hour or until just firm to the touch. Remove and

allow to stand 5 minutes before turning out onto hot serving dish.

**Chartreuse**

## Veal Olives

*Take the bone out of the fillet and cut thin slices the size of the leg, beat them flat, rub them with the yolk of an egg beaten, lay on each piece a thin slice of boiled ham, sprinkle salt, pepper, grated nutmeg, chopped parsley, and bread crumbs over all, roll them up tight, and secure them with skewers, rub them with egg and roll them in bread crumbs, lay them on a tin dripping pan, and set them in an oven; when brown on one side, turn them, until sufficiently done.*

| | |
|---|---|
| 10 slices, very thin, | 2 packages frozen |
| veal scalloppini | peas, or 2 cans of |
| ½ pound finely ground | concentrated |
| lean raw veal | cream of pea soup |
| 20 thin strips of boiled | 2 tablespoons flour |
| tongue | 2 teaspoons potato |
| 10 green olives stuffed | flour |
| with pimento | 1 teaspoon tomato |
| 3 egg whites | paste |
| ¾ cup light cream | 1 teaspoon meat glaze |
| 2 teaspoons salt | 1 teaspoon red |
| ½ teaspoon finely | currant jelly |
| ground white | 1¼ cups chicken stock |
| pepper | ¼ cup dry white wine |
| ⅓ cup brandy | ¼ cup dry sherry |
| 3 ounces salt butter | |

Put thin slices of veal between two pieces of waxed paper, and beat with a cleaver until they are extremely thin. Remove the paper, and brush the meat with a little brandy; season with a little salt and freshly ground white pepper.

Spread with the following veal mousse:

Put ground veal into a mixer bowl with egg whites and beat until smooth. Slowly add the light cream, drop by drop; season with salt, pepper, and 1 tablespoon of brandy. Spread this mixture on top of each of the thin veal slices about ¼-inch thick, and in the center of each put 2 fingers of tongue, and in the middle a stuffed olive. Roll up carefully. Fasten each end with a piece of butcher's string.

Now heat 1 ounce of butter in a shallow heavy skillet. Quickly brown the veal olives in this butter all over. Flame them with the rest of the brandy; then remove the veal from the pan and add two tablespoons of butter, then stir in two tablespoons of flour.

Off the stove, stir in tomato paste, meat glaze, and potato flour. When smooth, mix in chicken stock, white wine, and sherry, the rest of the brandy, the red currant jelly. Set back on low heat, stir continuously until it comes to a boil. Remove the strings from the veal olives, and put them into the gravy.

Next, place them on the top shelf of oven preheated to 375°F without a cover, and let them braise for ½ hour, basting occasionally. Remove, and carefully cut the veal olives in half in center. Arrange them on the top of a pea puree (made of 2 cans of concentrated cream of pea soup, heated and stirred until smooth), or with a bowl of cooked peas.

**Veal olives on a pea puree**

**Wine jelly**

## Wine Jelly

*Take 4 calves feet, & wash them well without taking off the hoofs. (or instead of that 1 oz. isinglass, or 1 oz. of deers horns) These feet must be well boiled the day before they are wanted. Let them cool in order to take off the greese. After taking off the greese put the jelly in a casserolle. Put there 4 oz. sugar, cloves, nutmeg. Boil all together. Take 6 whites of eggs, the juice of 6 lemons, a pint of milk, a pint of madeira. Stir all together. Pour it into the jelly & boil it. Taste it to see if sweet enough, if not, add powdered sugar. Strain it 2 or 3 times thru' flannel till clear. Put it in glasses or moulds.*

| | |
|---|---|
| 2 envelopes unflavored gelatin | pinch of salt |
| ½ cup cold water | 1 pint wine (Madeira, red Burgundy, or sherry) |
| 2 cups strained fruit juice (grape, cranberry, or raspberry) | strained juice of 3 lemons |
| ¾ to 1 cup sugar | fresh fruit for garnish |

Dissolve 2 envelopes of gelatin in ½ cup of cold water. Add this to the fruit juice, which has been brought to a boil. Add sugar to taste and a pinch of salt. Let cool. Next, add the pint of wine and lemon juice.

Pour into mold that has been chilled. Set into the refrigerator for at least 2 hours. Unmold and serve cold. Decorate with fresh fruits that have been rolled in powdered sugar.

## 10

*Proportion of a Plumb Pudding*

Four spoonfuls of brown sugar, 1/2 lb currants, 1 lb of raisins, 1 lb of suet, 3 spoonfuls of flour, the crumb of a penny loaf of bread grated, 12 eggs, 1 nutmeg, mace & cinnamon 1 spoonful, citron, 1 tea spoonful of salt, 1 wine glass of brandy.   Monticello.

Wyeth's English
Plumb Pudding

2 lbs best muscatel raisins, 1 lb currants, 1 lb sultana raisins. Rub the currants & sultanas through a dry cloth; pick out the stalks & pebbles which may be in them; 1 qt grated bread crumbs; 1 qt beef suet chopped fine; 8 oz citron cut thick; 2 oz candied orange peel; & dit lemon, both cut thin; 1 large tea spoonful of

grated nutmeg; dit grated ginger, green ginger best; 1 teaspoonful of salt. Mix all in a dry state, well; beat up 12 eggs and stir into the fruit; add half a pint of the best fourth proof brandy; if not moist enough add as much milk as will make it so. Boil in a thin cloth, four or five hours, the water must be boiling when the pudding is put into the pot. The pudding is much better boiled in a tin form. When all is done, before you turn out the pudding, plunge it in a pail of cold water for 4 or 5 minutes, this will make it turn out firm.   Wyeth, an English Hotel keeper

\* Mrs G. W. R. says 1 nutmeg.

**Manuscript cook book by Virginia Randolph Trist**

## Wyeth's English Plum Pudding

| | |
|---|---|
| 2 pounds seedless raisins | 2 ounces candied lemon peel, cut fine |
| 1 pound currants | 1 grated nutmeg |
| 1 pound sultana raisins | 1 teaspoon salt |
| 1 quart grated bread crumbs | 1 teaspoon ginger |
| 1 quart beef suet, chopped fine | 12 eggs, beaten whole |
| ½ pound citron, cut fine | 1 cup brandy |
| 2 ounces candied orange peel, cut fine | milk |
| | spray of holly, for decoration |

Mix the dry ingredients together well. Beat the eggs, and stir in the dry mixture. Add 1 cup brandy; if not moist enough, add as much milk as will make it cling together.

Put into closed tin forms, making sure that the cover is on tight. Put into boiling water, and boil 4 or 5 hours. The water must be boiling when the pudding is put in. When the water boils away, add boiling water, to keep the tin forms covered.

Before turning out the pudding, plunge the closed pudding form into cold water for a few minutes. Serve with hard sauce in a separate dish. Decorate with a small sprig of holly.

## Hard Sauce

| | |
|---|---|
| ⅓ cup butter | brown, or maple) |
| 1 cup granulated sugar (sugar may be powdered, | 1 teaspoon flavoring (vanilla, almond, or rum) |

Cream the butter until it is very soft, then stir in the desired kind of sugar, and the desired flavoring. Set in a cool place until required for use. Optional: May be put into a star tube and squeezed out in rosette form.

**Wyeth's English plum pudding**

*James Madison*

*Dorothea Payne Todd Madison*

# James
# MADISON

THE MOST famous hostess the White House has ever had came from the unlikely background of a devout Quaker family. The orderly, quiet routine of her childhood in Virginia and her girlhood in Philadelphia had given her no training in the art of hospitality. Indeed at the time she married James Madison in 1794, as the young widow Todd, with one child, her life and personality seemed already set into the traditional Quaker mold. But the gay, warmhearted Dolley inside the Quaker mold adapted quickly to her new life and loved every minute of it.

During the first years of Dolley's marriage to James Madison, they lived in Philadelphia where he served as Member of Congress from Virginia and was active as the spokesman for the Republican Party. As his hostess Dolley served a demanding social apprenticeship. Madison's home was open for entertainment during the entire Congressional session. Dolley received graciously the great and small of every phase of government as well as distinguished foreign visitors. Hospitality at the Spruce Street house was never limited to political

sympathizers. Madison personally disliked the social atmosphere of a partisan circle and Dolley's non-political background made her feel even more strongly averse to it.

Dolley soon adapted herself to the worldly customs of the new life she was leading. She found herself delighted with the colorful silks, satins, and brocades in which she could now dress. She let her sisters enter conventional society and even allowed the girls to dance. Anna, the sister who made her home with Dolley, was one of the charming belles of the time. Dolley's rare gift of common sense helped her to assume her new role without any outward confusion, despite all the frolics of the gay life in Philadelphia.

Madison retired from Philadelphia at the end of President Washington's administration, and he and Dolley spent the four years of the Adams administration at their home in Virginia. At Montpellier Dolley took over as a competent mistress of the plantation with all its attendant duties. It was a busy, happy life reminiscent of her girlhood days at Scotchtown but it was not destined to last long. With the election of Thomas Jefferson as President, the future of the Madisons was to be spent in the city of Washington.

There the Madisons arrived in May 1802, and the very next day James Madison was sworn in as Secretary of State. Living conditions were difficult in the new city and the Madisons were not able to rent a house that pleased them until they came back from the summer which they spent at Montpellier. They then settled in a comfortable and convenient rented house on F Street, midway between the President's house and the Houses of Congress. Here Dolley remained on call for the social needs of both the President and the Secretary of State.

In 1802 an admirer writes of Dolley "Her smile, her manners are so engaging, that it is no wonder that such a young widow with her fine blue eyes and large share of animation, should be indeed, a Queen of Hearts."

Before long she was the recognized leader of Washington society, described in a diary of that day as "leader of everything fashionable in Washington." Her dominion even extended to the field of fashion as Dolley emerged from her drab Quaker background to become the best dressed woman in Washington. In the small official society the usual entertainments were card playing, dining, and formal visiting. Highlights of the social year were the Dancing Assembly and the horse races. Dolley attended both but, as she never learned to dance, she reigned at the assembly simply by her gracious presence.

At the hospitable home of the Secretary of State on F Street there was always a warm welcome, and usually a circle of charming women and attractive men gathered around the hostess. It was during her first years in Washington that Mrs. Madison began a social career that lasted, with some brief interruptions, for over forty years. She entered into the life of the new capital with enthusiasm, bringing to her task a natural taste for company, tact, charm, good humor, and a young heart. The years as wife of the Secretary of State were happy ones for Dolley, perhaps even happier than those as First Lady with their unavoidable cares and responsibilities.

Madison's dinner table was immortalized by Mrs. Merry, the aggrieved wife of the British Minister, who said it was "more like a harvest home supper than the entertainment of a Secretary of State." To which Dolley replied pleasantly, "The profusion of my table so repugnant to foreign customs arises from the happy circumstance of abundance and prosperity in our country."

The inauguration of President Madison was celebrated with great rejoicing. Salutes of cannons from the Navy Yard and Fort Warburton greeted the day, and troops of militia from the surrounding area assembled in Alexandria and Georgetown, marched to the city, and escorted the President to the Capitol. That night an elegant ball, the first Inaugural Ball in Washington, was held at Davis' Hotel. "Upwards of four hundred persons graced the scene, which was not a little enlivened by the handsome display of female fashion and beauty." Dolley was Queen, resplendent in a gown of buff color velvet, ropes of pearls, and a stylish turban

**Mrs. Madison's china**

which was ornamented with a bird-of-paradise plume.

The Madison administration brought a restoration of some of the protocol and ceremony of the days of Washington and Adams, yet the most lasting impression of White House visitors was not the formality but the easy grace and warmhearted Virginia hospitality that characterized the First Lady's drawing rooms and dinners.

At the crowded Wednesday evening receptions known as "Mrs. Madison's levees," Dolley made a point of greeting everyone. "Sometimes sitting in familiar conversations and sometimes standing or moving from place to place, or, when the levees are full, from room to room," she passed from one delighted guest to another. The fame of her drawing rooms spread throughout the country.

Washington Irving heard of the levees in New York and went to one as soon as he arrived in Washington. Of it he wrote: "In a few minutes I emerged from dirt and darkness into the blazing splendor of Mrs. Madison's drawing room. Here I was most graciously received; found a crowded collection of great and little men, of ugly old women and beautiful young ones, and in ten minutes was hand and glove with half the people in the assemblage. Mrs. Madison is a fine, portly buxom dame, who has a smile and a pleasant word for everybody . . . but as to Jemmy Madison—ah poor Jemmy! —he is but a withered apple-john."

Mrs. Seaton, whose husband was one of the editors of the *National Intelligencer,* described a drawing room she attended in November of 1812: "On Tuesday, William and I repaired to the palace between four and five O'clock, our carriage setting us down after the first comers and before the last. It is customary, on whatever occasion, to advance to the upper end of the room, pay your obeisance to Mrs. Madison, courtesy to His Highness and be taken to a seat. . . .

"The dinner was certainly very fine; but still I was rather surprised as it did not surpass some I have eaten in the Carolina. There were many French dishes and exquisite, I presume, by the praises bestowed on them; but I am so little accustomed to drink, that I could not discern the difference between Sherry and rare old Burgundy Madeira. . . . Ice creams, macaroons, preserves and various cakes are placed on the table which are removed for almonds, raisens, pecan-nuts, apples, pears, etc. Candles were introduced before the ladies left the table; and the gentlemen continued a half-an-hour longer to drink a social glass."

**Madison's state china**

At dinner parties, Mrs. Madison also gracefully took the reins. She presided at the head of the table with guests on her right and left, Madison at the side and his secretary at the foot of the table. This saved him from the effort of serving the guests, drinking wine, and leading the conversation. Again Dolley's social ability smoothed the path of her distinguished husband and her famed conversational abilities assured the success of her parties.

Many stories are told of Mrs. Madison's quickwittedness and ready tact which smoothed the path of many a shy or awkward stranger. Stories have come down even to the present day which prove that much of the secret of Dolley's success lay in the warmth of her heart and the quickness of her perceptions.

Visitors to the capital were expected to leave their cards at the White House. In a letter to a friend Mrs. Madison expressed regrets that some of her Philadelphia friends had not left cards as she wished to invite them to dinner and she did not know where they were staying. She even called at several of the "principal taverns" to try to find them. No friend or acquaintance was neglected; all were asked to the White House and made to feel at home.

Dolley's chief assistant was the steward she was fortunate to acquire directly from his duties at the British Embassy. Jean Pierre Sioussat, born in Paris, made his way in America and eventually ended up in Washington. He became Dolley's most loyal and devoted servant and was an invaluable assistant in keeping the domestic and social life of the administration running smoothly. It was "French John," as he was called by the Negro servants, who was by the side of the First Lady as she hurriedly packed and prepared to leave the White House only hours before the British marched into

Washington in 1814 and burned the Executive Mansion.

With the declaration of the War of 1812, the country was split into many factions. Through it all Dolley's social regime continued unchanged. The usual Wednesday evening levee was held the very evening before war was declared. New Year's Day 1813 was celebrated with the customary reception, and after the inauguration in March a contemporary account relates that the President "was accompanied on his return to the palace by the multitude."

The pleasures of Mrs. Madison's drawing room were immortalized in the message sent to her by the British Admiral in the Chesapeake Bay in 1813 that he "would soon dine in Washington and make his bow in Mrs. Madison's drawing room."

His threat was put into action in August 1814 when the British marched into the city unopposed and fired all the public buildings including the President's House. The First Lady had fled only hours before.

When President and Mrs. Madison returned to Washington after an absence of forty-eight hours, they found the White House a smoking ruin. Thereupon they first occupied the home of the Cutts on F Street, and then moved to the Octagon House. It was while they lived in this attractive house that news came of the signing of the Treaty of Peace at Ghent.

On February 14 the signed treaty was received in Washington. The city went wild with joy. That night the Octagon was ablaze with lights and citizens crowded in regardless of party. Dolley welcomed all impartially; the guests laughed and cried and drank freely; Madison's famous wine stores were put to a severe test. It was a celebration long remembered.

In less than a year the Madisons moved from the celebrated Octagon House to a very much less elegant house at the corner of 19th Street and Pennsylvania Avenue.

It was a house without any privacy, built right on the street. In this small residence the First Lady continued her official entertaining. Her receptions were more crowded than ever, the chief entertainment of Washington society. The greatest of all was the reception the Madisons gave for General Andrew Jackson, the hero of the hour. The guests crowded into the place and crammed it to overflowing. The General in full uniform received the adulation of the crowd.

It was to add to the festivities and provide light for the drawing room that Dolley on this occasion had Negro servants standing before each window holding lighted candles and torches. In this way the crowds assembled in the streets could also enjoy the gaiety within the house. Despite Federalist criticism of the "Egyptian" grandeur, Dolley had again shown a fine consideration of the people over whom she reigned.

It was the last of her elegant parties. In March President James Monroe was inaugurated and the Madisons retired to their estate in Virginia and took up the duties of plantation life.

At her last reception as the President's wife, before the inauguration of the Monroes, Dolley Madison wore a gown of rose-colored satin with a white velvet train that swept the floor for several yards. This she completed with a golden girdle, gold necklace and bracelets, a white velvet turban trimmed with white ostrich tips, and a gold-embroidered crown.

After their retirement the hospitality of Montpellier was Dolley's chief occupation. Everyone traveling in the vicinity of their home stopped casually at the Madisons' and sometimes stayed for days. Ten years after they left Washington Dolley speaks casually of twenty-three house guests at one time as if it was nothing unusual. The usual routine followed by the guests was breakfast at nine, dinner about four, tea at seven, and retiring at ten.

Dinner at Montpellier was an elaborate affair. The food on the table was always luxurious. Food for a party would include three or four kinds of meat, three or four kinds of bread, fresh vegetables, fruit, pastry, champagne and ice.

To a visitor, who once arrived between meals, "wine, ice punch, and delicious pineapples were immediately brought."

The routine of their life changed very little in the 20 years which the Madisons spent together at Montpellier.

After the death of her husband, Dolley came back to Washington to live. Here she took her place in society just as if she had never left the city. In her house on Lafayette Square she received her visitors with the same warm hospitality she had dispensed at the White House. Her house was open to all on New Year's Day and the Fourth of July, and it became the custom for those who attended the official reception at the White House then to cross the square to greet the unofficial leader of Washington society, a custom that continued until she died in that city in 1849.

◀ **Williamsburg pound cake**

▲ **Macaroni soup à la Napeoliatine**

◀ **Madison cakes (rolls)**

# *Favorite Recipes*

## *Macaroni Soup à la Napeoliatine*

*Take a rich shin bone and boil the same in three qts of water and when thoroughly done strain the broth, so as to exclude every particle of meat or bone—then pour the liquor into another vessel and put it in one lb of pure imported Italian maccaroni. Watch the process of cooking carefully and stir the contents of the pot frequently until the liquid is almost entirely absorbed. Then line the inside of your Tureen with the finest and freshest butter and pour the contents of the pot into it. Sprinkle over the whole a quarter of a lb of parmesan cheese grated with the third of a nutmeg. To render the dish worthy of the palate of a Julius Caesar there should be added gravy gathered from the drippings of a roast turkey or in the absence of that admired specimen of the ornithological kingdom an equal amount of the unadulterated juice of roast beef or mutton.*

| | |
|---|---|
| Shinbone of beef or mutton | 1½ cups gravy from roast turkey drippings, or |
| 1 pound macaroni | |
| 1 cup diced celery | 1½ cups juice of roast beef or mutton (unadulterated) |
| ½ cup chopped onion | |
| ¼ cup chopped parsley | |
| ¼ teaspoon nutmeg | |
| ½ pound salt butter | 3 large onions, cut into rings, and fried in butter |
| ¼ pound Parmesan cheese, grated | |

Simmer the shinbone in 3 quarts of water 2 to 3 hours. Remove bone, dice the meat and set it aside. Skim all fat from broth. Bring broth to a boil and put in the macaroni. Watch the process of cooking carefully and stir contents of the pot frequently until the liquid is almost entirely absorbed and the macaroni is tender. This will take 10 to 15 minutes. Now add the celery, onion, parsley, and nutmeg. Line the inside of a casserole with butter and pour the contents of the pot into it. Over the whole sprinkle the grated Parmesan cheese. Add either the turkey gravy or the roast beef or mutton juice. Bake in a moderate oven (350°F) for 20 to 30 minutes.

**Williamsburg pound cake**

Before sending the casserole to the table, cover the top of the mixture with French fried onion rings.

## *Madison Cakes*

| | |
|---|---|
| 2 medium-size white potatoes | 4 tablespoons butter |
| | 2 teaspoons salt |
| 1 yeast cake crumbled over 1 tablespoon granulated sugar | 1 tablespoon sugar |
| | 2 eggs, beaten whole |
| | 6 cups flour |

Boil potatoes well in 1¼ cups boiling water, until tender. Strain, and save 1 cup of the potato water. Mash potatoes into a bowl, add butter, sugar, and salt. When potato-water and potato are cooled to lukewarm, mix dissolved yeast cake in potato-water, and then combine with mashed potato mixture. Beat well. Sift in flour, beating continuously. Knead until smooth and spongy; then return to a well-greased bowl. Cover with a damp tea towel and place away from draft. Let double in bulk for about 3 hours, depending on heat and humidity.

Turn out on a floured board and roll 1-inch thick. Cut into rounds with a biscuit cutter. Place on buttered cookie sheets placed far apart. Let rise until light. Bake at 350°F in moderate oven until golden brown. Brush tops lightly with butter, and serve at once.

## *Williamsburg Pound Cake*

| | |
|---|---|
| 1 pound butter | ½ pound of pitted dates |
| 1 pound granulated sugar | |
| 12 eggs, separated and beaten | 8 large almonds, with skins removed |
| 1 pound flour, sifted twice | honey (for glazing) |

Cream the butter and sugar together. Add the well-beaten yolks and the stiffly beaten whites, and the flour alternately to the sugar and butter mixture. Beat until very light. Pour the mixture into a well-greased and floured round pan, large enough to hold it with about 1 inch left on top. Bake in a moderate oven (325°F) until golden brown. Allow to cool in the pan. When cooled, decorate the top of the cake with the dates and almonds, glazed with honey. The secret of this cake lies in slow, careful baking.

James Monroe

Elizabeth Kortright Monroe

# James
# MONROE

THE NATURAL successor to the Presidency when James Madison left office in 1817 was James Monroe. He had spent forty of his fifty-nine years in the service of his country. As a boy of 19 he had commanded a company of Virginia volunteers during the Revolution. In the years following he served in the United States Senate, as Governor of Virginia, and, at the very important formative period of our country, he was our Minister to England, France, and Spain.

Elizabeth Kortright Monroe had been a belle in New York society in her girlhood. She was only 17 when James Monroe married her in New York City. Her father was a successful merchant who tried to protect his fortune by becoming a Tory during the American Revolution. James Monroe, veteran of the war with a scar to prove it, and member of the Continental Congress, made no reference to his wife's Tory relatives. He was content to present the lovely girl he had married and he let her make her own impression. That the consensus was approval is found in the contemporary account of a fellow Congressman who described her as "the smiling little Venus."

Throughout his long public career James Monroe retained the prerogative of setting the social style for his home and his position, which was faithfully followed by his devoted wife.

During their years abroad the Monroes' oldest daughter, Eliza, spent much of her time at a girls' school near Paris where her closest friend was Hortense Beauharnais, daughter of Josephine, the wife of Napoleon Bonaparte. It was a friendship which lasted a lifetime. The Monroes' youngest daughter was born in Paris and was not brought to her native country until a few years later.

The ceremonies attending the inauguration of President Monroe were held on the unfinished portico of the Capitol for the first time. A journal of the day called the ceremonies "simple but grand, animating and impressive." A reception at the Monroe home followed and the evening ended with an Inaugural Ball attended by the President and his family.

That first spring and summer the White House was not yet ready for occupancy. The Monroes used their own handsome home on I Street in Washington as the Executive Mansion. When the newly furnished White House was ready it was opened to the public for the first time on New Year's Day 1818.

The *National Intelligencer* reports the party in the following words: "The President's House, for the first time since its re-aerification, was thrown open for the general reception of visitors. It was thronged from 12 to 3 O'clock by an unusually large concourse of ladies and gentlemen, among whom were to be found the Senators, Representatives, Heads of Departments, Foreign Ministers and many of our distinguished citizens, residents and strangers. It was gratifying once more to salute the President of the United States with

**Monroe's state china**

the compliments of the season in his appropriate residence and the continuance of this Republican custom has given, as far as we have heard very general satisfaction. The Marine Corps turned out on the occasion and made a very fine appearance."

Mrs. Monroe's long training as a diplomatic hostess and her years in Washington as wife of the Secretary of State had made her admirably fitted for the role of First Lady.

It was becoming evident that, with the increase of congressional representation and the numbers of visitors from home and abroad, the social duties of the White House were growing unmanageable. Almost as soon as the administration began Mrs. Seaton was reporting:

"It is said that the dinner-parties of Mrs. Monroe will be very select. Mrs. Hay, daughter of Mrs. Monroe, returned the visits paid to her mother, making assurances, in the most pointedly polite manner, that Mrs. Monroe will be happy to see her friends morning or evening, but her health is totally inadequate to visiting at present!"

Even the acceptable Margaret Bayard Smith, who had been intimate at the White House during both the Jefferson and Madison administrations, wrote "Although they have lived seven years in Washington both Mr. and Mrs. Monroe are perfect strangers not only to me but to all the citizens." By this she meant to indicate that the city's free and easy social life had come to an end, to the great distress of the Washington social circle.

Another said, "Mr. and Mrs. Monroe's manners will give a tone to all the rest. Few people are admitted to the great house and not a single lady has as yet seen Mrs. Monroe."

It was clear that Mrs. Monroe was not to be tempted to follow in the footsteps of the gregarious Dolley Madison. To make her position even clearer, the Secretary of State for the administration, John Quincy Adams, drew up a code of social etiquette for the First Lady and the White House —a code which, with a few modifications, has governed the social life of the nation's capital from that day.

Under the system outlined, Presidents would receive foreign ministers only at private audiences requested by them, at the drawing room, and at diplomatic dinners once or twice a winter.

The President's wife decided that she would neither pay nor return calls. This was bitterly resented by both the diplomatic corps and the elite of Washington society—but the lady was adamant. At the height of the social struggle, the drawing room of Mrs. Monroe was boycotted. However, social Washington needed the White House more than the White House needed Washington society so it was decided to accept the situation without further struggle. Soon the people returned in droves to the weekly receptions.

The curious crowds which attended were described by one of the less friendly newspapers in the following terms: "In addition to the secretaries, senators, foreign ministers, consuls, auditors, accountants, officers of the Army and Navy of every grade were farmers, merchants, parsons, priests, lawyers, judges, auctioneers and nothingarians, all with their wives and some with their gawky offspring, some in shoes, most in boots and many in spurs; some snuffing, others chewing and many longing for their cigars and whiskey punch at home."

A contemporary account of a dinner at the White House during Monroe administration states: "I think I told you we were to dine at Mrs. Monroe's the day before yesterday. We had the most stylish dinner I had been at. The dishes were silver and so heavy that I could hardly lift them to my mouth and the spoons were very heavy. You would call them clumsy things. Mrs. Monroe is a very elegant woman. She was dressed in a very fine muslin, worked in front, and lined in pink and black velvet. The turban was close and spangled."

It was at this time that Mrs. Edward Livingston said that Mrs. Monroe "looks more beautiful than any woman of her age I ever saw."

Still another account records that "To illumi-

**Gumbo**                     **Mock turtle soup**

nate their drawing room according to her taste she spent $100 per night on wax lights alone and her refreshments and service displayed her foreign culture and French cooking prevailed much to the disgust of many prominent officials."

Mrs. Monroe's oldest daughter, Mrs. Hay, moved with her husband into the White House so that Mrs. Hay could assist her mother with her social duties. The younger daughter, Maria, at 14 was also ready to share in the fun and social life of the President's house. Perhaps the gayest event of the administration was Maria's marriage at the age of 17 to her cousin, Samuel L. Gouverneur of New York, who was one of her father's secretaries. The wedding was conducted in what the local residents called "the New York Style" which apparently referred primarily to the exclusive guest list limited to relatives, the attendant bridesmaids and groomsmen, and a few old friends of the family. One of the bridesmaids wrote to a friend in Philadelphia that the wedding was the most absorbing topic of conversation in the capital.

A drawing room was held at the White House a few days after the wedding to allow society to pay its respects to the bride. It ushered in a round of festivities which was abruptly ended by the death of Commodore Stephen Decatur in a duel only a few days after a delightful ball which the Decaturs had given in honor of the bride and groom. As Mrs. Seaton so aptly put it, "The murder of Decatur . . . will prevent any further attention to the President's family."

The Monroe administration ended in a final burst of glory with the visit of General Lafayette to this country. His formal reception in Washington at the end of 1824 was a spontaneous outburst of affection on the part of the people as well as of the officials of the government. The city of Washington welcomed him with a group of twenty-five young girls who represented the States of the Union and the District of Columbia. The young ladies were uniformly dressed, carried long blue scarfs and wore wreaths of eglantine in their curling hair. The 11-year-old who represented the District of Columbia recited a message of welcome to Lafayette and the General returned the compliment by kissing the hand of each of the young ladies. The White House honored Lafayette with a state dinner and he was also present at the New Year's Day reception in 1825.

When the eight years of the Monroe administration ended, the Monroes were pleased to retire to their beautiful home at Oak Hill in Virginia. The handsome house, erected while the President was in office, had been designed for him by President Thomas Jefferson.

Unfortunately, the Monroes, too, faced financial difficulties. The President even took in a few law students to help with family finances.

The Monroes did not live to enjoy their retirement very long. Within five years Mrs. Monroe died at Oak Hill. This was in 1830. James Monroe then moved to New York to live with his daughter's family. He died at the home of Mrs. Gouverneur a year later on July 4, 1831.

**Monroe's compotes and candelabra**

# Favorite Recipes

## Gumbo

*Cut up two chickens, fry slightly with a little onion and a few slices of pickled pork. Put in 3 to 4 quarts of boiling water, together with pepper, salt, eighteen okras, ½ peck of tomatoes, stew one and a half hours.*

| | |
|---|---|
| 2 spring fryers, cut up (about 4 pounds) | peeled, diced, fresh tomatoes |
| 1½ pounds of fresh or frozen, sliced okra | 1 teaspoon salt |
| | coarse black pepper |
| 1 large onion, chopped | 2 to 3 tablespoons flour |
| 5 tablespoons bacon drippings, or half butter and half lard | 2 cups water |
| | 3 stalks celery with tops |
| | 1 bay leaf |
| 2 No. 2 cans solid-pack tomatoes, or 5 cups | ½ teaspoon basil |
| | 1 cup rice |

Put the chicken giblets in cold water with celery, bay leaf, basil, salt and pepper to taste, and add backs and necks. Simmer gently while preparing the gumbo. In a paper bag, put flour, salt, and coarse black pepper. Shake up the chicken pieces, a few at a time, until each piece is well covered with the flour and seasoning mixture. Fry in fat in heavy skillet until brown and transfer to a soup kettle; do not use iron, as the okra will discolor the entire dish and turn it an unappetizing gray. Next add the onions to the fat and brown until clear over low heat. Add several tablespoons flour to make a roux. Strain the broth from the giblets over this, stir well, and pour over chicken. Add tomatoes and okra, and simmer over low heat for about 2 hours. Rectify seasonings. Serve in soup plate over mounds of fluffy rice. Serves 8 to 10.

## Mock Turtle Soup

*One pint of black beans soaked overnight in four quarts of water, two onions, one large carrot grated, half pound of fresh beef, half pound of pork; boil all day. When ready for dinner strain through a colander in a tureen; add one wineglass of port wine or not according to fancy, one hard boiled egg, one lemon slice.*

| | |
|---|---|
| 1 pint black beans | pod |
| 4 quarts cold water | salt |
| ½ pound of beef plus one shinbone | coarse black pepper to taste |
| ½ pound salt pork | 1 wineglass port |
| 2 onions, chopped | 3 hard cooked eggs, sliced |
| 2 carrots, grated | |
| 1 small red pepper | 12 thin slices of lemon |

Pick over beans, add water, and soak overnight. Add meat, vegetables, and seasonings and simmer about 4 to 5 hours. Remove meat. When cool, dice the beef and return to kettle. Puree soup through a colander, add port, and reheat. This will make at least 12 cups or plates. Serve with a slice of egg and a slice of lemon in each cup or plate.

*Louisa Catherine Johnson Adams*

# John Quincy
# ADAMS

Perhaps never in the history of the White House have a President and First Lady moved into the mansion who were more practiced in politics and more experienced in the duties of official social life than President John Quincy Adams and his wife Louisa. John Quincy Adams' public career began at the age of 11 when he accompanied his father on a diplomatic mission to Europe. In France he met for the first time his future wife, then a little girl of 4. Louisa Catherine Johnson was a London-born American, the child of a British mother and a father from Maryland. Joshua Johnson had gone to England to represent the Maryland tobacco planters in the commercial market and there he had met and married his British wife. Because of the Revolutionary War, the Johnsons moved to France, where Congress asked him to act as bookkeeper for accounts of Americans traveling abroad on official business.

Through this official connection, John Quincy Adams was in and out of the Johnson home until he returned to America to complete his education

at Harvard. When in 1795 he renewed the acquaintance in London he was a full-fledged diplomat.

John Quincy Adams had just been appointed American Minister to the Court of Prussia in 1797 when he and Louisa were married in London. Their married life began with Adams engaged in official business for his country and Louisa acting as its official hostess. This pattern continued without change until they arrived at the White House.

In the interim they had lived in Washington, in St. Petersburg, and in London—always in the role of public servants, a role which they performed gracefully and with competence.

On their return to Washington in 1817 for John Quincy Adams to accept the position of Secretary of State under President Monroe, they were well equipped for Washington social life.

For the eight years that John Quincy Adams was Secretary of State, Louisa was a leading hostess in Washington society. Surrounded by numerous members of her own family who already lived in Washington her drawing rooms on her "Tuesday evenings" were a pleasant combination of American hospitality and cosmopolitan sophistication. In her home on F Street she provided a dignified background for her husband and a comfortable home for her children.

The Adams home became a rendezvous for young and old, for diplomatic and political circles, and the "era of good feeling" became a reality in the drawing room as well as the conference room.

Louisa was an excellent hostess. As she had

lived in France until she was 7, French was for her a second mother tongue. She loved music and played both the harp and the spinet. Her appreciation of the arts—sketching, music, and literature —was above average and her letters and writings could rival those of her brilliant mother-in-law, Abigail Adams.

The home of the Secretary of State was the scene of a most unusual and elegant ball in January of 1824. The guest of honor was General An-

**Baked codfish pie**                    **Chowder**                    **Chicken croquettes**

drew Jackson who had lately come to Washington as Senator from the State of Tennessee. The occasion was the anniversary of the Battle of New Orleans. It was an event of significance as the courtly recognition of the Secretary of State helped to advance the personal ambitions of his political rival, Jackson. Ultimately the two men became the bitterest of personal and political enemies. But for that night they stood side by side, host and honored guest, in the house on F Street. Eight rooms of the house were stripped of superfluous furniture and elaborately decorated for the party with tissue paper and evergreens. The floor of the ballroom was chalked with pictures and slogans—eagles, flags, and "Welcome to the Hero of New Orleans." Festoons of laurel and wintergreen bedecked the ceiling and the lamps were decorated with evergreens and wreaths of artificial roses. An eight-piece orchestra provided music for dancing. Mrs. Adams received her guests resplendent in a gown of steel-colored llama cloth with cut-steel ornamentation. Her husband in his blue nankeen

**John Quincy Adams' state china**

seemed plain and undistinguished in the glittering assemblage of military and diplomatic uniforms. It was a gay and brilliant occasion, the most ambitious and successful party given in Washington up to that time, and it was the most talked of affair in the city. The occasion was even commemorated in a lengthy poem which was published in the *National Journal* and widely quoted:

"Wend your way with the world tonight?

Belles and matrons, maids and madames
All are gone to Mrs. Adams'. . . ."

The bitterness of the political campaign in which President John Quincy Adams was elected, plus the fact that General Jackson forced him into a campaign for the next election as soon as he was inaugurated, helped to keep to a minimum the social life of the administration of President John Quincy Adams.

President Adams' life in the Executive Mansion was as close an approximation to his previous existence as he could arrange. He rose at five A.M., went for a walk or a swim, read his Bible, wrote letters or in his diary, had breakfast, met with his Cabinet, ate dinner with his family and guests, wrote, read, counseled and enjoyed his sons, and retired as early as he could excuse himself. His geniality in private life is attested to by none other than Martin Van Buren who said, "In a small and agreeable party, he was one of the most entertaining table companions of his day."

Louisa continued to play her role as hostess with her usual capability. She made it a rule that no one, friend or enemy, should be excluded from the White House drawing room. It became necessary to issue cards of admission for the large receptions to control any possible drunken revelry, but men and women of every party were welcomed. Louisa, standing in a circle of Cabinet ladies, received all without question. Her background and experience of official life at European courts had fitted her well for the role of First Lady.

She held the usual weekly levees and served refreshments to the guests in attendance. Everyone assembled at 8 o'clock and all had retired by 11. Music, dancing, pleasant conversation, and card playing enlivened these evening receptions.

A distinguished visitor was honored at the White House early in the Adams' occupancy. The aged Lafayette had arrived in 1824. He was still present in 1825 when his long-time friend took the oath as President of the United States. Lafayette stayed in the White House for a short visit, then he and President Adams journeyed together to Montpellier to visit aging James Madison. When finally Lafayette was ready to return to France, the United States fitted out for his personal use a frigate which President Adams named the "Brandywine," and Adams himself was "launched" in it at the Navy Yard.

The final parting between the President and

the General was like that of father and son. Louisa had given a splendid farewell dinner which was followed by the good-byes on the portico of the White House. Lafayette and Adams embraced many times. Lafayette, in tears, recalled the beginnings of their friendship, when John Quincy as a small boy had accompanied his father to France; the President recalled, for all, the bravery and assistance of Lafayette during the days of the American Revolution. Then the Frenchman kissed Mrs. Adams' hand, bade a fond farewell to the younger members of the family, and finally entered his carriage. The bald-headed, sturdy Adams stood on the portico waving until the carriage disappeared from sight.

Josiah Quincy of Massachusetts, who visited Washington in the winter of 1826, tells of a state dinner of forty covers he attended at the White House which was "very splendid and rather stiff."

There is one thing of which we can be sure, and that is that the food was Continental in flavor as the Adams were accompanied to the White House by the French chef Michael Anthony Guista, who had been a devoted member of the Adams family since he joined their menage in Amsterdam in the year 1814.

The White House years brought sorrows as well as joys. On July 4, 1826, the aged John Adams, father and mentor of the President, died at his home in Quincy. Louisa's health was poor for much of the administration with one long illness of weeks in bed and sleepless nights while John Quincy read to her by the hour. But before the end of the administration she was up and about again. Her family needed her, so she got well.

Perhaps the most joyous event of the administration was the White House wedding in February 1828. John Adams, Jr., who acted as private secretary for his father, had courted his cousin Mary Hellen for several years, with a bit of teasing competition from his older brother, George. John's suit was brought to a happy ending with their wed-

**John Quincy Adams family china**

ding which took place in the Blue Room. An account of the gay affair has been left for us by another young member of the Adams family who was visiting from Boston. She says that "the Bride looked handsome in white satin, orange blossoms and pearls." The four bridesmaids, one of whom was the chronicler, Abigail, and the groomsmen hung garlands of flowers and ribbons in the circular room. The day after the wedding everyone assembled in what Miss Abigail called "the yellow room" for a ball at which even the austere President unbent to join in the family fun and dancing. "The Virginia Reel" was specifically mentioned as one of the dances enjoyed by the guests.

Again, on a day late in December 1828 the mansion of the President of the United States presented a scene of unusual brilliancy. In the great audience chamber, musicians played gay airs while the dancers enjoyed the fine floor and excellent music. Louisa was present, never more charming; her ability as a hostess never more plainly demonstrated. Instead of receiving in the usual fixed circle of Cabinet ladies, Louisa passed from group to group pleasantly welcoming her guests. The President stood in the audience chamber taking the formal bows. It was a ball to celebrate their departure from the White House. The popular Andrew Jackson had won the election and Adams had become the second member of his family to fail in his bid to succeed himself.

Of this party, that fascinating but prejudiced chronicler of Washington society, Mrs. Samuel Harrison Smith, wrote: "At Mrs. Adams' drawing-room last week everyone attached to the Administration as well as members of the Cabinet appeared with their best looks and best dresses. Mrs. Adams never on any other former occasion was so social, attentive and agreeable. Instead of standing in one place, making formal courtesies, she walked through the rooms conversing with everyone in the most animated manner. To add to the gaiety and brilliancy of the evening, the great audience chamber was lit up, the band of music stationed there and dancing took place. Most people think this was going rather too far. To appear cheerful would be consistent with dignity and self-respect. But as one of the members observed they meant to march out with flying colors and all the honors of war!"

The Adams left the White House to begin a life which Louisa hopefully believed and John Quincy bitterly expected to be one of complete retirement from public activities. It did not last long. For John Quincy Adams soon returned to Washington as Congressman from his home district in Massachusetts. In that capacity he served seventeen years, and life assumed a pleasant routine of Washington in the winter and Quincy in the summer, surrounded by their family and congenial friends. Louisa was at the side of her husband when he died in the Capitol Building in 1848 from the effect of a stroke which felled him while he was on the floor of the House of Representatives. She remained the elegant hostess and devoted wife all her life.

## *Favorite Recipes*

### *Chicken Croquettes*

| | |
|---|---|
| 2 to 3 cups of cooked chicken, cold | 1 teaspoon mustard |
| 3 to 4 slices of ham, cold | 1 tablespoon catsup |
| 2 cups grated stale bread or bread crumbs | ⅛ pound of butter |
| salt and pepper | 1 egg yolk, beaten |
| grated nutmeg | drippings, for frying |
| | parsley sprigs for garnishing |
| | radish roses for garnishing |

Take cold fowl or cooked meat of any kind, with slices of ham, fat and lean, and chop them together very fine. Add half as much stale bread grated, or bread crumbs, salt, pepper, grated nut-

Chicken croquettes

meg, mustard, catsup, and butter. Knead all together well till it resembles sausage meat. Make the mixture into cakes of the desired size, dip them in the yolk of an egg, beaten, cover them thickly with the rest of the grated bread, or bread crumbs, and fry them in drippings till they are light brown. Serve hot, garnished with sprigs of parsley and radish roses.

## Baked Codfish Pie

| | |
|---|---|
| 1 large codfish | ¼ cup chopped parsley |
| stale bread, grated, | grated nutmeg |
| or bread crumbs, | pepper, to taste |
| double the | 1 teaspoon mustard |
| quantity of the | butter, melted |
| fish | piecrust dough |
| milk, heated | |

Soak the fish, boil it, and take off the skin. Pick the meat from the bones, and mince it very fine. Take double the quantity of your fish of grated stale bread, put into a large bowl and pour over it as much fresh milk, boiling hot, as will wet it completely; add parsley, nutmeg, pepper, and mustard, with as much melted butter as will make it sufficiently rich, the quantity of butter to be determined by that of the other ingredients. Beat all these together very well, add the minced fish, mix it all, cover the bottom of the baking dish with piecrust paste. Pour the fish in, cover the top with more of the piecrust dough and bake in a hot oven (425°F) until well browned, about 45 minutes.

## Fish Chowder

| | |
|---|---|
| ½ pound salt pork | sliced potatoes, raw |
| 1 onion, sliced | 1 tablespoon butter |
| large fresh cod or | 1 tablespoon flour |
| haddock | ¼ cup chopped parsley |
| pepper, to taste | 1½ pints cold water |
| biscuits, or crackers, | |

Take the salt pork, and having half-boiled it, cut it into strips, and with some of them cover the bottom of a 3-quart pot. Next strew on the sliced onion. Have ready a large fresh cod, or an equal quantity of haddock, or any other firm fish.

Cut the fish into large pieces, and lay part of it on the pork and onions. Season with pepper. Then cover it with a layer of biscuits or crackers that have been previously soaked in milk or water.

**Chowder**

You may add also a layer of sliced potatoes. Next proceed with a second layer of pork, onions, fish, etc., and continue as before until the pot is almost full, finishing with soaked crackers on top. Pour in the cold water. Cover it close, and allow to simmer for 1 hour. Then skim it, and turn it out into a deep dish. Leave the gravy in the pot till you have thickened it with 1 tablespoon butter rolled into 1 tablespoon flour, and some chopped parsley. Then give it one boil-up, and pour it hot into the dish.

## Clam Chowder

| | |
|---|---|
| 1 quart shucked | 2 tablespoons butter |
| clams | 2 tablespoons flour |
| 1 quart whole milk | |

Chowder may be made of clams, first cutting off the hard part of 1 quart of shucked clams. Strain clam liquor. After simmering chowder 15 minutes, add 1 quart whole milk, and set aside to ripen. Reheat and thicken with 1 to 2 tablespoons butter rolled in equal parts of flour.

*Andrew Jackson*

*Rachel Donelson Robards Jackson*

# Andrew JACKSON

THE too often accepted picture of Andrew Jackson as the uncouth, illiterate frontiersman is belied by the elegant home, the Hermitage, which he built for his beloved wife in Tennessee. It is forgotten that this was a man who had studied law and been admitted to the North Carolina bar before he came to Tennessee at the age of 21. Although he had been born in comparative poverty, after the death of his widowed mother he was left to live with people of distinction, who provided the boy with a home in the midst of a prosperous and cultured Southern family.

Andrew Jackson came into Tennessee territory as the State's Attorney for North Carolina and settled in 1788 in the Nashville community. Here he met the attractive young Rachel Donelson Robards. Rachel was at the time living at home with her mother to escape the insane jealousy of her husband, Lewis Robards, who remained in Kentucky. Despite the honest efforts for reconciliation made by Rachel, Robards advised her that he was going to get a divorce. A year later in 1791 she married the energetic young lawyer who lived in the same community as her mother. They were an ideal couple with a love and devotion that lasted for all the thirty-seven years of their life together. Unfortunately they had neglected to check on the divorce proceedings before their marriage and they found that no divorce had actually been granted. This made Rachel technically guilty of bigamy. Another marriage was performed in 1794 after the Kentucky divorce was granted but the unusual aspects of the Jacksons' marriage were to haunt Andrew Jackson's political future.

Jackson was soon established in the Nashville area as a man of affairs. His energy and ambition had involved him in the multifarious activities incidental to practicing law, holding public office, cultivating a farm, and operating a general store. Before 1800 he had served in both the House of Representatives and the Senate of the United States. Then he became judge of the Superior Court and at the same time major-general of the state militia. In 1804 Jackson met severe financial reverses and retired from public life to recoup his fortune.

60

He had again established himself financially when he was called into active military duty with the Tennessee Militia. This was the beginning of a successful military career which culminated in Jackson's being appointed a Major-General in the United States Army and, during the War of 1812, in the victory of the United States troops under his command in the Battle of New Orleans.

The Battle of New Orleans brought Jackson national fame and the adulation of the American people. There began to converge on his home in Tennessee great numbers of friends, admirers, and casual visitors who were passing through the neighborhood. The Hermitage became the goal of everyone of prominence who came into its vicinity. It is from these days that we get the first accounts of the generous hospitality of General and Mrs. Jackson.

One of Andrew Jackson's neighbors said of the General that he was "the prince of hospitality" not only because he entertained a great many people but because the poor, belated peddler was as welcome at the Hermitage as was the President of the United States and put so much at his ease that he felt as though he had at last got home. Thus was Jackson celebrated by his neighbors for his hospitality in a country where hospitality was a common virtue.

An early visitor to the Hermitage has left us his observation concerning Jackson, the host: "Had we not seen General Jackson before we would have taken him for a visitor, not the host of the mansion. He greeted us cordially and bade us feel at home, but gave us distinctly to understand that he took no trouble to look after any but his lady guests. As for the gentlemen, there were the parlor, the dining-room, the library, the sideboard and its refreshments, there were the servants; and if anything was wanting all that was necessary was to ring. He was as good as his word. He did not sit at the head of the table, but mingled with his guests, and always preferred a seat between two ladies obviously seeking a chair between different ones at various times. He was very easy and graceful in his attentions; free and often playful, and always dignified and earnest in his conversation."

As on most Southern plantations, all foodstuffs except coffee and tea were grown on the place. Among the references to food at the Hermitage we find that barbecued pig was the feature of a dinner given there for the notorious Peggy O'Neill Eaton and her husband, Major John Eaton, in 1830.

In 1819 President James Monroe visited the old log Hermitage while he was on a presidential tour. General Jackson had gone to Augusta, Georgia, to act as his official host on the journey to Nashville. The President and his party stopped at the Hermitage for two days.

But perhaps the most famous guest of the Hermitage in the days before Jackson became President was General Lafayette. The two generals had met in Washington in 1824 and in fact had lived in the same boarding house in Washington. Lafayette had promised that he would not leave the country without having an opportunity to express to Andrew Jackson in person his "high regard and sincere friendship." After his official visit in Nashville the party boarded the steamboat there and proceeded up the river to the Hermitage to have dinner with General Jackson. Dinner in those days was a big meal served about 3 o'clock in the afternoon. Lafayette's secretary left an interesting account of the visit: "At one o'clock we embarked, with a numerous company, to proceed to dine with General Jackson whose residence is a few miles up the river. We there found numbers of ladies and farmers from the neighborhood whom Mrs. Jackson had invited to partake of the entertainment she had prepared for General Lafayette. The first thing that struck me on arriving at the General's was the extreme simplicity of his house. Still somewhat influenced by my European habits, I asked myself if this could really be the dwelling of the most popular man in the United States, of him whom the country proclaimed one of her most illustrious defenders; of him, finally who by the will of the people was on the point of becoming her chief magistrate."

The guest was at the home only a few hours as he had to return to Nashville for the grand banquet given in his honor that night.

It was said that during the campaign for the Presidency the Hermitage was more like a hotel than a home, "so numerous were the guests whom curiosity, friendship and political business" had brought there.

Jackson had become the man of the people and as their champion he rode into the office of the Presidency of the United States in 1828. Unfortunately the campaign had been bitter and vicious, and the account of the irregularities in the marriage of the Jacksons became a campaign weapon in the hands of the General's opposition. After the General's election Rachel faced her life in Washington with misgivings yet prepared bravely for

**Burnt cream**    **Pease pudding**    **Savory jelly**    **Roast leg of pork**

the move. Unfortunately she did not live to get
to Washington. In December she died of a heart
attack brought on, the General believed, by the
slanders of the campaign.

Though Rachel Jackson never entered the
President's House as its First Lady and mistress,
it is doubtful if the wife of any other President
ever exerted so powerful an influence over an
administration in life as she did in death. In death
she became the tutelary saint of the White House.
Wherever the President went he wore her miniature. No matter what the duties or pleasures of
the day may have been, when the President came
to his room, Rachel's Bible and her picture kept

him company. From the hour of her death Andrew
Jackson seemed motivated by a desire to avenge
her wrongs and to honor her memory. Probably
in few administrations have personal feelings had
so much to do with official appointments.

The "lovely Emily" Donelson, niece of Mrs.
Jackson and wife of Andrew Jackson Donelson,
Mrs. Jackson's nephew and adopted son, together
with Mrs. Andrew Jackson, Jr., the wife of another
adopted son, shared the social honors of the
administration.

The President solved the delicate problem of
precedence between the ladies by telling Mrs.
Jackson, "You, my dear, are mistress of the Her-

mitage and Emily is hostess of the White House."
In reading his letters one gets the feeling that he
considered it more of an honor to preside at the
Hermitage as successor to his beloved Rachel than
to be First Lady of the White House. However
after 1836 Sarah Yorke Jackson had an opportunity to act as First Lady when Emily had to return
to Tennessee ill with tuberculosis and died there
that same year.

Probably the most unrestrained White House
reception in history followed upon the inauguration ceremonies of President Jackson on March 4,
1829. The mansion had been thrown open to the
immense throng of people who had come to the
city to see their hero sworn into office. The dignity
of the occasion disappeared under the pressure of
the rabble, a mob of "boys, Negroes, women and
children, scrabbling, fighting, romping." It was
said that damage amounting to several thousand
dollars was done to the glass and china in the
crush to reach the refreshments. It finally became
necessary to carry out the punch and food in tubs
and buckets to supply the crowd estimated at
20,000 persons. One contemporary description continues: "But had it been in hogsheads it would
have been insufficient ice creams and cakes and
lemonade. . . . Ladies fainted, men were seen with
bloody noses and such a scene of confusion took
place as is impossible to describe—those who got
in could not get out by the door again but had
to scramble out by the windows." Eventually even
the President had to escape from his admirers
through the kitchen of the house.

After the wedding of Andrew Jackson, Jr.,
and Sarah Yorke in Philadelphia, they had come
to Washington where they were received with delight by the members of the family at the White
House. A family letter says: "In the first place
there was a large dining given to them of about
forty persons, the Cabinet and the diplomatic corps
—The dinner party were invited at 5 O'clock and
at 8, three hundred were invited to spend the
evening—We had all the fashion in the city—
the band of music and dancing—the party was
very brilliant and everything went off well."

There is a charming account of an evening at
the White House in the early part of the Jackson
administration.

"The large parlor was scantily furnished; there
was light from the chandelier and a blazing fire
in the grate; four or five ladies sewing around it;
Mrs. Donelson, Mrs. Andrew Jackson, Jr., Mrs.
Edward Livingston. Five or six children were

playing about, regardless of documents or work
baskets. At the farther end of the room sat the
President, in his arm chair, wearing a long, loose
coat, and smoking a long reed pipe, with bowl of
red clay—combining the dignity of the patriarch,
monarch and Indian chief. Just behind was Edward
Livingston, the Secretary of State, reading a dis-
patch from the French Minister for Foreign Affairs. The ladies glance admiringly, now and then,
at the President, who listens, waving his pipe
toward the children when they become too
boisterous."

During the Jackson administration, huge-scale
invitations to the White House made their debut.
Besides holding general levees, President Jackson
staged invitation receptions attended by as many
as 1,000 persons. At these affairs, a lavish supper,
prepared by the French chef, Michael Anthony
Guista, was provided.

Jessie Benton, daughter of Senator Thomas
Hart Benton, described one of these "great supper
partees" she attended at the White House during
the Jackson administration:

"I have the beautiful recollection of the whole
stately house adorned and ready for the company
—the great wood fires in every room, the immense
number of wax lights softly burning, the stands
of camellias and laurentia banked row upon row.
After going through all this silent waiting fairy-
land, we were taken to the state dining room where
was the gorgeous supper table shaped like a horseshoe, covered with every good and glittering thing
French skill could devise, and at either end a
monster salmon in waves of meat jelly."

Perhaps the most vivid description of the
White House during the Jackson administration
was left for us by Harriet Martineau, the English
journalist and social reformer, who visited Wash-

**Emily Donelson**                    **Sarah Yorke Jackson**

ington in the winter of 1834-1835:

"One of the most remarkable sights in the country is the President's levee. Nothing is easier than to laugh at it. There is probably no mode in which a number of human beings can assemble which may not be laughable from one point of view or another. The President's levee presents many facilities for ridicule. Men go there in plaid cloaks and leather belts, with all manner of wigs, and offer a large variety of obeisance to the chief magistrate. Women go in bonnets and shawls, talk about the company, stand upon chairs to look over people's heads and stare at the large rooms. There was a story of two girls, thus dressed, being lifted up by their escorting gentlemen and seated on the two ends of the mantel-piece, like lustres, where they could obtain a view of the company as they entered. To see such people mixed in with foreign ambassadors and their suites, to observe the small mutual knowledge of classes and persons who thus meet on terms of equality, is amusing enough. But, amidst much that was laughable, I certainly felt that I was seeing a fine spectacle. If the gentry of Washington desire to do away with the custom, they must be unaware of the dignity which resides in it and which is apparent to the eyes of a stranger, through any inconvenience which it may have. I am sorry that the practice of distributing refreshments is relinquished; though this is a matter of less importance and of more inconvenience. If the custom itself should ever be given up, the bad taste of such a surrender will be unquestionable. There should be some time and place where the chief magistrate and the people may meet to exchange their respects, all other business being out of the question: and I should like to see the occasion made annual again.

"I saw no bad manners at the President's levee, except on the part of a silly, swaggering English-man. All was quiet and orderly; and there was an air of gaiety which rather surprised me. The great people were amused at the aspect of the assembly: and the humbler at the novelties that were going on before their eyes. Our party went at eight o'clock. As we alighted from the carriage, I saw a number of women well attended going up the steps in the commonest morning walking-dress. In the hall, were parties of young men, exhibiting their graces in a walk from end to end: and ladies throwing off their shawls, and displaying the most splendid dresses. The President, with some members of his cabinet on either hand, stood in the middle of the first room, ready to bow to all ladies and shake hands with all the gentlemen who presented themselves. The company then passed on to the fire-place, where stood the ladies of the President's family attended by the Vice President and the Secretary of the Treasury. From this point, the visitors dispersed themselves through the rooms, chatting in groups in the Blue-room or joining the immense promenade in the great East Room. After two circuits there, I went back to the reception room; by far the most interesting to the observer. I saw one ambassador after another enter with his suite; the Judges of the Supreme Court; the majority of the members of both Houses of Congress; and intermingled with these, the plainest farmers, storekeepers and mechanics with their primitive wives and simple daughters. Some looked merry; some looked busy, but none bashful. I believe there were three thousand persons present. There was one deficiency—one drawback, as I felt at the time. There were no persons of colour. Whatever individuals or classes may choose to do about selecting their society according to rules of their own making, here there should be no distinction. I know the pleas that would be urged. The levee being held in a slave district; the presence of slave-holders from the south; and many others; but such pleas will not stand before the plain fact that this levee is the appointed means by which citizens of the United States of all degrees may, once in a time, meet together to pay their equal respects to their chief magistrate. Every man of colour who is a citizen of the United States has a right to as free an admission as any other man; and it would be a dignity added to the White House if such were seen there."

After his second term of office President Jackson retired to the Hermitage in Tennessee in 1837. Here he lived comfortably with his adopted son and daughter-in-law, Mr. and Mrs. Andrew Jackson, Jr., and their family of children. The constant stream of visitors began anew and young Mrs. Jackson proved as equal to the duties of dispensing the hospitality of the mansion as had Rachel in the days before the Presidency.

When a regiment of Texas volunteers arrived 900 strong to pay their respects to the General, sheep, beeves, and chickens from the plantation were hastily prepared for the unexpected guests, in such quantity that every fireplace on the plantation was pressed into service and a wagonload of bread had to be purchased in Nashville as the Hermitage ovens could not bake that much bread on short notice.

# Favorite Recipes

## Roast Leg of Pork

*Skin the pork, then place it in water for one hour. Throw off the first water. Wipe the pork perfectly dry and put it on a spit. Set it before a clear steady fire. Sprinkle some salt on it and, when it becomes hot, baste it for a time with salt and water. Then put a good spoonful of lard into the dripping pan and when melted continue to baste with it. When the meat has been cooking this way for sometime, but before it begins to look brown, cover it with paper and baste on it, and when it is partly done take off the paper, dredge it with flour, turn the spit for a few minutes very quick and baste all the time to raise a froth, after which it is ready to serve.*

| | |
|---|---|
| 1 leg of pork weighing 8-10 pounds | freshly ground white pepper |
| 2 pints beer | a few peppercorns, black or white |
| 1 cup light brown sugar | ½ teaspoon ground sage |
| 10 long young sprigs of broccoli | 2 white cloves, whole |
| a little butter, melted | 1 small piece of root ginger |
| salt | 1 level teaspoon cornstarch |

Skin the leg of pork and put it in a large deep crock. Crush the ginger root; add it to the beer, with the whole cloves and ground sage, salt, pepper, and peppercorns. Warm this mixture gently for a few minutes; then pour it over the pork. Cover and leave to marinate for 24 hours in a cool place. During this period, turn the pork over once. Remove and place pork on a roasting rack over a fairly deep roasting pan. Strain over the pork the juices it has been marinating in and roast in a preheated oven (350°F) for 3½ to 4 hours, basting every 20 minutes. Each time it is basted, add ¼ cup cold water. About ¾ of an hour before it is roasted, pour off 1 cup of the juices and mix in the brown sugar. Carefully cover the top of the leg with this mixture and it will give it a beautiful glaze. Now, carefully slice ten very thin slices of the pork and set them aside, keeping them hot. When the pork is done, arrange on a hot, flat platter. Mix the cornstarch with a little cold water, add it to the pan juices, and stir well. Reheat and strain a little of this gravy over the pork. Serve the rest in a sauceboat. Cover the bone on the leg with a large paper frill, and garnish the dish as follows:

Put the sprigs of broccoli in the boiling salted water and cook until only just soft. They must retain their bright green color and be a little crisp. Drain them carefully, and sprinkle them with a little diced sage and melted butter. Make large cornucopias out of the thin slices of pork and place in each a cooked sprig of broccoli; garnish around the leg of pork.

## Pease Pudding (Pea Pudding or Pea Puree)

*Get small, delicate peas, work them well, and tie them in a cloth, allowing a little room for swelling, boil them with some pork, then mash and season them, tie them up again and finish boiling it, take care not to break the pudding in turning it out of the cloth onto a dish.*

| | |
|---|---|
| 1 pound dried peas | 2 ounces of butter |
| the skin from the leg of pork | 1 level teaspoon nutmeg |
| 1 onion stocked with 2 cloves | ½ cup sour cream |
| 1 small carrot | salt, sugar, freshly ground white pepper, to taste |
| 2 pieces of celery | |

Put the dried peas in a large deep bowl. Cover with cold water and leave in a cool place overnight. Strain, and pour over more fresh cold water. Strain again, and put them into a large deep kettle, together with the skin from the leg of pork, cover with cold water so that the water comes up above the peas about 2 inches. Bring very slowly to a boil and carefully remove all the skin. Add the onion, carrot, celery, and the nutmeg and season with 2 teaspoons salt, 1 teaspoon white pepper, and 1 teaspoon sugar. Simmer all this together slowly until the peas are very soft and also have absorbed all the water. Stir frequently. Put all through a fine strainer. Then beat in the butter and sour cream and correct the seasoning. Arrange in a flat dish, and serve with the pork.

## Savory Jelly (Meat Jelly)

| | |
|---|---|
| 6 cups strong chicken and beef stock (cold and free from fat) | 3 egg whites, beaten |
| | 2 tablespoons tomato paste |
| 1 cup port wine | 5 packages of plain gelatin |
| ½ cup dark sweet sherry | salt |
| ¼ cup red currant jelly | freshly ground black pepper |

Put the stock into a large tin-lined saucepan of stainless steel with the port wine, sherry, currant jelly, tomato paste, gelatin, salt and pepper to taste, and the egg whites beaten to soft peaks. Over a slow fire beat with a large whisk until mixture comes to a rolling boil. Draw aside at once, and allow it to stand without moving for 15 minutes. Now line a cheap strainer or colander with a cloth which has been wrung out in cold water, and slowly and carefully pour the jelly through this cloth, taking extreme care not to allow any of the egg white to get into the strained clear jelly. Then cool. Rinse out a fancy jelly mold with cold water —large enough so that there is a rim of about ½ an inch when the jelly has been poured into the mold. (Measure ahead of time!) Now pour in the jelly and put to set in the refrigerator. To unmold, first slide a thin-blade pointed knife around the edge of the mold. Then turn it upside down on a well-chilled, round flat dish. Rub the top of the mold with a hot damp cloth, and carefully lift up the mold.

### Burnt (Custard) Cream

*Boil a quart of milk, and when cold mix with the yolks of eight eggs, stir them together over the fire a few minutes, sweeten it to your taste, put some slices of savory cake in the bottom of a deep dish and pour on the custard; whip the whites of the eggs to a strong froth, lay it lightly on the top, sift some sugar over it and hold a salamander over it until it is a light brown; garnish the top with raspberry marmalade, or any kind of preserved fruit.*

| | |
|---|---|
| 6 eggs, separated | 12 tablespoons coarse |
| 2 cups light cream | granulated sugar |
| 8 heaping tablespoons | 2 teaspoons almond |
| confectioners' | extract |
| sugar | |

Add 6 heaping tablespoons of the superfine sugar to the egg yolks and beat until very light and creamy. Scald the cream with the almond extract and mix it into the beaten egg yolk mixture. Mix thoroughly. Pour into a round deep earthenware dish which is large enough so that the cream comes about ½ an inch from the top of the dish. Stand the dish in a shallow pan half filled with hot water, and put to set in a 300°F oven for 1 hour. Remove and cool a little. Now beat the egg whites to soft peaks and slowly add the coarse granulated sugar, beating all the time, and continue to beat until it is thick and holds its shape. Cover the dish with this meringue and pile it up so that it comes up

1½ inches above the dish. Set the rest of the meringue into a pastry bag with a small rose tube and decorate the side of the dish only. Sprinkle the top with what is left of the confectioners' sugar and put to set in a 325°F oven for 10 to 15 minutes. Get a skewer red hot and make criss-cross markings on the meringue. Serve hot.

**Blanc mange**

### Blanc Mange

*Break one ounce of isinglass into very small pieces; wash it well, and pour on a pint of boiling water; next morning, add a quart of milk, boil it till the isinglass is dissolved, strain it, put in two ounces sweet almonds, blanched and pounded; sweeten it, and put it in the mould—when stiff, turn them into a deep dish, and put raspberry cream around them. For a change, use other flavorings.*

| | |
|---|---|
| 1 cup blanched | ½ cup sugar |
| almonds | 1 drop almond extract |
| 2 cups water | 2 tablespoons kirsch |
| 1½ tablespoons gelatin | (optional) |
| ¼ cup cold water | candied cherries, for |
| 1 cup cream | garnish |

Make 2 cups almond milk by grinding the almonds several times with the 2 cups of water, until the liquid becomes milky. Strain through a sieve lined with cheesecloth.

Soften the gelatin in ¼ cup cold water for 5 minutes, and combine it with 2 cups of almond milk, 1 cup cream and the sugar. Slowly bring the mixture to a boil, but do not boil, stirring continuously to dissolve the sugar and the gelatin. Cool and stir in the almond extract and the kirsch (optional).

Pour the mixture into an oiled mold, reserving some for garnish. Chill until firm. When ready to serve, loosen edges and unmold onto a large serving dish.

Pour the remaining blanc mange into a pastry bag with rose tube, and garnish the dish, topping each rosette with a candied cherry.

Martin Van Buren

Hannah Hoes Van Buren

# Martin VAN BUREN

Martin Van Buren moved into the Presidency with the blessing and support of the retiring President, Andrew Jackson. So pleased was Jackson with the inauguration of his protegé that he attended all the ceremonies despite the fact that he had to leave a sickbed to be present. He even remained in residence at the White House for two weeks after President Van Buren moved in.

There was a huge reception at the mansion immediately following the inauguration, but the pushing, scrambling crowd went home disappointed because no refreshments had been served to them. In the late afternoon the President at a special audience received the congratulations of the diplomatic corps.

That night President Van Buren attended the elegant ball at Carusi's Hall, where all the social world had gathered to celebrate the inauguration. An elaborate and plentiful banquet was served the guests, with champagne in abundance, compensating those present at both events for the

lack of hospitality at the White House earlier that same day.

An account of the first "drawing-room" held by President Van Buren after his inauguration, the night of March 8, 1838, is given us by a visiting Englishman who tells us:

"The President received his visitors standing in the center of a small oval room, the entrance to which was directly from the hall on the ground floor. The introductions were made by the City Marshal, who announced the names of the parties; and each, after shaking hands with the President and exchanging a few words of courtesy, passed into the adjoining rooms to make way for others . . . (The President) was dressed in a plain suit of black; the Marshal was habited also in a plain suit, and there were neither guards about the gate, nor sentries within, nor a single servant or attendant in livery anywhere visible.

"The party, though consisting of not less than 2,000 persons, was much less brilliant than a drawing-room in England or than a fashionable soirée in Paris, but it was far more orderly and agreeable than any party of an equal number that I ever remember to have attended in Europe."

One of President Van Buren's tasks on coming to the Presidency was to dispose of a large cheese which had been given to President Andrew Jackson two years before. The cheese was to be sold at public auction, and the announcement read as follows:

"A cheese weighing 700 pounds is now at the store of Mr. William Orme, near the corner of Eleventh Street and Pennsylvania Avenue, where it will remain entire for one day and will afterwards be sold in quantities to suit purchasers. It is from the dairy of Colonel Meachem of Orange County, New York, by whom it was presented two years ago to the President of the United States, and has been preserved with great care. Having been made expressly for the President and by a gentleman whose cheeses are in high repute, it may be supposed to be of the very best quality."

President Van Buren moved into the White House together with his four bachelor sons. His wife had been dead for eighteen years. The public soon found out that the urbane and sophisticated man had his own ideas of the social life suitable for that historic mansion. No longer was the public permitted access to the President's house. He abolished the morning receptions and did away with the weekly levees to which the public had been encouraged to come.

Soon one formal levee for the people on New Year's Day was all that was allowed, and contrary to all former precedent, no ices, wines, or refreshments of any kind were offered to the guests. No eating or drinking was permitted the populace within the palace walls on state occasions. The people had to be content to listen to the Marine Band, to exchange formal civilities, or to discuss the weather.

More to President Van Buren's taste were

**Huguenot torte**    **Salade à la Volaille**

**Angelica Singleton Van Buren**

elegant dinners which he gave for small parties of select friends.

An English novelist tells about the restrictions President Van Buren placed on his public receptions:"It is remarkable that although at the head of the Democratic party, Mr. Van Buren has taken a step striking at the very roots of their boasted equality, and one on which General Jackson did not venture, i.e., he has prevented the mobocracy from intruding themselves at his levees. The police are now stationed at the door to prevent the intrusion of any improper person. A few years ago, a fellow could drive his cart, or hackney coach, up to the door, walk into the saloon in all his dirt and force his way to the President that he might shake him by one hand while he flourished his whip with the other. The scenes which took place when refreshments were handed around, the injury done to the furniture, and the disgust of the ladies may well be imagined. Mr. Van Buren deserves great credit for this step, for it was a bold one; and I must not praise him too much, or he may lose his next election."

Jessie Fremont, writing of the city of Washington at this period, says that President Van Buren brought over from London, where he had been our Minister, a fine *chef,* and that his dinners were as good and delicate as possible; but it was a formal household—none of the large hospitality of General Jackson, who regarded it as "the People's House" and himself as their steward.

Mrs. Fremont says that the city of Washington

was addicted to the easy and graceful habit of impromptu and small dinner parties. This was in part possible because in those days there were well-trained servants who did not often change positions. She remarked that there had always been admirable French cooks in Washington: "The foreign ministers all brought them; when they returned—if not sooner—the cooks deserted and set up in business for themselves. These not only went out to prepare fine dinners, but took as pupils young slaves sent by families to be instructed. In that way a working knowledge of good cookery of the best French school became diffused among numbers of the colored people—and for cookery they have natural aptitude."

Another writer of the Washington scene at the time expressed it this way: "There are mysteries in cooking unattainable to any but the elect, and of the elect were the sable priestesses of the Washington kitchens."

The new President had begun a thorough renovation, systematic cleaning, and refurnishing of the Mansion as soon as he moved in. He was determined to bring the house up to the standards that he felt were suitable for the residence of the President of the United States. Carpets were renovated, hangings and draperies cleaned, and damaged and worn furniture repaired and recovered. The designation of the oval reception room at the White House as the "Blue Room" dates from this administration, when President Van Buren had the gold furniture in the room re-upholstered in blue instead of the red which had been used from the time of its purchase by President Monroe.

The President's personal attire, the magnificence of his coach with its silver-mounted harness

**Van Buren's china**

**Salade à la Volaille**

and liveried footmen were considered bad enough, but it was his elaborate household and table appointments of gold and silver that really brought down the wrath of the people. Representative Ogle of Pennsylvania was the voice of the criticism heaped on the President, and it was for the President's table service that he saved his harshest invective.

"How delightful it must be to a real genuine locofoco to eat his *paté de foie gras, dinde desosse* and *salade à la volaille* from a silver plate with a golden knife and fork. And how exquisite to sip with a golden spoon his *soupe à la Reine* from a silver tureen."

This criticism by a bitter political opponent must be considered quite unjust, as the gold and silver in question had been purchased, not by the present inhabitant of the White House, but by President Monroe.

These select dinners which were under criticism were served to political foes as well as friends. As a matter of fact, Mr. Ogle himself had been one of the President's frequent guests. When Mr. Van Buren was asked if Ogle was correct in referring to those "gold spoons," he replied, "He ought to know; he has often had them in his mouth."

During the Van Buren administration Dolley Madison returned to Washington to live in her house on Lafayette Square. She was troubled to find the White House operating as a bachelor establishment, and soon determined that this was a state of affairs not to be long endured. When one of her attractive young Southern relatives, Miss Angelica Singleton of South Carolina, arrived in Washington to spend the social season of 1837-1838, Dolley arranged for her to meet the President's sons. When Angelica returned home in the summer of 1838 she was engaged to the President's oldest son, Major Abraham Van Buren. In November of that year they were married in South Carolina and Angelica made her first appearance as mistress of the White House at the New Year's Day reception in 1839.

Her success as a hostess was recorded in the Boston *Post* of that year:

"The Executive Mansion was a place of much more than usual attraction in consequence of the first appearance there of the bride of the President's son and private Secretary, Mrs. Abram Van Buren. She is represented as being of rare accomplishments, very modest, yet perfectly easy and graceful in her manners and free and vivacious in her conversation. She was universally admired and is said to have borne the fatigue of a three hours' levee with a patience and pleasantry which must be inexhaustible to last one through so severe a trial."

In the spring of 1839 Angelica and Abraham went abroad on a belated honeymoon. In London they visited Angelica's uncle, who was Minister to Great Britain. They were received with great ceremony at both the British and the French courts.

Angelica came back from Europe devoted to the ceremonies surrounding court life, and the only criticisms we can find of this charming and efficient hostess are that she tried to adapt some of the customs of the royal court to her White House receptions, which caused dismay to many of her republican guests.

Angelica's first baby, a little girl, was born at the White House but lived only two hours, much to the distress of her young parents and the surrounding circle of interested relatives.

The combined effects of a financial depression and the publicity given to his gold spoons prevented Van Buren's reelection. He met defeat calmly, however, and was seen on Inauguration Day 1841 placidly walking down the streets of Washington, a demoted civilian spectator to the spectacle of the Log Cabin victory parade of his successor, William Henry Harrison.

Van Buren now retired to his home in New York where he played the role of senior politician for the next two decades.

## Favorite Recipes

### Salade à la Volaille

| | |
|---|---|
| 2 large chickens, roasted or boiled, or | olives, ripe and green |
| 1 small (7-pound) turkey | small artichoke hearts |
| hearts of lettuce, lettuce shredded, watercress, capers, stuffed | anchovy fillets salt mayonnaise wine vinegar |

Remove all skin from fowl. Cut into suitably sized pieces. In a large, chilled, earthen salad bowl make a mound of shredded crisp lettuce. Season with a little salt and wine vinegar. Over it arrange the sliced choice portions of the cold fowl. Cover with a good mayonnaise and smooth it. Decorate with the olives, anchovies, capers, and tiny artichoke hearts, in an attractive pattern. To these add very small hearts of lettuce, or quartered portions of lettuce heart. When ready to serve, toss lightly, and serve on individual plates. A platter of peeled tomatoes, sliced thin, is a good accompaniment, but the tomatoes should not be added to the principal dish.

### Huguenot Torte

| | |
|---|---|
| 2 eggs, whole | 4 tablespoons flour, mixed with |
| ½ teaspoon salt | |
| 1 cup peeled and chopped tart cooking apples | 2½ teaspoons baking powder |
| 1 cup coarsely chopped pecans | 1 cup whipped cream, lightly sweetened and flavored with |
| 1 teaspoon vanilla | 1 teaspoon almond flavoring |
| 1½ cups white granulated sugar | |

Beat eggs and salt with rotary beater until light and fluffy, then gradually beat in sugar. Fold in apples and pecans with a whisk. Add vanilla, flour, and baking powder. Pour into well-greased baking pan about 8x12 or 9x9 inches and at least 2 inches deep. Bake in 325°F oven for 45 minutes, until crusty and light brown. The torte will swell up and form a crust on top and liquid batter may ooze over the edge unless you open the oven occasionally and prick with a cooking fork to allow steam to escape. When done, the torte will shrink into the pan, and the texture is that of a macaroon rather than of a soufflé which it seems to resemble. This may be served warm cut into squares. However, it is best when chilled overnight, cut into 8 squares which can be lifted out with a pancake turner, and served with the sweetened and flavored whipped cream. Here is a variation in which the dessert is baked in three layers:

**Three-layer Huguenot torte**

### Three-layer Huguenot Torte

| | |
|---|---|
| 6 eggs, whole | powder |
| ½ teaspoon salt | ½ pound apricot jam |
| 4½ cups powdered sugar | 3 cups sliced tart |
| 3 cups chopped | apples |
| skinned tart | 3 cups whipped cream, |
| apples | lightly flavored |
| 3 cups coarsely | with |
| chopped pecans | 3 teaspoons almond |
| 3 teaspoons vanilla | flavoring, and |
| extract | 3 tablespoons |
| 12 tablespoons flour, | confectioners' |
| mixed with | sugar |
| ½ teaspoon baking | |

Beat whole eggs with salt until light and fluffy. Gradually add the powdered sugar and continue beating until stiff. Fold in apples and nuts with a rubber scraper. Add vanilla, flour, and baking powder, and pour into 3 well-greased baking pans measuring 8x12 inches at least 3 inches deep. Bake in 325°F oven for 45 minutes until crusty and light brown. During the baking, open the door once or twice and prick with fork to allow steam to escape. Allow to get cold in the pan overnight. Turn out. Take one layer, place on jelly roll pan. Strain the apricot jam, and brush top of layer with a little of the jam. Cover the top, overlapping with thin slices of peeled apple. Sprinkle with a little sugar and hold under broiler to singe the edges of the apples. Remove, cool, and glaze with rest of the apricot jam. Sandwich three layers with whipped cream, reshape and stick around the edge with the following meringue:

### Meringue

| | |
|---|---|
| 3 egg whites, beaten | ¼ cup granulated |
| to soft peaks | sugar |
| 1 cup powdered sugar | |

Beat 3 egg whites to soft peaks, gradually add the powdered sugar, and continue beating until stiff. Fill into pastry bag with a large plain tube about the size of a quarter. Line a jelly roll pan with waxed paper, and pipe out the meringue in small egg shapes. Sprinkle top with granulated sugar and put to bake in 325°F oven for ½ hour or until it is firm to the touch. Remove. Pour a little cold water underneath the paper and slide with spatula to loosen the meringue from the paper. Put the rest of the whipped cream in pastry bag with small star tube, pipe rosettes of whipped cream around the edge of the cake, and stick meringues around the sides.

*William Henry Harrison*

*Anna Symmes Harrison*

# William H. HARRISON

GENERAL HARRISON called at the White House to pay his respects as soon as he arrived in Washington on February 9, which was also his 68th birthday. President Van Buren and his whole Cabinet returned the call on the President-elect at his hotel.

The day of the inauguration was cold and stormy. President-elect Harrison rode up the avenue in the midst of a hollow square of his friends, mounted on a white horse and followed by an enthusiastic procession of people, many of them wearing coonskin caps and hauling wagons on which were displayed log cabins. After the oath of office he proceeded to give the longest inaugural address on record. It lasted for one hour and forty-five minutes. That night the President and his relatives paid visits to each of three inaugural balls held in his honor. *The National Intelligencer* reported that for the inauguration a pound-cake had been made in the model of the Capitol of the United States. This marvelous creation was nine feet long, eight and a half feet wide, and six feet high, and weighed eight hundred pounds.

Mrs. William Henry Harrison was not present for the inauguration. As she had been ill that winter, she was unable to make the long trip from Ohio to Washington at that time of year. She planned to await better weather, and hoped to arrive in Washington about May.

For the interim the President-elect had asked his daughter-in-law, Mrs. William Henry Harrison, Jr., widow of his eldest son, to come to Washington with him. This young woman was the niece and adopted daughter of General and Mrs. James Findlay of Cincinnati. Mrs. Findlay decided to act as chaperone and to help guide her niece through the social maze of Washington. She herself had spent several years in Washington in the 1830's when General Findlay was a member of Congress. The Washington newspaper records that "Mrs. Findlay of Ohio . . . almost invariably occupied the right hand of the President at his table." Undoubtedly, had they had the opportunity, these two ladies could have created a social atmosphere at the White House equal to the most severe test.

President Harrison considered himself the head of the household at the White House, and frequently he could even be found doing his own marketing in the early morning, wearing an old hat, and with a market basket slung over his arm. It must have been a real pleasure for one as interested in food as he was to visit the sources of supply in Washington.

Mrs. Roger Pryor, writing of life in Washington before the war, tells us: "The market in Washington was abundantly supplied with the finest game and fish from the Eastern Shore of Maryland and Virginia and the waters of the Potomac. Brant, ruddy duck, canvasback duck, sora, oysters and terrapin were within the reach of any housekeeper. Oysters, to be opened at a moment's notice, were planted on the cellar floors, and fed with salt water, and the cellars, as far as the mistress was concerned, were protected from invasion by the large terrapins kept there—a most efficient police force crawling about with their outstretched necks and wicked eyes.

"Such dainties demanded expert cooking."

The hospitality to be found wherever the Harrisons lived was a family tradition, with contemporary accounts to substantiate the legend. In 1807 William Henry Harrison, then living in Vincennes, Indiana, where he served as Governor of the Northwest Territory, was sending back to

Philadelphia for coffee, sugar, tea, Madeira wine, and rice. Game was plentiful on the frontier and it is said that the Governor was an excellent shot, who spent an occasional afternoon hunting for partridge, geese, wild pigeon, deer, and turkey. Fish were always available from the Wabash River, which flowed directly in front of the Governor's Mansion.

A letter of that same period refers to Harrison's old gardener, who had been asked to come and live in Vincennes. The importance of the gardener evidently arose from Mr. Harrison's love of fresh vegetables. When he went to Bogota in the 1830's as United States Minister, he wrote home: "I have a very excellent garden, beans, peas, cabbages, cauliflower, celery and artichokes in abundance, and we shall soon have beets." The clerk of the legation adds further evidence in one of his letters: "Most of our common vegetables were never known here until introduced by General Harrison. When a dinner is given by any of the Diplomatic Corps he is always called upon for his vegetables; his celery, turnips, radishes, salads, etc., are the finest I ever beheld, and he says they grow faster and are more easily cultivated than at home."

Timothy Flint, writing of the Harrisons' home at North Bend, describes the table loaded with abundance and with substantial good cheer, "especially with the different kinds of game." Flint was enthusiastic about the food and the hospitality he found there. "On a fine farm, in the midst of the woods, his house was open to all the neighbors, who entered without ceremony, and were admitted to assume a footing of entire equality."

Campaign literature, admittedly biased, assures us that the General "always prepared and set his table with the expectation and hope of having guests at it—that he had made it a rule through life not to suffer any person to go from his house hungry—that this was a feeling brought with him from Virginia, his Mother State."

A politician recorded his visit to North Bend

in 1840: "Our supper was soon served, at an early hour, before six o'clock, the usual supper hour of the country, and we had on the table the good and plain fare of all substantial farmers, the best of butter made in General Harrison's own house, cornbread and flour bread, with milk in abundance and rich as cream; and when this tea was over, Mrs. Harrison herself, though not unattended by domestics, seemed to prefer the superintendence of the disposal of the affairs of her own table."

It is said that Sunday dinner at the Harrisons' was usually shared with fifty guests and that in the course of a year over three hundred hams were needed to provision the table.

Upon assuming the office of President, Harrison was deluged with office seekers. The Whig party had been out of power for twelve long years and party members were demanding the spoils. Already fatigued from the strenuous campaign, the President had been exhausted by the journey to Washington and the celebration of the inaugu-ration. Cares of office gave him no rest. He caught a severe cold in the last week of March, and died of pneumonia on April 4, 1841, exactly one month after his inauguration.

For the first time in the history of our country, the chosen leader of the people lay dead in the White House. The city and the country went into mourning. Elaborate funeral services attended by all of official Washington were held in the East Room. A procession two miles long and numbering 10,000 persons escorted the cortege to the temporary vault where the body would await removal to Ohio. An eyewitness account says of the ceremony: "It was more imposing and better arranged than that of the inauguration."

Anna Harrison received word of her husband's death in North Bend, where she was getting ready for her trip to Washington. Though she had been the wife of one President and was to be grandmother of another, she died many years later without ever having been in the White House or even in the city of Washington.

## *Favorite Recipes*

### *Roast Wild (or Domestic) Duck*

*When the ducks are ready dressed, put in them a small onion, pepper, salt, and a spoonful of red wine; if the fire be good, they will roast in twenty minutes; make gravy of the necks and gizzards, a spoonful of red wine, half an anchovy, a blade or two of mace, one onion, and a little cayenne pepper; boil it till it is wasted to half a pint, strain it through a hair sieve, and pour it on the ducks—serve them up with onions and sauce in a boat; garnish the dish with raspings of bread.*

| | |
|---|---|
| 2 ½-pound wild ducks, or | four, with the skin on |
| 2 4-pound domestic ducks | garlic cloves |
| ½ lemon | red wine |
| ground white pepper | lump of butter |
| salt | 1 cup orange juice |
| large orange, cut in | orange marmalade |

Remove gizzards, livers, hearts, and necks. Scrub fowl thoroughly inside and out, then rub half a lemon all over inside and out. Dry well on paper towel. Season inside with salt and pepper. Stuff quarters of orange into each duck. Add bruised clove of garlic, a small lump of butter. Tie up duck carefully and arrange on a rack. Brush with melted butter. Pour a little red wine in the bottom of the roasting pan (save the rest for basting). Roast *wild* ducks 25 to 30 minutes in a 450°F oven; duckling, or domestic duck, should be roasted in a medium slow oven (325°F) for 35 minutes a pound (2½ to 3 hours for a 4 or 5 pound duckling). Only wild ducks are cooked at a high temperature and served rare.

Baste occasionally with a mixture of orange juice and red wine. Each time you baste, brush the fowl with melted butter. Turn it on its breast for part of the cooking time. Ten minutes before it is roasted, brush duck with orange marmalade to get a nice glaze.

For ease of serving, carve 1 duck carefully and arrange the pieces on a hot platter beside the uncarved duck, which may be carved at the table.

## Sauce for Duck

| | |
|---|---|
| 2 teaspoons salt butter | shredded |
| ¼ cup calvados | 2 teaspoons finely |
| 1 teaspoon tomato | chopped garlic |
| paste | ½ cup red wine |
| 2 teaspoons potato | ¾ cup strong chicken |
| flour | stock |
| 1 teaspoon meat glaze | ¼ cup sherry |
| ⅓ cup salt butter | 2 teaspoons guava |
| ½ cup sweet orange | jelly |
| marmalade | a little pepper |
| juice of 2 oranges | 2 or 3 navel oranges, |
| 2 orange rinds, finely | segmented |

Brown the livers in two teaspoons hot salt butter. Flame with ¼ cup calvados. Remove the livers from the pan and add another tablespoon of butter. Add finely shredded rind of the 2 oranges and the chopped garlic. Cook slowly, without browning, for 3 minutes. Stir in, off the fire, the tomato paste, potato flour, meat glaze, one third cup butter, ½ cup sweet orange marmalade, juice of 2 oranges, red wine, chicken stock, sherry, guava jelly, a little pepper, but no salt. Stir over fire until it comes to a rolling boil. Put back the livers, simmer gently for ½ hour. Cut livers into thin slices and put back into sauce. Add the skinned sections of the oranges. (*Note:* Do not cook any more after adding orange sections as they will disintegrate.) Pour all this sauce over ducks and garnish with little orange baskets.

**Roast duck**

*Letitia Christian Tyler*

*John Tyler*

*Julia Gardiner Tyler*

# John TYLER

THE DEATH of President William Henry Harrison ushered in the administration of the tenth President, John Tyler. From the social aspect it was an active four years even if it was somewhat controversial politically. The tone of its social life was perhaps best captured by Jessie Benton Fremont, who described the hospitality of the administration of President John Tyler as being that of an "open house, where there were many young people who kept to their informal, cheery, Virginia ways."

Tyler did not continue at the White House the ceremonious etiquette of the Van Buren administration; his personal style of living might be characterized as the simplicity of a country gentleman. Attended by his family slaves, the President lived at the Executive Mansion just as he had been accustomed to live on his Virginia plantation. He and his family even used a second-hand carriage, and at state dinners some of the waiters were in liveries that had been purchased at the sale of the effects of a foreign Minister.

This does not mean to imply that President Tyler lived economically, for the type of informal, cordial hospitality that he dispensed actually cost a great deal. He always summoned his guests to the dining room where they were invited to help themselves "from a sideboard well garnished with decanters of ardent spirits and wines, with a bowl of juleps in the summer and of egg-nog in the winter."

President Tyler himself cared little for eating and drinking. Politics was his love, his meal and drink. Food was simply sustenance, and his servants at the White House were so aware of the fact that when he was alone they made little provision for him. A fellow Virginian tells of dining with the President unexpectedly and finding that the menu was ham and turnip greens—that and no more. The President was chagrined at being caught in such a predicament; as compensation he sent for the keys of the White House wine cellars and let his friend go down there and take his choice. For the rest of his days the Virginia gentleman retained the memory of that afternoon's entertainment. He declared it was the only

78

time in his life when he had "more good liquor than he could drink and not as many people as he wanted to divide with him."

But the social functions of the administration were a different matter. During the whole four years the social life of the White House was extremely successful and was praised by all, even by Tyler's bitterest enemies. This was possible because of the good taste, common sense, and social experience of the President and the ladies of his household.

The city of Washington in 1841 was still in many respects a small town. Charles Dickens, who visited Washington, called it a "City of Magnificent Intentions, with spacious avenues that begin in nothing and lead nowhere; streets, miles long, that only want houses, roads and inhabitants." Pennsylvania Avenue was the only street that was paved, and during the Tyler administration it was also provided with street lamps; the rest of the city was muddy or dusty depending on the weather, and at night the streets were dark and deserted.

The President's wife, Letitia Christian Tyler, had had a severe paralytic stroke several years before Tyler became President; so she was not able to assume the duties of the mistress of the White House. The President had two attractive single daughters who might have helped him, but one was quite young, and the other one married and left Washington the first year. His daughter-in-law, Mrs. Robert Tyler, wife of his oldest son, was living at the White House, and so most of the social duties fell on her shoulders. Priscilla Cooper Tyler, daughter of the tragedian, Thomas A. Cooper, and herself a professional actress before her marriage, was well equipped for the role of hostess at the Executive Mansion. She had both the social qualifications and the social experience, and she was fortunate to have as her adviser the experienced and accomplished Dolley Madison, who was on friendly terms with the family.

Until early in 1842 it was the practice to have open house every evening for the reception of all family friends, members of Washington society, and visitors to the city. The house was thronged every night, and entertaining these crowds soon proved to be too big a burden for the family. It became necessary to limit the evening receptions to Thursday and Saturday nights.

Also, while Congress was in session, President Tyler gave two formal dinners a week. One was a stag affair, while the other included both men and women. Tyler seems to have entertained without regard for political animosities. The *New York Herald* describes the first dinner as follows: "Entertainment was magnificent, the wines superb, and whatever diversity of sentiment might exist respecting a bank or other questions of public policy, there was a concurrence of opinion as to the grace and dignity with which the President presided, and the genuine benevolence and simplicity of his character."

In addition to the dinners and receptions, a public levee was held once a month, and the usual general receptions were given on New Year's Day and the Fourth of July.

In 1841, the visit of the Prince de Joinville, son of the French King, was the occasion for much entertaining. The President gave a dinner in his honor to which were invited the Cabinet, foreign Ministers, and high naval and military officers. Mrs. Fremont's description of the gala evening says that the President rightly thought a dance would best please a young navy man and a Frenchman, so there was "a charming and unusually brilliant ball" following the dinner.

"The Prince was tall and fine-looking, and Miss Tyler and himself opened the ball, while those of us who knew French well were assigned to his officers.

"We had remained in the Oval reception room until the company assembled, and then, the President leading, the whole foreign party were taken through all the drawing rooms, ending by our taking places for the *Quadrille d'honneur* in the East Room; that ceremony over, the dancing became general."

Also worthy of mention was a reception given in honor of the two literary figures, Washington Irving and Charles Dickens, at which the number of people in the East Room alone was about 3,000.

Of the dinner given for Lord Ashburton in 1842, John Quincy Adams said, "The courtesies of the President and of Mrs. R. Tyler to their guests were all that the most accomplished European court could have displayed." High praise

**Tyler's china**

**Sally Lunn**         **Tyler pudding**

indeed from one who had known European court life intimately.

There is an account of a charming fancy dress ball given by the President for his eldest granddaughter, Mary Fairlee Tyler. The little girl was dressed as queen of the fairies, with gossamer wings, a diamond star on her forehead and a silver wand in her tiny hand, and she stood at the door of the East Room to welcome all of her delighted little friends to Queen Titania's realm. The guests were dressed in costume and in the crowds were to be seen flower girls, gypsy fortune tellers, an Aztec princess, and an Albanian boy.

The sociable Tyler family introduced the custom of having music in the White House grounds on Saturday afternoons, which made a pleasant rallying-point for the Washington world.

The social gaieties of the President's house were interrupted in September 1842 by the death of the invalid Mrs. Tyler.

That winter one of the belles of Washington society was Miss Julia Gardiner, daughter of a wealthy Senator from New York. Her raven black hair, expressive dark eyes, and stylish hourglass figure, combined with her vivacity and flirtatiousness made her the sensation of every gathering. She became, in fact, with her attractive personality and social background, the marriage catch of the season. President Tyler could scarcely resist

the challenge. That winter he began to court the young lady. The romance did not reach any formal conclusion then, probably because of the great age difference between the 23-year-old debutante and the 53-year-old President.

The tragedy of the gun explosion aboard the *Princeton,* which caused the death of two members of the Cabinet and Julia's father, seems to have helped Julia to make up her mind to accept her ardent though older suitor. Four months later, in June 1844, Julia Gardiner and the President were married at a very quiet ceremony in New York City.

Julia Gardiner Tyler served as First Lady for eight months, enjoying her position immensely. Her beauty, youth, enthusiasm, social experience, and intellectual brilliance were excellent preparation for the position.

Two days after the wedding there was a wedding reception in the Blue Room of the White House which was attended by all of official and social Washington. The President and his bride received the guests. In the center of the Oval Room was a table on which was a wedding cake surrounded by wine and bouquets. The young bride cut the cake with the help of John C. Calhoun, Tyler's new Secretary of State. The bride wrote home that the party was "very brilliant— brilliant to my heart's content. I have commenced my auspicious reign and am in quiet possession of the Presidential Mansion."

"This winter," Julia wrote her mother, "I intend to do something in the way of entertaining that shall be the admiration and talk of the Washington world." There were to be weekly White House levees, the usual formal receptions, and several special grand functions to be the marvel of all Washington.

That year Christmas was celebrated with abandon at the White House. The holiday feast placed on the table was "à la Virginia (with) immense hams, rounds of beef, veal, etc." The room and the table were decorated with wreaths of evergreens. The portrait of Washington framed in holiday greenery looked benignly down on the gaiety. "We commenced the day with Egg Nog and concluded with apple Toddy."

Julia's fondness for display occasioned some criticism, as had President Van Buren's two administrations earlier. Mrs. Fremont remarked that the new Mrs. Tyler was very handsome. She records that: "There was some amusement at her driving four horses (finer than those of the Russian Minister) and because she received seated in her large armchair on a slightly raised platform in front of the windows in the oval room. She also wore three feathers in her hair and a long trained velvet dress, which were commented on by the elders who had seen other Presidents' wives take their state more easily."

The grand finale of the Tyler administration was an elegant ball held at the White House in February, 1845, as a farewell party. Julia's sister, writing of the affair, says that it was attended by 3,000 persons. "The east room was brilliantly illuminated with some hundred additional lights, the floor highly polished and orchestra (with full band in scarlet uniforms) tastefully hung with blue satin drapery, above which floated the national flag. . . . The supper table, arranged under my own eye, was superb, and wine and champagne flowed like water—*eight* dozen bottles of champagne were drunk with wine by the *barrel*."

On March 1 President and Mrs. Tyler gave a dinner party for President-elect and Mrs. Polk, and two days later moved out of the White House.

The Tylers retired to their Virginia estate, "Sherwood Forest," where they lived in happiness and contentment, raising seven children to add to the President's first family of seven. Tyler died during the Civil War. Julia outlived him for twenty-seven years, but to the day of her death, when she spoke of "Mr. President," her reference was always to her devoted husband.

# Favorite Recipes

## Tyler Pudding

| | |
|---|---|
| ¼ cup butter | 1 teaspoon vanilla |
| 2½ cups sugar | ½ of a fresh grated |
| 3 eggs, whole | coconut |
| ¼ teaspoon salt | pastry for 2 9-inch |
| ½ cup heavy cream | pies |

Cream butter and half of the sugar well. Beat eggs well and gradually add the remaining sugar, beating constantly. Add salt. Mix in cream well and add vanilla. Stir in coconut and pour into partially baked pie shell. Bake in low (300°F) oven for about 20 minutes until set.

If you like lightly toasted coconut, reserve some of the coconut from the pie and sprinkle it on the top. If it has not browned sufficiently when the custard is set, run it under the broiler a few minutes with the oven door open.

## Sally Lunn

| | |
|---|---|
| 1 yeast cake | For decorating: |
| 1 cup milk, warm | glacé cherries |
| ½ cup butter | angelica |
| ⅓ cup sugar | glacé orange and |
| 3 eggs, beaten whole | lemon rind |
| 4 cups flour | |

Put yeast cake in 1 cup of warm milk. Cream together ½ cup of butter and ⅓ cup of sugar, add the 3 beaten eggs and mix well. Sift in flour alternately with the milk and yeast. Let rise in a warm place; then beat well. Pour into one well-buttered Sally Lunn mold, or two smaller molds. Let rise again before baking in a moderate oven (325°F) until light brown.

Can be decorated with glacé cherries and angelica, and thin slices of glacé orange and lemon rind.

*Sarah Childress Polk*

*James Knox Polk*

# James K. POLK

T HE INAUGURATION of President James K. Polk in 1845 was almost drowned in a deluge of rain. Only those few officials who had to be there huddled under their umbrellas to hear the inaugural address as it was shouted out into the driving downpour. On the platform to appreciate the highest moment of her husband's career was Polk's wife, the former Sarah Childress, who had been instrumental in making his success possible.

The inaugural ball that night proved to be equally out of the ordinary. A delightful contemporary account tells us that there was a $10 ball and a $5 ball. It had been intended that the $10 ball should be attended by all the highest society of Washington, both official and private. Unfortunately someone forgot to invite the diplomatic corps. To this oversight the diplomats retaliated by patronizing the $5 ball with the "rank and file" of the people. There resulted a strange mixture of people so that at one point a foreign Minister's lady found herself dancing in the same quadrille as her gardener.

The Polks helped put a damper on both balls.

On their arrival they ordered the dancing stopped. They stayed for two hours, greeted every guest, and only after they left was dancing resumed.

The Polks took their new duties with great seriousness. The President spent hours at his desk, as he considered himself "hired to work" for the country. The President's wife acted as his private secretary and worked by his side, leaving the social and household chores to the White House staff.

The new First Lady provided a great contrast to her predecessor. She frowned upon cards, dancing, and all such vanities. However, in every decision relating to White House social life she was supported by her husband.

The Polks came from conservative Southern families with similar social backgrounds. Their forebears, though decidedly simple folks, had amassed enough money to be able to live comfortably. James K. Polk was a member of the Tennessee Legislature at the age of 29 and shortly after his marriage to Sarah he moved up to a seat in the House of Representatives in Washington. The Polks were not extravagant and they had no financial problems to slow down James' political career.

Sarah Polk shared her husband's political interests avidly. The Polks, man and wife, worked as a team, and Polk himself said of her, "None but Sarah knew so intimately my private affairs."

When Polk was elected President as the first genuine "dark horse" candidate, he was at 49 the youngest man ever elected to the office. He was slender, dark-haired, and aristocratic looking, and his wife was a handsome, Spanish-looking woman of only 41. Together they were one of the handsomest couples to enter the White House.

Sarah made her presence felt as soon as the Polks arrived at the White House. She refused to pay any private calls. Entertaining was reduced to only those events which were so well established that they had become traditional. Twice a week they had state dinners and public receptions. The public gatherings were quite staid. There was nothing to do but promenade up and down the East Room and chat with the other promenaders. The First Lady not only banished drinking, she refused to serve food, too. That, like dancing, she proclaimed to be beneath the high dignity of the Presidential office.

A newspaper account describes one of these occasions: "The President held last evening one of his 'drawing rooms' (the name given to the mere opening of the doors of the White House to the public). Crowd thin—conversation stiff, frigid, hard, affected, and altogether so-soish." (September 6, 1846.)

A visitor to a reception reported, "The wife of the President was seated on the sofa, engaged with half a dozen ladies in lively conversation. Ill and clumsy as I am at millinery, yet for the sake of my fair readers, I will try to describe her toilet. A maroon colored velvet dress, with short sleeves and high in the neck, trimmed with very deep lace and a handsome pink head-dress was all that struck the eye. . . . Mrs. Polk is a handsome, intelligent and sensible woman, better looking and better dressed, than any of her numerous lady visitors present on the occasion."

One of Sarah Polk's innovations was a rigidly reverent observance of the Sabbath Day. No company was received at the White House on that day, and the first family attended church without fail. In the moralistic Victorian society then in ascendancy throughout the country, Sarah Polk's reforms were greeted with acclaim. Newspapers said, "All will agree that by the exclusion of frivolities and her excellent deportment in other

respects, she has conferred additional dignity upon the executive department of the government."

Despite the Polks' strict devotion to duty and their limited social activities, they were well liked personally. If the First Lady did not dance, she could talk. Sarah Polk was well informed and well read. She was also tolerant of those who did not share her own strict ideas. She was apt to pardon them with the observation, "You were not brought up in so strict a school as I was."

The Polks' first autumn in the White House seems to mark the first Thanksgiving dinner to be given there. As reported in the local newspapers: "The President had some friends to dinner— This new idea of a Thanksgiving in Washington was well observed and gave such general satisfaction as to lead to the deduction that it will be an annual custom hereafter."

The New Year's Day reception in 1846 was a success, with the foreign courts well represented. A visitor described Mrs. Polk on that occasion as "fittingly representing, in person and manner, the dignity and grace of the American female character."

Dolley Madison, widow of the fourth President, was one of the welcome guests at the White House throughout the Polk administration and most accounts of social affairs contain a reference to the aged Mrs. Madison and the courtesies shown her by the President and the First Lady. At the public receptions she is described: "You will probably find her (the First Lady) supported by an elderly lady in a black turban, who you will know at once is Mrs. Madison."

One of these contemporary reports gives a graphic account of the chief entertainment of a White House levee of this administration. The full account gives a description of the arrival of a guest at the White House and tells how he is received by the President and his official family. It continues: "To the East Room you repair, then, and find a spacious apartment splendidly furnished and brilliantly illuminated. There is comparative stillness here. . . . The great amusement of the evening now commences. . . . This popular court practice consists in solemnly promenading around the room in pairs. . . . Solemnly and without pause, they perform their slow gyrations, while a group of young men in the centre survey their motions, quizzing their dress and general appearance."

In the spring of 1846 a great National Fair was held in Washington. The event brought to the city even more people than came for a Presiden-

tial inauguration. The Fair opened on May 23, and in the afternoon the President and Mrs. Polk and members of the Cabinet visited the building. Mrs. Madison was also among the visitors, "a circumstance which did not diminish the crowd."

The Polks were the first occupants of the White House in many years who made an honest effort to live within the Presidential salary. The curtailment of entertainment at the Presidential Mansion proved beneficial to the family fortunes as well as a tribute to the strict principles of the First Lady.

The only thing about the Polk administration in which Mrs. Polk did not seem interested was the household details of the Executive Mansion. The details necessary to make the house neat and well appointed were left to the servants. She rarely directed or interfered with their arrangements for White House dinners. Once a guest remarked that there were no napkins on the table. Mrs. Polk had not even noticed it. The only thing about her dinner parties that she really enjoyed was the conversation. Often she got so involved in an interesting conversation that she forgot to eat. The steward would save dishes that she particularly liked so that she could enjoy them after the guests had left.

Mrs. Polk preferred to discuss serious politics with the gentlemen rather than participate in the social conversations of the ladies. This was the basis of a complaint that Mrs. Polk did not stay in the sitting room with the ladies but preferred to be "always in the parlor with Mr. Polk and other male guests." Franklin Pierce, who later became President, is quoted as saying that he would much rather talk politics with Mrs. Polk than anyone else, including her husband.

In his four years at the White House President Polk gave an incredible amount of time to his official duties. He felt that the people had a right to see their President and spent long hours every day receiving anyone who came to call on him. He rarely took a day off and never during his whole term took a long vacation. He considered himself "hired to work" and work he did. Often, after a reception, he and his wife would sit up, working for hours into the night to make up for the hours spent in social activities.

The Polks carried their political life into the drawing room during the Mexican War. A reception was often stopped so that the President could read to the assembly the latest dispatches from the battlefront. Sometimes an officer home from the

war "was encouraged to recount some thrilling incidents of those scenes." The war marked the height of the President's popularity. At the New Year's Day reception in 1847, the President shook hands from 11:30 in the morning until 3 in the afternoon.

Their last New Year's Day reception was even more brilliant than usual, despite the fact that "There were no refreshments, of course, and nothing to animate the crowd but the beauty of the women and a splendid band of music." The Mexican War heroes in the crowd were the lions of the occasion.

A few days before the end of the administration the Polks gave a dinner party for General

**Polk's state china**

Zachary Taylor and a farewell levee for their friends.

The Polks' return to Nashville became a triumphal journey from Washington all the way home. They were entertained lavishly and hoped to continue their tour to Europe. Unfortunately the strain proved too much for the former President. Polk died at Nashville only a few weeks after he reached home.

His handsome widow lived on for forty more years in the fine residence they had acquired for their retirement to Nashville. She made her home a memorial to the late President and in it she received prominent men of all classes and professions who lived in Nashville or came to visit there.

## *Favorite Recipes*

### *Tennessee Ham*

| | |
|---|---|
| 1 ham | meal or cracker |
| 1 cup dark molasses | crumbs |
| cloves | fruit preserves |
| 1½ cups brown sugar | |

Completely cover the ham in cold water; allow to soak overnight. Take out and remove any hard surface. Put in suitably sized pot with fresh water, skin side down, add molasses. Cook slowly (225°F), allowing 25 minutes to the pound. Allow to cool in the liquid. Pull skin off carefully. Score ham; stick a clove in each square. Sprinkle with paste made of brown sugar, meal or cracker crumbs, and sufficient liquid to make the paste. Bake slowly in moderate oven (320°F) for 1 hour.

Decorate the platter with thin ham slices cut from the roast ham, rolled into cornucopias, and filled with fruit preserve.

### *Hickory Nut Cake*

| | |
|---|---|
| 1 cup butter | powder |
| 2 cups sugar | ½ teaspoon salt |
| 4 eggs, separated | 1 cup milk |
| 1 teaspoon lemon | 1 cup chopped hickory |
| juice | nuts (pecans may |
| 3 cups flour, sifted | be substituted) |
| with | 1 teaspoon almond |
| 2 teaspoons baking | flavoring |

Grease an 8¼-inch tube cake pan or turk's head mold well, and flour it. Cream butter with 1 cup of the sugar. Beat egg yolks until light, beating in the remaining cup of sugar until light and lemon-colored. Then fold in lemon juice and combine with the creamed mixture. Next sift in dry ingredients alternately with the milk. Stir in nuts and flavoring. Beat egg whites light, but not dry. Fold in lightly. Pour into cake pan, bake in moderate (350°F) oven for about 1 hour.

This cake can be served unfrosted with spiced peaches or brandied peaches.

A caramel icing made with caramelized white sugar is recommended, sprinkled with nuts.

Hickory nut cake

### *Icing for Hickory Nut Cake*

| | |
|---|---|
| 1 cup sugar | 1 teaspoon vanilla |
| ½ cup cold water | 1 cup chopped nuts |
| 2 egg whites | |

Make a syrup of the sugar and water, cooking to 238°F, the soft-ball stage. Allow to cool, while egg whites are beaten. Now pour the syrup in a thin steady stream onto the beaten egg whites, beating the mixture until it is thick enough to spread over the top and sides of the cake. Add flavoring before spreading. Sprinkle with nuts on top and around the cake.

Margaret Smith Taylor

Zachary Taylor

# Zachary TAYLOR

WHEN GENERAL ZACHARY TAYLOR was elected President of the United States, he said with truth, "For more than a quarter of a century my house has been the tent and my home the battlefield." For all those years this house and home had been shared by his devoted wife, Margaret Smith Taylor.

From the beginning of his army career General Taylor had been a frontier officer. He and his family never had enjoyed official duty at an Eastern post like West Point or Washington. His life was spent on the borders of the United States, in swampy Florida, in Mexico, or on the Indian frontier; at every post his wife followed him and made a home for him. Her children were born in the wilderness and lived there until they were old enough to go back East to acquire a proper education for their future security.

At the Taylors' home in Baton Rouge, their home previous to the White House, the family had lived quietly. Mrs. Taylor took great pride in her garden. She raised the best table delicacies of that area and even owned a cow so that they might

have milk and butter for their table. The General was very particular about food. Plain fare was acceptable, but it must be well cooked.

The Taylors' daughter, Knox, writing to her mother in 1835 says, "How often, my dear Mother, I wish I could look in upon you. I imagine so often I can see you about your domestic concerns —down in the cellar skimming milk or going to feed the chickens." Always, from military post to military post, the General's lady looked after his welfare and dispensed the hospitality of her frontier home with the grace acquired in her childhood in tidewater Maryland.

Because most of Zachary Taylor's life had been spent on the frontier, there were many who expected that the social life of the Mansion would be marred by crudity. But this was not the case. The President was gentlemanly, inherently gracious, an affable and agreeable host. There was no doubt about his cordiality to his guests or the pleasant conversation at his board. In the courtesies he extended to ladies, in the hospitality of his home and his table, in his dignified simplicity of

manner, he reflected the Virginia-Kentucky traditions of his family background. His relatives included James Madison, Robert E. Lee, John Taylor of Caroline [county] and a roster of first families of Virginia. During Taylor's Presidency, George Washington Parke Custis, adopted son of George Washington, was one of his admiring intimates. Nellie Custis Lewis, his sister, considered President Taylor the most qualified man to become President since her beloved adopted father, George Washington. Rough as Taylor could be on the battlefield, these people accustomed to social refinement would not have accepted him unless he met their standards. Custis held him in such high regard that he gave him George Washington's writing case as a personal gift.

Nellie Custis Lewis was a distant cousin of Mrs. Taylor's, who had been born Margaret Mackall Smith in Calvert County, Maryland. Her socially prominent family was related to the best families of Virginia and Maryland, such as the Calvert, Lewis, and Conrad families. Peggy Taylor had known Nellie Custis when both were young girls, although there had been little opportunity to see each other in the years Mrs. Taylor spent as an Army wife. Small wonder that Nellie was pleased when Zachary Taylor, the husband of her girlhood friend, was elected President.

Retiring President Polk and incoming President Taylor rode up to the Capitol together as is customary for the inaugural ceremony. After the oath-taking, they went back down Pennsylvania Avenue together. Polk got out at the Irving Hotel and the new President continued on to the White House. The *National Intelligencer* reports that, "Followed by a vast concourse of people, the President entered the Mansion . . . and there received . . . the salutes of some thousands of persons, passing in a long array in front of him."

That night the President attended three inaugural balls, the most elegant of which was the one at the City Hall. Here, in the words of one of the guests: "The largest ballroom, the largest company, the most painful and dangerous pressure . . . I ever witnessed; from four to five thousand persons were present, each of whom seemed to think that he or she alone was entitled to be there; but it was nevertheless a grand affair."

At the ball the President's daughter—a bride of three months, Betty Bliss—was much admired. She wore a simple white gown and a single flower in her hair. Already it was known that Mrs. Bliss would act as First Lady for her father as Mrs. Taylor had neither the interest nor the health to undertake the responsibility.

Betty Taylor Bliss by birth and education was quite capable of assuming the role of First Lady. She possessed beauty, good sense, and quiet humor. As a hostess she was at ease and received her guests with grace, but like her mother she preferred a quiet role to that of a queen of society. Formal receptions and official dinners were not to their taste. Nevertheless this is part of the job which must be accepted by the First Lady, and there were murmurs of discontent at the lack of elegant affairs during the first year that President Taylor was in office.

After his election to the Presidency, Taylor's days were crowded not only with his official duties but also with the official levees and the constant stream of office seekers. Job-hunters, dignitaries, personal friends, and the merely curious flowed through the Mansion at levee time and at the evening receptions. The White House doors were open to all. Strangers marched unannounced into the East Room and introduced themselves to the President. The Washington *Whig* reported with approval that the President "mingles with the crowd in the most familiar manner. He has no personal attendants to stand between him and the people."

A good description of these afternoon levees has been left us by one who visited there. When Gideon Welles arrived at 12:30 he found about sixty or seventy persons already gathered—"some on the portico, some in the Hall, some in the oval room, the room east and the East Room." About half of them were women. The Cabinet was still in session. It was nearly 2 when the President came into the Oval Room. He shook hands with the people and spoke a few words to each; most of these people were office seekers. Welles accurately observed that the President seemed to be present not because he enjoyed it but simply because it was "one of his duties." Yet his manner was "kind and friendly."

The President was never free from pressure from these office seekers. The daytime crowds were followed by those who came at night. "At 8 P.M. office seekers go to his room, where himself and lady, Col. Bliss and lady receive company. . . . They 'sit it out' till the ladies retire, then they open their battery upon the President. . . . Last night he was unable to . . . go to bed till from 12 to 2 o'clock."

President Taylor gained a reputation for gra-

◀ **Wine jelly**

**Crabmeat on shells**          **Daube glacé**

cious and bountiful hospitality at his dinner table. Official dinners were held in the state dining room twice weekly during the congressional season, usually on Wednesdays and Saturdays at 6 o'clock. But Taylor apparently preferred the coziness of a small room, beyond the east-west corridor, where he took most of his meals informally surrounded by his family.

For the second winter the ladies of the family seemed ready to assume more prominently and publicly the social duties of their high position, and that fall the social schedule resumed without interruption. The President received European visitors, Indian chiefs, and miscellaneous callers. Receptions were held on Tuesday and Friday afternoons and on Friday evenings. Marine Band concerts were held on the grounds on Saturday afternoons. Elegant dinners were scheduled twice a week.

The President's flower garden was especially praised that fall. "The surpassing splendor of the President's garden elicits high admiration from every visitor. Dahlias, roses in many varieties and indeed every description of flowers and shrubbery appears in gayest attire."

The New Year's Day reception was the high point of the winter season. President Taylor "returned the salutations of thousands." People poured into the building without interruption from noon until 2 o'clock. The Marine Band added

gaiety to the party, and the visitors duly admired the fresh paint, the new rugs and curtains and china and glass.

In March there was a large reception held at the White House to celebrate the anniversary of the inauguration. A contemporary account tells us, "It was remarked that the ladies never appeared to better advantage. . . . Their influence began to be felt in political circles. . . . Mr. Webster began now to visit the White House and was treated with marked consideration by its female inmates."

On July 4th President Taylor accepted an invitation to sit on the platform at a big Independence Day celebration at the site of the Washington Monument. The day was hot and the President became ill shortly after his return to the White House. Four days later he was dead and his family lived through the agony of a state funeral, which was conducted with as much ceremony as such a funeral today.

The President's widow, accompanied by the Blisses and her son, returned to their Louisiana home. There she lived for two years before she died, and never in that time was she ever heard to mention the White House or her life in the Executive Mansion. When her husband was elected, she had declared it a plot to shorten his life and deprive her of his society, and time had proved her to be a true prophet.

# Favorite Recipes

## Crabmeat on Shells
### (Devilled Hard Crabs)

| | |
|---|---|
| 1 pound crab meat, well picked | 1 teaspoon fresh minced parsley |
| ¼ pound butter, melted | 1 teaspoon Worcestershire sauce |
| 12 salted crackers, crushed | 3 tablespoons dry sherry |
| 1 tablespoon mayonnaise, beaten with | salt and pepper to taste |
| 1 egg, whole | lemon wedges |
| ¼ teaspoon dry mustard | |

Clean and butter 6 to 8 large crab backs, or shallow shells or ramekins of ovenware. Over the cracker crumbs pour the melted butter, reserving some crumbs for sprinkling over the top of the crabs. Add mayonnaise which has been beaten with whole egg, the seasonings, and the sherry. Mix in crab meat lightly with fork, to prevent breaking the pieces. Fill the shells generously with the mixture, but do not pack down. Sprinkle with the remaining crumbs and bake in medium oven (350°F) for about 30 minutes. Serve at once with sprigs of parsley. Lemon wedges may be served separately.

## Wine Jelly

| | |
|---|---|
| 6 envelopes of gelatin (unflavored) (makes 3 quarts of jelly) | 1 pint fine dry sherry |
| 2 cups cold water | 3 tablespoons choice brandy |
| 6 cups boiling water | whipped cream, sweetened with a little sugar |
| 3 lemons (grated peel and juice) | vegetable food coloring |
| 2 cups sugar | |

Sprinkle gelatin on cold water to soften. Add sugar, salt, and lemon. Pour boiling water into it and stir well to dissolve thoroughly. When cool, stir in brandy, sherry, and food coloring, and place in molds that have been rinsed in cold water. Chill until set and serve with slightly sweetened whipped cream. Only the best Duff Gordon Amontillado or Bristol Cream Sherry is recommended. Garnish with orange slices and strawberries.

## Daube Glacé

| | |
|---|---|
| 5- to 6-pound round of beef | 4 tablespoons butter or shortening |
| ¼ pound salt pork cut into thin strips | ½ teaspoon cayenne |
| 2 veal knuckle bones, well cleaned | salt and pepper |
| 2 teaspoons mixed herbs (thyme, marjoram, savory, rosemary) | 1 clove garlic, minced |
| | 1 cup claret or other red wine |
| | 1 cup rich stock or bouillon |
| | can of peas |

Roll the strips of salt pork in the herbs and seasonings and, with a larding needle, insert into the meat, as in a sewing process. In a large heavy kettle, lightly brown the meat in the butter or shortening. Add the veal bones, 1 cup stock, and 1 cup claret. Cover with a tight lid, and simmer slowly in a 325°F to 350°F oven for at least 3 hours, turning the meat occasionally.

When the beef is tender, lift from kettle and set aside to cool. Strain the stock and reserve. Take a large mold or deep casserole. Cover the bottom of the mold or casserole to a depth of 1 inch with the stock, and chill until set.

Place the cooked beef onto this, and pour over the remaining stock, to which peas and carrots have been added. Chill overnight, to jell.

Serve on a large platter, garnished with green peas. If you prefer, the platter can be garnished with watercress and radish roses.

**Wine jelly**

Abigail Powers Fillmore

Millard Fillmore

# Millard
# FILLMORE

THE SUDDEN death of President Taylor brought to the White House a man and woman of simple domestic tastes and habits whose intelligence and tact helped them to become an acceptable addition to the Washington social scene.

Millard Fillmore, a handsome man, distinguished in appearance with dignified and courtly manners, had been Comptroller of the State of New York and a member of Congress from that state a number of years before he was elected Vice President.

Mrs. Fillmore, the former Abigail Powers, was a person of intellectual ability and culture. The President and his wife were accompanied by their son and daughter, Powers Fillmore, who acted as secretary to the President, and Mary Abigail, who assisted her mother with the social duties of the administration. Mrs. Fillmore was not well when she became First Lady, and it was sometimes necessary for her to remain in bed all day so that she might be able to receive her guests in the evening.

After President Taylor's death there was some talk about the White House being an unhealthy place in which to live, and there were rumors that, indeed, the new President would not live there. There was little ground for such a rumor. Within a month of Taylor's death, Millard Fillmore wrote from the White House to Salmon P. Chase, thanking him for a gift of wine: "Like yourself," he said, "I am chiefly a water drinker, but it will nevertheless be received by me with great pleasure and as soon as the removal of the habiliments of mourning from the White House will permit entertainment of my friends, it will be as you request, submitted to their criticism."

An appropriation from Congress for necessary modernizations at the White House leads us to this delightful contemporary record: "The old black cook who had served many years at the White House was greatly upset when a range of small hotel size was brought to his quarters. He had managed to prepare a fine State dinner for thirty-six people every Thursday in a huge fireplace, with the cranes, hooks, pots, pans, kettles and skillets; but he could not manage the draughts of the range, and it ended in a journey of the

President to the Patent Office to inspect the model and restore peace in the kitchen."

The Fillmores soon made a home of the President's House. Book-loving Mrs. Fillmore, a school teacher in her youth, secured money from Congress for a library. When she arrived at the White House there was not even a Bible or a dictionary in evidence. The books were installed in the oval room on the second floor and this room became a center for the family's activities. Visitors to the White House described the upstairs oval room as the most comfortable and cheerful room in the Mansion. It was in this room that Mrs. Fillmore received her personal friends in the evenings. In addition to the books, there was a piano for the First Lady and a harp for Mary Abigail, who was gifted in music. The mother and daughter especially enjoyed playing and singing duets for their friends.

Young Miss Fillmore was the sole social representative of her family for affairs outside of the White House. Not only was Mrs. Fillmore's health a problem, but she also felt that a public role for a lady was unseemly.

Mrs. Solomon G. Haven, whose husband had been the President's law partner in Buffalo, and who visited in the White House, has left us a delightful description of the pleasant atmosphere of the oval room: "Here Miss Fillmore had her own piano and harp, and here Mrs. Fillmore, surrounded by her books, spent the greater part of her time, and in this room the family received their informal visitors. The President had but little time to give to this library, but he usually succeeded in leaving the executive chamber at 10:30 at night, and spending a pleasant hour in the library with his family."

Shortly before Christmas 1850 Fillmore wrote to Mr. Haven: "The busy week is nearly ended, the last letter read—but not answered—and the last office-seeker politely bowed out of the room, and I seize the precious moment simply to say that I am anxious that you and Mrs. Haven should come and make us a visit this winter. Do come!—Come directly to the White House. We have one spare room in this temple of inconveniences, neatly fitted up—and just the thing for you and Mrs. H."

During the Fillmore administration, a reception was held at the White House each Tuesday morning, and a levee each Friday evening when Congress was in session. They had a large dinner on Thursday evenings in the State Dining Room, and more intimate dinners each Saturday in the family dining room of the White House.

One of the morning receptions was described by a guest: "Yesterday was a bright, windy day, and there were a good many ladies at the morning levee. Mr. Fillmore is in fine health and spirits, and I think it will be conceded by everybody that he is the best-looking of all the Presidents who have occupied the National Mansion. I have seen the greater part of them, but certainly for an unaffectedly polite and courteous gentleman none could compare with the present occupant. . . . He is a man among men in appearance, overtopping in his height the majority of the human family; finely formed, in good health, with a bright eye, erect in carriage, and sufficiently stout without being corpulent, he is the representative of the American gentlemen whom his countryman may take pride in."

There was great preoccupation with the President's good health probably because of the deaths of President Harrison and President Taylor within such a short space of time. President Fillmore himself explained it in these words: "I owe my uninterrupted bodily vigor to an originally strong constitution, to an education on a farm, and to lifelong habits of regularity and temperance. Throughout all my public life, I maintained the same regular and systematic habits of living to which I had previously been accustomed. I never allowed my usual hours of sleep to be interrupted. The Sabbath I kept as a day of rest. Besides being a religious duty, it was essential to health. On commencing my Presidential career, I found the Sabbath had been frequently employed by visitors for private interviews with the President. I determined to put an end to this custom, and ordered my doorkeeper to meet all Sunday visitors with an indiscriminate refusal. . . . My labors were also onerous and often excessive, but I never suffered an hour of sickness through them all."

The fact that some of the food for the White House table was bought outside of the city of Washington is documented by correspondence between the President and a Mr. Isaac Newton of Philadelphia. In one of the letters Mr. Fillmore sends thanks for two capons and a saddle of lamb and asks Mr. Newton to send more as they are available. From the correspondence it appears that Mr. Newton sent supplies regularly to the White House during the Fillmore administration.

The Fillmores extended every courtesy possible to incoming President Pierce when he arrived in Washington. William Makepeace Thackeray

**Roast capons**

was in Washington lecturing on English humorists, and Washington Irving was in town at the same time. President Fillmore invited Franklin Pierce to be his guest at the lecture. He also asked Pierce and Washington Irving to go on an excursion down the Potomac to view the steamship *Ericcson,* which was considered a great advancement in technology. The President and his wife also entertained Pierce, Thackeray, and Irving at dinner at the White House and at a public reception. Washington Irving has left a record of the visit: "I have been much pleased with what I have seen of the President and his family, and have been most kindly received by them.

"Yesterday I made a delightful excursion with

some of our household and some of the young folks of the President's family down the Potomac to Mount Vernon. We began by a pleasant breakfast at the President's.

"In the evening I was at the President's levee. It was very crowded. I met with many interesting people there, but I had no chance of enjoying conversation with any of them, for in a little while the same scene began which took place here, eleven years ago, on my last visit. I had to shake hands with man, woman and child."

It was said that Mrs. Fillmore caught cold the day of the inauguration standing on the cold, windy portico of the Capitol while her husband's successor, Franklin Pierce, was sworn in as Presi-

## *Favorite Recipes*

### *Roast Capons*

*Leave out the livers, gizzards and hearts, to be chopped and put into the gravy. Fill the crops and bodies of the capons with a force-meat, put them before a clear fire and roast them an hour, basting them with butter or with clarified dripping. Having stewed the necks, gizzards, livers and hearts in a very little water, strain it and mix it hot with the gravy that has dripped from the capons and which must be first skimmed. Thicken it with a little browned flour, add to it the livers, hearts and gizzards chopped small. Send the capons to table with the gravy in a boat, and have cranberry sauce to eat with them.*

| | |
|---|---|
| 2 capons | 2 breasts of chicken |
| ½ teaspoon salt | salt and pepper to |
| ¼ teaspoon pepper | taste |
| 2 egg whites, well | 1 cup bread crumbs |
| beaten | 1 cup milk |
| butter or drippings | ⅛ teaspoon mace |
| for basting | 3 tablespoons butter |
| flour, browned for | |
| gravy | |

### *Garnish*
**parsley sprigs**
**whole mushrooms,**
**cut into rosettes**

First, remove the livers, gizzards, hearts, and necks. Cut into small pieces. Stew the chopped-up pieces in a very little water until tender, and use in gravy.

Salt and pepper the capons. Fill the crops and bodies with a forcemeat made as follows: Chop and rub through a sieve the uncooked chicken breasts. Add salt and pepper. Boil together the bread crumbs, milk, and mace, until they are cooked to a smooth paste, about 10 minutes. Remove from fire, add butter, the seasoned chicken meat, and the well-beaten egg whites. Stir until thoroughly blended.

Roast the stuffed capons in a moderate oven (350°F) allowing 22 to 25 minutes to the pound, basting them often with butter or with clarified drippings.

Next, strain the liquid in which the livers, gizzards, hearts, and necks have been stewing, and mix this with the gravy that has dripped from the capons, which must first be skimmed. Thicken with a little browned flour, and add to the finely chopped pieces.

**Roast saddle of lamb**

dent and delivered his inaugural address. She was standing with Thackeray and Irving, their personal guests for the historic ceremony.

Mrs. Fillmore retired to the Willard Hotel in Washington that night with a severe chill and never left it. Bronchial pneumonia developed and the First Lady died there a few weeks later. The Fillmores had planned a European tour following their retirement from the White House. It would have been a glorious experience for the well-educated school-teacher First Lady, but fate did not permit her the pleasure.

After his term ended Millard Fillmore returned to his home in Buffalo and was an honored member of that community until his death in 1874.

Garnish capons with parsley, whole mushrooms cut into rosettes, and whole stuffed tomatoes. Serve the gravy in a gravy boat.

### Roast Saddle of Lamb

*Wash the meat, wipe it dry, spit it, and cover the fat with paper. Place it before a clear brisk fire. Baste it at first with a little salt and water, and then with its own drippings. Remove the paper when the meat is nearly done, and dredge the lamb with a little flour. Afterwards baste it with butter. Do not take it off the spit till you see it drop white gravy.*

*Prepare some mint sauce by stripping from the stalks the leaves of young green mint, mincing them very fine, and mixing them with vinegar and sugar. There must be just sufficient vinegar to moisten the mint, but not enough to make the sauce liquid. Send it to table in a boat, and the gravy in another boat. Garnish with sliced lemon.*

| | |
|---|---|
| saddle of lamb, 5 to 6 pounds | can of tiny carrots, heated |
| salt and pepper | potatoes, mashed |
| butter for basting | red pepper strips, for garnishing |
| flour for dredging | |
| can of asparagus tips, heated | |

Wash the meat, wipe it dry. Season with salt and pepper, and cover the fat with white paper. Put into an oven preheated to 300°F, and roast slowly, allowing 30 to 35 minutes to the pound. Baste it at first with a little salt and water, and then with its own drippings. Remove the white paper when the meat is nearly done, and dredge the lamb with a little flour. Afterwards baste it with butter. Do not remove from oven until you see it drop white gravy.

### Gravy

| | |
|---|---|
| 2 to 3 tablespoons flour | salt and pepper |
| 1 cup boiling water, if desired, seasoned with 1 bouillon cube | Worcestershire sauce (optional) |
| | 6-ounce jar of mint jelly |

To the drippings of the roast, add 2 to 3 tablespoons of flour gradually, stirring constantly to avoid lumps. Cook over low flame, continue to stir. Add boiling water or water seasoned with bouillon cube; continue to stir constantly. Season with salt and pepper. You may or may not add a flavoring of Worcestershire sauce.

Serve the saddle of lamb with asparagus tips, mashed potatoes, small boiled carrots, garnished with strips of red pepper. Mint jelly makes a nice accompaniment.

### Whole Stuffed Tomatoes

| | |
|---|---|
| 6 firm ripe tomatoes | ¼ teaspoon pepper |
| 1½ cups soft bread crumbs | 2 tablespoons butter or drippings |
| 1 teaspoon salt | butter in dabs |

Select tomatoes of equal size. Cut a piece from the stem end of each, and remove the centers, being careful not to break the walls. For the stuffing, use the centers of the tomatoes diced, crumbs, seasoning, and the butter or drippings. Mix well. Sprinkle each tomato with salt and pepper, and fill quite solidly with the stuffing.

Into a baking dish, place the tomatoes with a dab of butter on each. Bake in a moderate oven (350°F to 375°F) until tender, about ½ hour. Serve hot.

*Franklin Pierce*

*Jane Means Appleton Pierce*

# Franklin
# PIERCE

THE INAUGURATION of President Franklin Pierce was marred by the personal sadness of the new President, whose only son Bennie, a boy of eleven, was killed in a railroad wreck between the election and the inauguration. Mrs. Pierce was so prostrated by the loss that she stopped in Baltimore before reaching Washington, unable to bear the sight of the joyous ceremonials surrounding the inauguration of a new President. The inaugural ball had been canceled in the national mourning period for the Pierces' son, but great crowds did call at the White House to pay their respects to the new President.

President Pierce, after receiving visitors until past midnight of his inauguration day, went wearily upstairs to his private quarters only to find them in complete disarray. There was not even a bed made up for the President to sleep in.

Mrs. Pierce brought with her to the White House to assist in the social duties of hostess at the Mansion Mrs. Abby Kent Means, her long-time friend and relative by marriage. It was at a Means home in Amherst, nineteen years before, that Jane

Appleton and Franklin Pierce had been married. Jane Appleton was the daughter of a former president of Bowdoin College, and their romance dated from Pierce's college days.

Franklin Pierce was the son of a New Hampshire governor and had already been elected United States Congressman when they were married. His wife disliked political life intensely. Perhaps one reason was her husband's tendency towards alcoholism, which was evident even then. Another reason was her own poor health. At her persuasion Franklin Pierce, by then a United States Senator, retired to the life of a circuit lawyer in Concord in his home state. He became a leading citizen and won further distinction in the Mexican War, in which he attained the rank of General. The deadlock of the Democratic Convention in 1852 ended with the nomination for President of Franklin Pierce, a "dark horse" candidate. He was elected. Despite his wife's dislike of political life she took pride in the overwhelming vote which carried her husband into office, the youngest man so far elected President. The future looked bright for

the little family until the day when their son was killed right before their eyes in the railroad accident. It was a shock from which they never really recovered. Mrs. Pierce retreated still further into her invalidism, and President Pierce seemed to lose his self-confidence and his ability to lead. The Pierce who lived in the White House was not the same man as the dashing General of the Mexican War or the successful politician.

The President secured a New Hampshire hotel keeper and his wife to take over the running of the White House. By the end of March Mrs. Pierce was well enough to come to Washington with Mrs. Means.

The records show that at first the President did the social honors alone. By New Year's Day of 1855 Jane Pierce received beside her husband at the large annual reception, but she had been present at smaller affairs earlier in the administration.

Mrs. Pierce's first appearance in public was at a Presidential levee late in 1853. The tragic death of her son was still a subject of pitying conversation throughout the country, and Mrs. Pierce showed the effects of grief and shock. At this levee, she was clad in black velvet and diamonds, accentuating her natural pallor. Mrs. Clement Clay of Alabama said that "Mrs. Pierce's sweet graciousness and adaptability came freshly to me as I saw her assume her place as the social head of the nation."

Jessie Fremont said of Mrs. Pierce: "Her woebegone face, with its sunken dark eyes, and skin like yellowed ivory, banished all animation in others. She tried but constantly broke down in her efforts to lift herself, but her life was over in fact from the time of that dreadful shock. Mr. Pierce, too, felt their loss deeply, but his was a more genial

nature. He was a most amiable man whose friends remained always attached to him. He often received alone, and many a pleasant, gay circle gathered near the fireplace in the oval room and kept him amused."

A journalist's description of the White House during the Pierce administration says:

"The President's house had assumed a sombre, melancholy aspect, in consequence of the heavy dispensations of Providence which had fallen on Mrs. Pierce. Her efforts to entertain were forced and gave only pain to those who attended her receptions. Everything seemed to partake of her own serious melancholy and mournful feelings, and every echo of the merry laugh had died from the walls."

Mrs. Clay reported that a weekly occurrence in the city and one to which all Washington and every visitor thronged was the concert of the Marine Band which was given "within the White House grounds on the green slope back of the Executive Mansion overlooking the Potomac." Military uniforms were mixed among the black coats of the civilians, and often the President and his Cabinet were there, mingling democratically with the crowds of smiling citizens.

At one of these concerts an out-of-town visitor approached the President with shyness and, in a burst of courage, asked, "Mr. President, can't I go through your fine house? I've heard so much about it that I'd give a great deal to see it."

"Why, my dear sir!" responded President

**Pierce's state china**

Pierce kindly, "that is not my house. It's the people's house. You shall certainly go through it if you wish!" and, calling an attendant, he instructed him to take the grateful stranger through the House.

It is recorded that at state dinners during the Pierce administration a bouquet of camellias, from the White House greenhouse, wired to a lace paper doily was at the place of each lady. It was a style-setting note and Mrs. Clay wrote that "for an entire season the japonica (as the flower was called by the Southerners) was the only flower seen at the houses of the fashionable or mixing in the toilettes of the belles."

Mr. Amos Lawrence of Massachusetts leaves a charming description of dinner at the White House in his diary for the month of April 1854:

"At 6 o'clock I went with Sarah to dine at the President's. The company consisted of 25 persons besides ourselves. The servants seemed to know who we were, & ushered us into a handsome parlor where some of the guests were assembled. . . . Soon the President & Mrs. Pierce with Mrs. Means, & Miss Mary Mason came in. They greeted us cordially, & the President introduced all the company to Mrs. Pierce. Others arrived who were all introduced. Mrs. Pierce was handsomely dressed, & appeared well, tho. somewhat sad, as she always does. Dinner was announced. Judge Douglas, Senator of Illinois (of Nebraska memory) took Mrs. Pierce, Gen. Shields (of Mexican War celebrity & now Senator) took Sarah, & I had Mrs. Means. There were so few ladies that most of the gentlemen were obliged to go without; the private secretary Mr Sidney Webster having assigned the ladies as previously arranged. The dining room was splendid; so was the dinner. All in good taste, & after the modern fashion: No meats on the table, nothing but flowers and fruits. The servants handed each dish to all the guests in order. The head waiter was Peter who formerly lived with Mr. Copley Green: He seemed to be pleased to see us. The President & Mrs. Pierce sat on opposite sides of the table, & appeared well. After dinner we went into another room."

The First Lady began to receive at Friday afternoon receptions, at which she was assisted by Mrs. Means. Jane Pierce was always gracious, and the quietly elegant parties were popular with the people who lived in Washington. The strong affection felt for President Pierce and his wife by the many Southerners who made Washington their home is reflected in a letter Mrs. Robert E. Lee

**The Amos A. Lawrence diary describes a dinner ▶**
**at the White House on April 13, 1854**

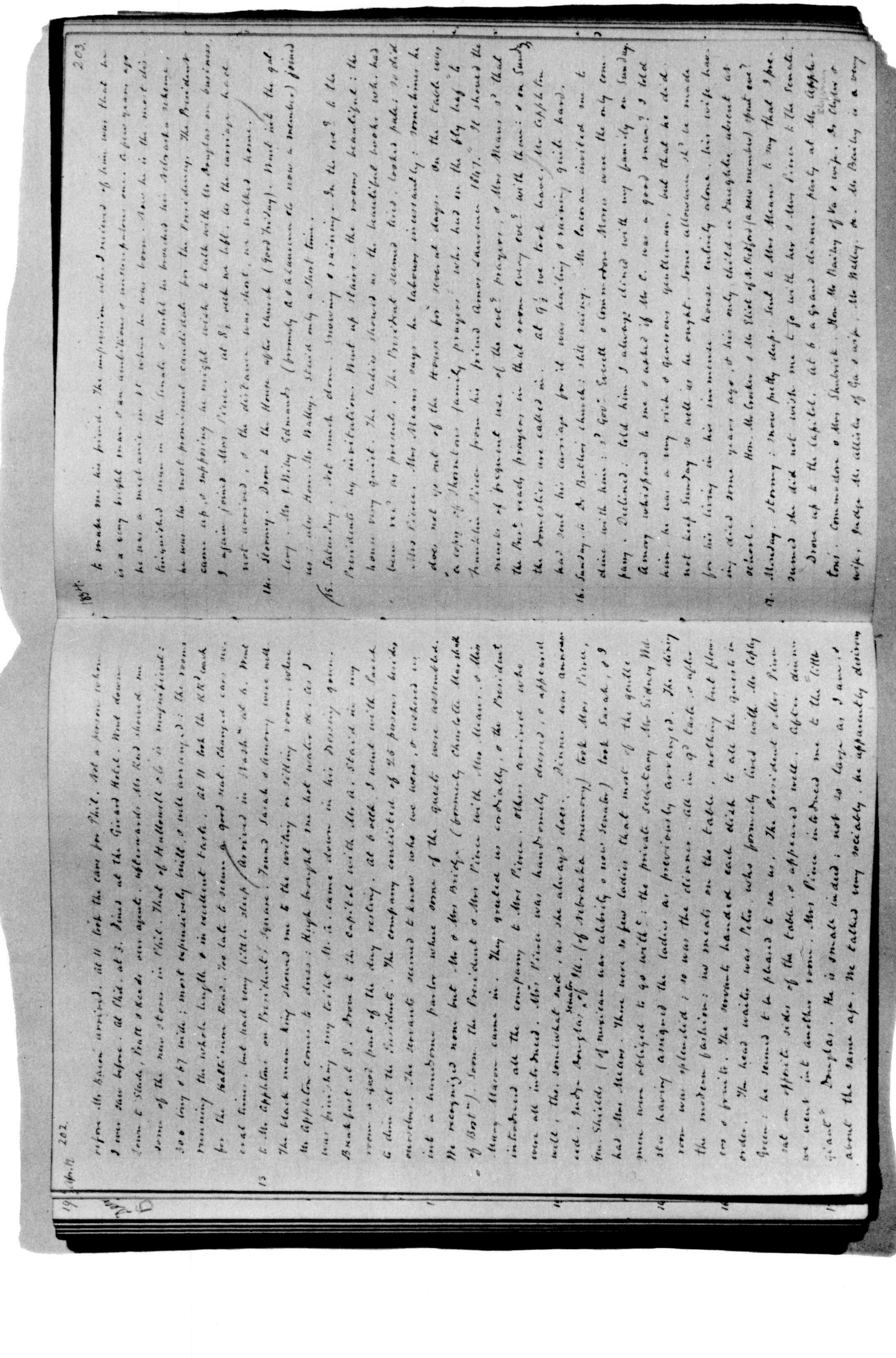

wrote at this time: "I have known many of the ladies of the White House, none more excellent than the afflicted wife of President Pierce. Her health was a bar to any great effort on her part to meet the expectations of the public in her high position, but she was a refined, extremely religious and well educated lady."

This kindly view is also reflected by those members of the White House staff who found her concern for their well-being rather unusual. She was especially anxious that all the young attachés attend church, and on their return she would ask about the sermon. Pierce's private secretary confessed that "Many a time have I gone from respect to her, when, left to my own choice, I should have remained in the house."

It was an administration which left town on the same subdued note on which it arrived. President and Mrs. Pierce moved out of the White House a bit early so that it could be cleaned up in preparation for the incoming President Buchanan. Pierce remembered too well the confusion of his own inaugural day and the indignity of there not being a bedroom ready for the President to sleep in.

After President Buchanan's inauguration, the Pierces returned to Concord with Mrs. Pierce now an admittedly sick woman. Despite a lengthy stay abroad in search of a climate where she could be comfortable, they returned home in 1860. Three years later she died, her husband still devotedly attentive at her side.

## *Favorite Recipes*

**Boiled lobster**

### *Boiled Lobster (or Crabs)*

| | |
|---|---|
| lobsters or crabs | cayenne pepper |
| salt water, boiling | salt |
| hard-boiled eggs | oil and vinegar |
| mustard | |

Lobsters, as well as crabs, should be boiled in strong salt and water. Have your pot of water boiling hard, put in the lobsters or crabs, and boil them for ½ hour, or if they are very large, a little longer. Take them out of the pot, and when they have drained, open them. Extract the meat carefully, putting it back into the shells for serving. Send the dish to the table cold.

Lobster or crabs are usually dressed at the table with mustard, hard boiled eggs, cayenne pepper, salt, oil, and vinegar.

### *Baked Clams*
### *(Whole or Minced)*

| | |
|---|---|
| 3 dozen clams | 2½ to 3 cups of grated |
| 1 teaspoon powdered | bread crumbs |
| mace | butter |
| 1 teaspoon powdered | |
| nutmeg | |

In taking out the clams, save several dozen of the largest and finest shells, which must afterwards be washed clean, and wiped dry. This is for minced clams.

Either chop the clams fine, or leave them whole, and mix with some powdered mace and nutmeg. Butter the sides and bottom of a large, deep dish, and cover the bottom with a layer of bread crumbs. Over this scatter some very small bits of sweet butter. Then, a layer of clams, minced or whole, next, another layer of bread crumbs and small dabs of butter. Proceed in this manner till the dish is full, finishing at the top with a layer of crumbs.

Set the dish in a preheated medium oven (375°F), and bake about ¼ hour. Have ready the clam shells, and fill them with the baked mixture, either leaving them open or covering each with another clam shell. Place them on a large hot dish, and send them to the table piping hot.

## Beef à la Mode

| 3 to 4 pounds round of beef | Dressing: |
| pepper and salt to taste | butter |
| flour for gravy | onion, chopped fine |
| watercress, for garnish | bread crumbs |
| | pepper and salt to taste |
| | pint of cold water |
| Optional: cloves, allspice | |

A round of beef is best for this purpose. With a sharp knife cut incisions in the meat about 1 inch apart, and within 1 inch of the opposite side. Season it with pepper and salt, according to the size of the piece of meat. Make a dressing of butter, onion, and bread crumbs, in the proportion of 1 pint of crumbs, 1 small onion finely chopped, and 1 ounce of butter with pepper and salt to taste. Fill the incisions with the dressing, put the meat in a pot, with about 1 pint of cold

**Beef à la mode**

water, and cover it tightly. Let it simmer 4 hours or until meat is tender.

Some stick in a few cloves, and those who are fond of spice add allspice. When the meat is done, dish it up, and thicken the gravy with a little flour. Let it boil once, and serve it in a gravy boat. Garnish the meat with watercress. A few slices may be carved in the kitchen, before the beef comes to the table.

*Harriet Lane Johnston*

*James Buchanan*

# James BUCHANAN

**W**ITH THE election of President James Buchanan, our only unmarried President, the Capital began the gayest social season in its history. The man in the White House was wealthy, an epicurean, a gay bachelor with a flair for society and impeccable knowledge of its ways. The First Lady was to be his niece, Miss Harriet Lane, a lovely young lady of twenty-five who had been well prepared and trained for her exciting new role.

Left an orphan as a child of 9, Harriet Lane picked her Uncle James as her choice of foster father and guardian. Uncle James, bachelor though he was, accepted the responsibility most seriously and began training her in deportment and educating her so that someday she might be able to serve as his official hostess. She spent two years at the convent school in Georgetown, D.C., and on the weekends she visited her uncle, who was then Secretary of State, to observe the ways of the fashionable world. After several seasons in society she accompanied Buchanan to Great Britain, where he was United States Minister to the Court of St.

James. Here they were welcomed in the highest social circles and the Court was so pleased with Harriet that the Queen granted her the full privileges of a diplomatic wife. The successful completion of their diplomatic duty set the stage for the next move by Buchanan and his beautiful niece. In March 1857 James Buchanan was inaugurated as President of the United States, and Harriet Lane assumed the duties of First Lady of the White House.

The Pierces graciously moved out of the White House a day early so that the house would be ready for President Buchanan and Harriet when they returned from the inaugural. Most of the staff had stayed from the previous administration, and President Buchanan soon hired a competent steward to take care of all the domestic arrangements. Miss Harriet was given complete freedom in matters of social protocol, with the steward handling the execution of details.

Only a few weeks after the inauguration, the President sent a note to his liquor merchants rebuking them for sending champagne in small bottles: "Pints are very inconvenient in this house, as the article is not used in such small quantities."

The domestic routine of the President's family was as follows: The household rose at 6:30 and was finished with breakfast by 8. The President then spent all morning in his second-floor office receiving visitors and attending to his mail. After lunch every day he met with his Cabinet, then went for an hour's walk in the vicinity of the White House. Harriet kept busy each morning planning or attending social functions. Many of her afternoons were spent riding on her beautiful white horse. Accompanied only by her groom she was a familiar and beloved sight in Washington.

In the evening the family gathered for dinner about 7. Buchanan invited one or two Cabinet families and a few friends to small weekly dinners at which rarely more than fifteen were present. Once a week there was a state dinner for forty persons that would include members of Congress, Supreme Court Justices, the diplomatic corps, service personnel, and important visitors from both home and abroad. Buchanan prepared the guest list, Harriet arranged the table according to protocol and Buchanan Henry, the President's nephew and secretary, paired the guests for dinner. Harriet's task was most delicate for she had to seat all guests in the right order of precedence without offending anyone and had to be careful to avoid the personal and political feuds that have always been an undercurrent in Washington social life. It speaks well for her London training and her own intelligence that she was so successful as an official hostess.

The White House receptions again became gorgeous displays of finery. Harriet Lane's personal beauty and her full figure were displayed to advantage in the hoop skirt and low bodice of Victorian fashions. Mrs. Clement Clay of Alabama describes the brilliant scene: "Low necks and lace berthas, made fashionable because of their adoption by Miss Lane, were worn almost universally, either with open sleeves revealing inner ones of filmy lace, or sleeves of the shortest possible form, allowing the rounded length of a pretty arm to be seen in its perfection. . . . Jewels were conspicuous even in men's dressing, and gentlemen of fashion were rare who did not have varieties of sparkling studs and cravat-pins to add to the brightness of their vari-coloured vests. The latter not infrequently were of the richest satin and velvet, brocaded and embroidered. They lent a desirable note of colour, by no means inconspicuous, to the swallow-tail eve-

ning dress of that time, a note, by-the-bye, which was supplemented by a tie of bright soft silk and ample proportions. President Buchanan was remarkable for his undeviating choice of pure white cravats."

The White House again took on the air of a European court. Titled travelers made it a stopping place as most of them were personal friends of the President whom he had met and gotten .to know during his diplomatic appointments at the Russian and British courts. All the expenses of this entertaining President Buchanan paid personally.

Buchanan was so particular about the quality of his food that he had fresh butter sent him regularly from Philadelphia in a locked brass-bound kettle. Once, when Harriet Lane wished to correspond with an old friend in Philadelphia who had become a political enemy of her uncle, she had two keys copied from that on the ring of the White House steward. With one key in her possession and the other sent to Philadelphia the two ladies corresponded for the last years of the administration "via the kettle," as they wrote on the envelopes.

A rather exciting event took place during the administration of President James Buchanan at the time of the annual visit of the Indian delegation, which was always an exciting affair. Mrs. Clay says that in the fifties these delegations usually numbered several hundred. They camped in a square in the Barracks, where, with almost naked

**Buchanan's china at Wheatland**

**Gooseberry tart**                    **Shoulder of pork**

bodies, scalps at belt and tomahawks in hand, they were viewed daily by crowds of curious visitors as they beat their drums, danced, or threw their tomahawks into the air. A single chain separated the Indians from the curious crowds. "To see the copper-hued sons of the Far West clad in buckskin and moccasins, paint and feathers, stalking about in the East Room of the White House was a spectacle not easily forgotten." The assembled chiefs, through their official interpreter, expressed to the

President their pleasure at being there and told him of their desire for continued peace. They said they needed farm implements and a grist mill. In the midst of this friendly exchange "a . . . younger redskin sprang from the floor, where with others of the delegation he had been squatting. . . . The muscles of his upper body, bare of all drapery, glistened like burnished metal. His gesticulations were fierce and imperative, his voice strangely thrilling. 'These walls and these halls belong to the redman!' he cried. 'The very ground on which they stand is ours! You have stolen it from us and I am for war that the wrongs of my people may be righted!' His motions became so threatening that the guests started to panic, but 'our dear old Mr. Buchanan, with admirable diplomacy' assured the young brave that the White House belonged to the Indians just as it did to all the people of the country and that he but welcomed the 'red brothers' to their own on behalf of the country."

The social life of the Buchanan administration reached its peak in 1860, as it was about to end. In May there was a visit by a large delegation of Japanese dignitaries who had come to the United States for the signing of the first commercial treaty to be negotiated with the mysterious Oriental empire. The visitors were the consuming topic of conversation in Washington and throughout the country. Harriet Lane wrote to a friend, "They are really a curiosity. All the women seem to run daft about them."

The Japanese delegation bowed low to Miss Lane and the other Cabinet wives, the only women they considered to be of a rank high enough for them to meet personally. President Buchanan gave a state dinner for them, arranging them in small groups at separate tables, at which members of the Cabinet presided. They left at the White House a whole room full of gifts which were placed on public view: ". . . saddles beautifully embroidered and embossed in gold and silver, bed curtains and screens, two princely swords, kimonos, lacquered ware, writing cases and a superb tea set inlaid with pearls and gold and valued at $3,000."

In October of that same year the Prince of Wales concluded a visit to Canada with a tour into the United States and a stopover in Washington. It was the first visit to the United States of a member of the British royal family and it created great excitement in top social circles.

Harriet wanted to have a huge ball for the Prince, but the President stated, "No dancing in the White House," in deference to many people throughout the country who believed dancing to be sinful. Instead the President held a grand state dinner. Towards the end of it the President grew fidgety and told the waiters to hurry up the courses because he thought the young man was falling asleep at the table. Later, guests played cards—a great concession by Buchanan, as he had never before allowed cards to be played in the White House. That night, after putting all the guests to bed, Buchanan discovered that all the beds were being used and he had to spend the night on the sofa. The Prince made a special trip to Mt. Vernon to place a wreath on the grave of George Washington. The party traveled to Mt. Vernon aboard the revenue cutter the *Harriet Lane*. An elegant lunch was catered by Gautier's of Washington, and on the return trip there was music and dancing. The Queen of England was delighted at the warm reception to her son in this country and sent the President and his niece her personal thanks and gifts of appreciation. This visit seems to mark the beginning of the strong ties which were to bind the British nobility and American high society for the next half century.

The last days of President Buchanan's administration were not happy ones. With the election of Abraham Lincoln the country started falling apart, with President Buchanan unable to stop the inevitable trend to war. His efforts to maintain the Union angered his Southern friends while the Northerners considered him to be partial to the South. He was happy to be able to turn the turmoil of a country on the brink of war over to the next President on March 4, 1861. At last he was to be relieved of the crushing cares and anxiety which he had borne for four years. Buchanan was out of politics at last. Now he was free to go home to his beloved Wheatlands in Lancaster, Pennsylvania. But his longed-for retirement was tormented by those who believed him responsible for the Civil War and those who believed him a Southern sympathizer. His consuming purpose in life became a defense of his policy, his character, and his reputation. In 1868 he died at Wheatland, having lived to enjoy Harriet Lane's marriage to Henry Elliot Johnston of Baltimore, a banker, of whom he highly approved, and to see their first child born. In a quieter era James Buchanan's many talents might have made him a great President, but he was overpowered by the events leading to the Civil War and overshadowed by the towering personality of the President who followed him.

Dining room, Wheatland

## *Favorite Recipes*

### Pennsylvania Dutch Stuffed Shoulder of Pork

| | |
|---|---|
| 5- to 6-pound shoulder of pork, boned | 1 tablespoon brown sugar |
| salt | Garnish of cinnamon apples, tiny |
| pepper | boiled carrots, |
| 4 cups fresh sauerkraut | mashed potatoes |
| flour | |

Sprinkle the meat inside and out with salt and pepper. Fill the shoulder with the sauerkraut, which has been drained. Sew or skewer the opening. Score the top lightly in a diagonal pattern as for baked ham.

Dredge with flour and brown sugar.

Preheat the oven to 450°F, and start the roast in this hot oven for 10 minutes. Reduce the heat to 350°, and bake 30 to 35 minutes to the pound, basting occasionally. Half an hour before the roast is done, pour off most of the drippings. Then place the remainder of the sauerkraut in the roaster around the meat, and complete the roasting.

Garnish the platter with cinnamon apples and mashed potatoes put through a pastry bag with rose tube; add small boiled carrots.

If the sauerkraut is not desired, it can be omitted as shown in the picture. In this case, carefully roll up the boned shoulder of pork and tie securely with string. Follow the other directions given.

### Mashed Potatoes

| | |
|---|---|
| 3 large Idaho potatoes | 2 eggs (used |
| 1 tablespoon salt | separately) |
| ¼ teaspoon pepper | pastry bag |
| 2 ounces butter | |

Peel the potatoes and cut in half. Place in a pan and cover with cold water. Add 1 tablespoon salt, bring to a boil. Let the potatoes simmer until they are soft; drain, return to pan to dry a little. Beat until smooth, adding butter and 1 egg. Season to taste with salt and pepper.

Fill pastry bag with the potato mixture. Use rose tube. Pipe large rosettes on buttered baking dish, sprinkle with beaten egg. Brown under the broiler, watching carefully so that they do not get too brown. Garnish the platter holding the shoulder of pork with these potato rosettes.

### Gooseberry Tarts Crust

| | |
|---|---|
| 1½ cups flour | ½ cup shortening |
| ¾ teaspoon salt | 3 tablespoons water |

Measure the flour into a mixing bowl and mix the salt thoroughly through it. Next, with a pastry blender cut in half the shortening finely until the mixture looks like meal.

Cut in the remaining shortening coarsely with particles the size of giant peas.

Sprinkle with water, 1 tablespoon at a time, mixing lightly with a fork until all the flour is moistened. Gather the dough together, press into a ball, then roll out on lightly floured pastry board. Fit pastry over the backs of fluted tart pans. (If you are making pie, line the bottom of a pie plate or bread pan.) Lay the tart pans upside down on a baking sheet. Bake at 475°F for 8 to 10 minutes.

### Filling

| | |
|---|---|
| 2 cups gooseberries | 2 tablespoons |
| 1 cup boiling water | cornstarch |
| ⅔ to 1 cup sugar, | 1 tablespoon butter |
| according to the | |
| acidity of fruit | |

Cook gooseberries and water until tender. Drain off the juice and add sugar and cornstarch, then add fruit, and cook 10 minutes. Stir in butter, chill, and pour into baked tart shells or pie shell.

### Cinnamon Apples

| | |
|---|---|
| 8 Rome Beauty apples | 2 cups water |
| (of equal size) | ½ cup cinnamon drops |
| 1 cup sugar | |

Pare and core the apples.

Boil sugar, water and cinnamon drops. When cinnamon drops dissolve, slowly add the apples, one at a time. Cook over low flame until tender. When tender, remove apples from syrup.

Boil syrup until it falls heavily from a spoon. Then pour over the apples.

**Shoulder of pork**

*Mary Todd Lincoln*

*Abraham Lincoln*

# Abraham
# LINCOLN

ABRAHAM LINCOLN rode up Pennsylvania Avenue to his inauguration in an open carriage, seated beside the outgoing President Buchanan. The air was tense with the fear of violence and the street was protected by guns at street corners and a line of sharpshooters on the roofs of adjacent buildings to protect the carriage as it passed. At the Capitol Mary Todd Lincoln and her family party were waiting to witness the stirring event. The day was sunny and the Capitol Plaza was crowded with a "sea of upturned faces representing every shade of feeling, hatred, discontent, anxiety and admiration."

At the close of the ceremony President and Mrs. Lincoln rode together back down the avenue to the White House. The door was opened to them by "Old Edward," doorkeeper of the Mansion since the administration of President Taylor. That night there were seventeen people at dinner, counting the family, the Todd cousins, and Springfield friends. They all attended the Inaugural Ball that evening, giving social Washington its first glimpse of the President and his First Lady. No wonder Mary needed the support of her Springfield family to face the eyes of the hostile city. They marched into the ballroom in twos while the band played "Hail Columbia." Mary's escort for the Grand March was Senator Stephen Douglas of Illinois, a long-time acquaintance and one of her serious suitors. Mary later danced the quadrille with him. Though the President retired before 12 o'clock, the rest of the White House party stayed on enjoying the dance.

The next morning Mary was up and at breakfast before 8 o'clock. A visitor who had that early morning appointment writes of her in the upstairs sitting room dressed in a "cashmere wrapper quilted down the front" and a "simple headdress." She was again surrounded by her Springfield family, most of the ladies in "morning robes."

The day was spent getting settled and inspecting their new home. Mary was very much disappointed and dismayed at the condition of the mansion. Except for the state rooms on the main floor the house seemed shabby. Everything needed to be redone, and Mary immediately decided that it would be her project to improve the house. Like many other things she attempted, the project was a worthy cause, her intentions were good, but her judgment was questionable.

In the household arrangements finally adopted by the family, the east side of the White House was devoted to business and public affairs, while the west side, except for the State Dining Room, was reserved for the family. Upstairs over the East Room were the President's office, the waiting room, and the offices of the President's secretaries. On the west end were the family bedrooms and guest rooms.

We find that Mrs. Lincoln especially liked the Red Room, which she used as her sitting room. Here she received private calls every evening of the week when she was in town, and in that room the President often met his friends socially after dinner.

One of the Springfield cousins related that before the first day in the White House was half over the place was mobbed with office seekers who filled waiting rooms, halls, and corridors and were even found pushing into the family quarters. This throng continued and increased during the ensuing war years. The house was in a continual turmoil, and for a person of Mrs. Lincoln's nervous disposition, there appeared to be no escape.

The first of the regular Friday evening receptions was held very soon after the inauguration, on March 8. Mrs. Keckley, the White House seamstress, was surprised at the new First Lady's poise. She had not expected it. She had heard Mrs. Lincoln being discussed in the city as ignorant, vulgar, and unused to polite society. Nothing could have been further from the truth. The hostess who greeted the crowd was dignified, calm, and completely charming.

Mary Todd Lincoln came from a proud, prosperous Southern family. She was well educated and accustomed from the time of her childhood in Kentucky to being in the center of the social circle. Only after her marriage to a poor lawyer in Illinois was her social life curtailed. The match of the pretty young social butterfly with the tall, rawboned lawyer, ten years older than she, was undoubtedly a love match. It had been opposed by her family. With the marriage, Mary for the first time faced the practicalities and responsibilities of life. Despite the rocky road their marriage traveled, Abraham Lincoln's career moved steadily ahead, and by the time the Lincolns arrived at the White House Mary felt she was well able to cope

with the social life of the White House. Unfortunately she stepped into a city which was predominantly Southern in sympathy and, as one who had rejected her own Southern background, Mary immediately became the target for all the cruelty and malice to which people could subject her. Few women have been placed in as difficult and lonely a position as Mrs. Abraham Lincoln, and she was both mentally and physically poorly equipped to accept it.

Mrs. Lincoln had brought to her position as First Lady excellent qualifications: the family background of a gentlewoman, a good education, a bright mind, a vital if somewhat mercurial personality, a desire to help her husband, and a natural enjoyment of social affairs. It was her misfortune that many of her social customs were provincial as compared with the greater sophistication of Washington society, and she was never allowed to forget it. She compensated for the critical attitude all about her with orgies of spending for an elegant home and an elaborate wardrobe.

Endless official duties crowded on the Presidential couple, including military reviews and visits to encampments.

On one occasion when a hamper of choice wines was sent to Mrs. Lincoln, she sent it on to a military hospital with the remark, "I never use any and Mr. Lincoln never touches any." It was not their custom to serve alcoholic beverages at White House entertainments.

With the beginning of the Civil War the Lincolns found that they were being criticized for continuing official entertaining, yet an attempt on their part to curtail social affairs was equally criticized.

During the first years of the Lincoln adminis-

**Lincoln's home, Springfield, Illinois**

Election cake        Fricasseed chicken        Scalloped oysters

tration the White House was open for the usual Friday evening levees, and in addition there were regular Saturday afternoon receptions. These receptions were more democratic than those of previous administrations, with an attendance which mixed Eastern elegance with frontier crudeness. Every class and condition from all sections of the country were cordially welcomed by the President and First Lady. These receptions were an ordeal, as each guest expected to shake hands with the President. In order to save his wife from this an arrangement was worked out by which Lincoln stood to the front, with his two secretaries introducing him to the people who filed past, while Mary stood behind her husband further back in the room. In this position she could be seen by all and was available to personal friends and special guests.

There was also continued the custom of music on the White House grounds on Wednesday and Saturday evening, with the public having free access to the area. The Marine Band played and the guests promenaded with an occasional appearance by the President on the balcony.

At an official dinner for the diplomatic corps in June that first year, Mrs. Lincoln introduced something new. The *Washington Star* describing the occasion says, "Through the good taste of Mrs. Lincoln, the stiff, artificial flowers, heretofore ornamenting the Presidential tables, were wholly discarded and their places delightfully supplied by fragrant, natural flowers." The conservatory at the White House was a real source of pleasure for Mrs. Lincoln. She loved flowers and delighted to send bouquets to her friends, including men to whom she wished to accord special recognition.

That August the French Prince Napoleon came to Washington and was entertained at a formal dinner at the White House. As the day was Saturday the Marine Band was just concluding its regular concert on the South lawn when the royal guest arrived. He consented to step out on the balcony so that he could see the crowd and, in turn, the crowd could see him. He was in full dress, "his breast a flame of decoration," over which crossed a crimson sash. It must have been an unforgettable experience for Mrs. Lincoln when she entered the State Dining Room on the arm of the Prince. And it was an equal satisfaction that, thanks to boarding school in Kentucky, she was able to join in the conversation, which was largely in French.

It was the local gossip that Mrs. Lincoln asked to charge the entertainment of the Frenchmen to the government and that Seward said no. About the time of the entertainment, wagonloads of manure were delivered to the White House for the lawn. According to the story, Mrs. Lincoln sold it and used the money to pay for what was crudely called "the manure dinner."

Before long Mrs. Lincoln decided to drop the costly state dinners from the White House social program. Her argument was wartime economy, but Mrs. Keckley says she won her point by saying, "Public receptions are more democratic than stupid state dinners—are more in keeping with the institutions of our country."

Much as Mrs. Lincoln enjoyed the social life of the White House, her husband and their sons

were the most important things in her life. After their son Willie died in 1862 the grief-stricken mother was inconsolable. She banned flowers from the White House because Willie had so loved them. She put an end to the concerts on the lawn because she could not stand the gay music. But grief did not stop her shopping trips to New York. It seemed that more and more they became the addiction which brought her comfort and the illusion of security. By 1863 her bills were so huge that she began to worry lest because of them her husband should not be reelected.

Summers during the Lincoln administration were spent at the Soldiers' Home on the outskirts of Washington. Here the air was fresher and the family could have privacy from the hordes of people who continued to haunt the White House.

With Lincoln's reelection in 1864 and his

**Lincoln's state crystal, champagne glass**

Lincoln's state crystal, dinner wine goblet

Keckley and little Tad, so distraught that she could not face the dreadful reality. She stayed in that room for five weeks before she was sufficiently composed to leave the White House.

During those five weeks the public had almost unlimited access to the White House. In the words of Washington correspondent Mary Clemmer Ames, who was an eyewitness, "The rabble ranged through it at will. Silver and dining ware were carried off, and have never been recovered. It was plundered not only of ornaments but of heavy articles of furniture. Costly sofas and chairs were cut and injured. Exquisite lace curtains were torn into rags and carried off in pieces." All the efforts Mrs. Lincoln had made to improve the White House turned to naught in the final tragedy.

When Mary Lincoln moved from the house

**Lincoln's state crystal, sherry glass**

inauguration in 1865 swiftly followed by the end of the war, it seemed that family fortunes would take a turn for the better.

The second inauguration was truly a victory celebration. On inauguration night the President and Mrs. Lincoln received for four hours at the White House while 15,000 people came through the line. This was Saturday evening, and on Monday night the Patent Office was the scene of an elaborate Inaugural Ball. Mrs. Lincoln wore a $2,000 dress, shimmering white silk and lace, with an elaborate fan and headdress. It was a moment of triumph.

Scarcely more than a month later the President was dead at the hands of an assassin and laid in state in the East Room of the White House.

The bereaved widow was in a bed upstairs at the White House, attended by the faithful Mrs.

Lincoln's state china

a confused mass of clothing, accessories, presents, and miscellaneous belongings were boxed and sent with her. It was the size and number of these boxes which led to the oft-repeated story that Mrs. Lincoln was robbing the White House, an unjust accusation that is sometimes still heard today.

The remainder of Mrs. Lincoln's life was spent in the shadows as both her physical and mental health deteriorated and as she lost one by one the persons dearest to her.

She died in Springfield, Illinois, at the home of her sister in 1882, the same house in which she had been the happy bride of the frontier lawyer destined to become one of the greatest of our Presidents.

# Favorite Recipes

## Fricasseed Chicken

| | |
|---|---|
| 2 to 3 fryers, cut up | parsley |
| salt | ¼ teaspoon nutmeg |
| pepper | ¼ teaspoon mace |
| flour, for dredging | a little butter rolled |
| ½ pint cream | in flour |
| lard or butter, for | parsley sprigs |
| frying chicken and | |

Cut up your chickens into pieces of the desired size. Wipe the pieces dry, season them with pepper and salt, and dredge lightly with flour. Fry them in lard or butter until they are brown on all sides. When they are quite done, take them out of the frying pan, and keep them hot in a covered pan on an asbestos pad over a low flame.

Skim the gravy in the frying pan, and pour the cream into it. Season with a little nutmeg, mace, salt, and pepper, and thicken it with a small bit of butter rolled in flour. Stir carefully to be sure that the mixture is smooth. Give it a boil, and then pour it over the pieces of chicken which have been kept hot and which must be served hot. Put some lard or butter into the pan. Fry the parsley sprigs in it to garnish the chicken; the fried parsley must stay green and crisp.

A variation is white fricassee of chicken.

## White Fricassee of Chicken

| | |
|---|---|
| 2 to 3 fryers, cut up | sweet marjoram |
| salt | ½ pint cream |
| pepper | butter rolled in flour |
| ¼ teaspoon nutmeg | Optional: small |
| ¼ teaspoon mace | forcemeat balls |

To make a white fricassee of chicken, remove skin, cut them up into pieces of the desired size. Season with salt, pepper, nutmeg, and mace, and strew over the pieces some shredded marjoram. Put them into a stewpot, and pour over them the cream, or whole milk. Add some butter rolled in flour, and if you choose, some small forcemeat balls. Set the stew pan over a low flame. Keep it tightly covered, and stew or simmer it gently till the chicken is quite tender, but do not allow to boil. Serve hot.

## *Scalloped Oysters*

| | |
|---|---|
| ¼ cup butter, melted | 2 tablespoons sherry |
| 2 cups coarse cracker crumbs | 1 teaspoon Worcestershire sauce |
| 2 dozen oysters (drained, save the liquor) | ⅓ cup cream mixed with oyster liquor |
| ¼ teaspoon coarse black pepper | |

Mix butter and cracker crumbs. Butter shallow baking dish and put ⅓ of the mixture on the bottom. Add layer of oysters. Mix cream, oyster liquor, sherry, Worcestershire sauce, and pepper. Cover layer of oysters with half of sauce. Add another ⅓ of the crumbs, place remaining oysters on top, and add remaining sauce. Sprinkle with the remaining ⅓ of the crumbs. Bake in hot oven (425°F) for 10 or 15 minutes until crumbs are lightly browned.

**Election cake**

## *Election Cake*

| | |
|---|---|
| 1 cup currants, soaked overnight in a tightly closed jar in ½ cup brandy | 1 cup sugar |
| | 2¾ cups sifted flour |
| | ½ teaspoon salt |
| | ¾ teaspoon mace |
| 1 tablespoon sugar | 1 teaspoon cinnamon |
| ¾ cup scalded milk | 1 egg, whole |
| 1 yeast cake | 1 teaspoon grated lemon rind |
| ¼ cup warm water | |
| 1 cup flour, unsifted | 2 teaspoons lemon juice |
| ½ cup butter | |

To the scalded milk add 1 tablespoon sugar; cool. Dissolve the crumbled yeast in warm water, and add to milk. Add the unsifted flour, and beat until well blended. Let rise in warm place until it has doubled in bulk, about 1 hour.

Cream butter and sugar until very light. Drain brandy from currants. Place sifted flour, salt, mace, and cinnamon in sifter. Add egg to creamed mixture and beat until light. Stir in lemon rind and juice. Add yeast mixture and beat thoroughly. Add currants, retaining the brandy for later. Sift in flour, add brandy, beat well. Place in tube pan or 9x5 loaf pan that has been well greased. Cover with a cloth and place in warm place away from draft. Allow to rise until double in bulk. This mixture rises very slowly and may take 4 to 6 hours to double in bulk.

Bake at 375°F for about 45 minutes. Cool in pan briefly. Turn out on rack, allow to cool further. Then brush with lemon or orange glaze.

## *Lemon or Orange Glaze*

| | |
|---|---|
| 1 cup confectioners' sugar | ¼ cup lemon or orange juice |

Mix the sugar with the lemon or orange juice. Beat well. Then spread thin on top of cake. Let it drizzle down the sides, but do not ice the cake sides.

Eliza McCardle Johnson

Andrew Johnson

# Andrew
# JOHNSON

THE SIMPLE ceremony at which Andrew Johnson took the oath of office of President of the United States took place in his rooms at the Kirkwood House in Washington on the morning that President Lincoln died.

The new President did not want to disturb the sorrowing widow in the upstairs room at the White House, so he set up temporary executive offices in the Treasury Building on the side adjacent to the White House. Here he worked at his desk daily from 9 until 5. Secretary of the Treasury McCulloch relates, "His luncheon, when he had one, was like mine—a cup of tea and a cracker."

For his temporary home, the new Chief Executive accepted the offer of Representative Samuel Hooper's house on Massachusetts Avenue. The first morning, there was actually no food in the house and he had to send to market before he could have his breakfast.

The new President wished to be as considerate of the widow of the late President as possible. On April 25 Robert Todd Lincoln had written

him, "My mother is so prostrate that I must beg your indulgence. . . . Mother tells me she cannot possibly be ready to leave here for two and a half weeks." The Lincolns finally left the house with great reluctance early in June.

It was June 9 before President Johnson could move into the big, empty house. His family was still in Nashville. That entire first month he was so immersed in work that he did not leave the house a single time.

On the Fourth of July, he was at last persuaded to take a boat trip down the Potomac. His daughter, Mrs. Patterson, and her children, who had arrived in Washington by that time, accompanied him. The first year was to be as happy a season as Johnson would be permitted to spend in the White House.

In August two carriages arrived at the mansion bringing the rest of the Johnson family. In one was the President's wife Eliza, weak from continuing attacks of tuberculosis. She came from Tennessee in company of her other daughter, Mrs. Stover, with her three children, and the

President's sons, Robert and Andrew Junior. With his son-in-law, Senator Patterson, the household numbered twelve. Robert acted as his father's secretary, Andrew entered school, Mrs. Johnson retired to a quiet bedroom on the southwest of the Mansion, leaving Martha Johnson Patterson to assume the role of First Lady for the administration.

The grandchildren with their many activities transformed the White House into a happy home. The President was devoted to children, and it was for them that he reserved most of his infrequent smiles. It is reported that at one of the White House New Year's receptions, "his affectionate, ample greeting to the children in the throng was particularly noticeable, and was remarked by all. Big-hearted people afterward remarked, as they gathered in the East Room, that the President's success in putting little people at their ease was a sure indication of his excellence as a man."

There were many children's parties at the White House that first summer, special fetes as well as informal entertainments. A young friend of Andrew Junior once lunched at the President's table when the table conversation turned to pirates. Sixty-three years later, the guest could still recall Johnson's wonderful smile.

The children coaxed the President away from his work to take long walks with them in Rock Creek Park and drives into the country. One afternoon, returning from Rock Creek in a thunderstorm, the President saw a poor woman carrying her baby and walking toward town in the rain. He stopped his carriage, picked up the ragged and wet creature and took her back to her home.

In spite of their simplicity, White House social activities during this administration were not uncouth or rude. Mrs. Patterson was a woman of dignity and taste, as were her mother and sister. Senator McCulloch said of the Johnson ladies, "More sensible and unpretending women never occupied the White House." The White House dressmaker, Mrs. Keckley, tells of going to the Mansion one day with some dresses and finding Mrs. Patterson busily at work at the sewing machine. One of the secretaries says that Mrs. Patterson "made all the butter that was used in the White House during her father's term of office."

Martha Johnson Patterson was no stranger to the White House. As a schoolgirl at the convent in Georgetown she had visited in the White House on weekends during the administration of President Polk, a fellow Tennessean.

In the days of uncertainty following the Lincoln assassination, one of Martha's first statements was obviously calculated to set the people at ease. She said, "We are plain people from the mountains of Tennessee, called here for a short time by a national calamity. I trust too much will not be expected of us."

The first job facing the new First Lady was to get the house cleaned up and made presentable after the hard usage it had received during the war years. It took soap, water, mending, patching, and a $30,000 appropriation from Congress to do the job. Martha supervised the work closely, even giving up her summer vacation to do so.

To quote Mary Clemmer Ames, the New York reporter who wrote in her *Ten Years In Washington:* "The result of this ceaseless industry and self-denial was the President's house in perfect order and thoroughly renovated from top to bottom. When it was opened for the winter season, the changes were apparent and obvious, even to the dullest eyes, but very few knew that the fresh, bright face of the historic house was all due to the energy, industry, taste and tact of one woman, the President's daughter."

The house was first reopened to the public on New Year's Day 1867. The rooms had been newly and strikingly repapered; the floors were carpeted with rich velvet carpets which were covered to prevent soil. After the guests were received, they made their exit from the Green Room, through the hall to a bridge constructed at a hall window, and from thence to the north lawn. The East Room was still being worked on.

Martha Patterson used flowers in natural arrangements to enhance the beauty of the rooms. Most of these came from the White House conservatory. A severe fire in the conservatory that same year caused $20,000 worth of damage and destroyed one third of the White House collection of rare plants, including a Sago palm which had been imported by George Washington. Fortunately, however, the new decorations were not damaged.

It was said that White House dinners in this administration were well planned and well served. Martha was liked by the White House servants who were careful to carry out all her suggestions.

During his term of office Johnson stayed close to his task, always hard at work. He got up at 6 in the morning in the summer; at 7 in the winter.

**Saddle of lamb à la duchesse**          **Stuffed eggplant, Spanish style**

He would write, study, or read until 10. For the next hour he saw visitors. At 11 came lunch, and in the next hour he met with his Cabinet or special visitors. Often at 3 he took a walk if he could get away; 4 was his dinner hour and relaxation. At 5 he was back at his desk, often working until midnight, with a cat and a coffeepot for company. At 8 he stopped briefly for refreshments with his family. This, for year after year, was a usual day for the President so that it was a wonder he endured it physically. He was an omnivorous reader and was especially fond of history, though lists of books he read include poetry and novels.

All in all the White House during this administration seemed to be "an old-fashioned, hospitable, homelike, farmhouse," with the President of the United States "one severely earnest laborer."

All during the bitter days of President Johnson's impeachment trial Mrs. Patterson went on with the social events regularly scheduled at the White House, and the family faced the curious public with cheerfulness. Diplomats were impressed when the President and his daughter serenely presided at a diplomatic reception from 8 until 11 without any indication of the trouble that faced them. There was an air of confidence about the family that impressed all who came to the White House.

The months after the acquittal were, naturally, a bit more relaxed. The President now seemed eager to get what pleasure he could out of entertaining his friends. The White House began a brilliant and popular season. On December 29, the President's sixtieth birthday, there was a great children's party at the Mansion to which children all over the city were bid by engraved invitations from "The President of the United States." Johnson stood at the entrance of the Blue Room and greeted his small guests with cordial hospitality. Mrs. Patterson and Mrs. Stover were beside him. Even his wife came downstairs on this occasion to view the happy throng. The Mansion was brilliantly lighted and wonderfully decorated so that it "looked like fairy land." Dancing in the East Room was led by the students of Marini's Dancing Academy, and included the Highland fling, the Spanish fandango, and the Virginia reel. Afterwards the President led the way to the dining room for refreshments. One little guest reported "gorgeous refreshments of ice cream and cakes and beautiful glacé fruits."

New Year's Day was the scene of another huge reception. The people came in such a throng that the crowd was hardly able to move. From 11 in the morning until late afternoon the President shook hands with thousands. The only person absent was the President-elect; his absence was so noticeable that President Johnson took it as a personal affront.

On Washington's Birthday another large reception was held at the White House. And on the evening of March 3 the house was packed with friends and officials who had come to say good-bye. The occasion was a personal triumph for

President Andrew Johnson.

The next day the President did not ride up to the Capitol to attend the inauguration of his successor. Instead, he stayed at the Executive Mansion until noon. Then he shook hands with his Cabinet members and the White House staff and was driven off in his carriage, only a few minutes before the new President, Ulysses S. Grant, drove down Pennsylvania Avenue and into the White House grounds to become the next resident of that historic house.

Johnson's trip home to Greeneville, Tennessee, two weeks later was a series of receptions. His friends and neighbors demonstrated their confidence in him by returning him to Congress as their Senator in 1874. He served less than a year and died six months before his invalid wife.

# *Favorite Recipes*

## *Stuffed Eggplant, Spanish Style*

| | |
|---|---|
| 4 small eggplants | 1 cup chopped celery |
| 1 No. 2 can solid-pack | heart, including |
| tomatoes, or | tops |
| 2½ cups peeled chopped | 1 teaspoon basil |
| fresh tomatoes | butter |
| 1 onion, chopped fine | salt and pepper to |
| herb-seasoned bread | taste |
| crumbs, or | ½ teaspoon sugar |
| prepared dressing | |
| mix | |

Select small firm eggplants, and wash well. Cut in half lengthwise, leaving stem if any. Using a curved grapefruit knife, cut out the center, leaving about ½ inch in the shell. Butter the shells well, and place them in shallow baking dish or casserole containing about ½ inch water. Cut the centers of eggplant that you have removed into small pieces into a saucepan, discarding any coarse seedy portion. Add celery, tomatoes, basil, and seasoning, and simmer over low heat. Sauté onion in butter, and add to mixture. Stir constantly until tender and until mixture is thick. Place mixture in shells, sprinkle with crumbs, and dot generously with butter. Bake at 325°F for about 15 minutes. Drain water, if any, from bottom of casserole and serve from it. Serves 8.

Large eggplants may be used if small ones are not available. Cut each in half, and serve to make

8 portions. Garnish with thin slices of fresh tomatoes and a strip of broiled bacon on top of each serving.

## *Saddle of Lamb à la Duchesse*

| | |
|---|---|
| 8-pound saddle of | ¼ cup flour, for |
| lamb | dredging and |
| 1 teaspoon salt | gravy |
| ½ teaspoon pepper | hot water, for gravy |
| 5 or 6 strips of bacon | |

If saddle of lamb is not available, get a 6-pound loin of lamb, and have butcher crack the bones between the joints for easier carving and serving.

Rub the lamb with salt, pepper, and flour. Place on rack in open pan with a few slices of fat bacon on top. Roast at 300°F, allowing 30 to 35 minutes per pound. Americans prefer it well done; the French prefer it rare. Pour off surplus fat, add flour to drippings, stir carefully to avoid lumps, brown slightly, add hot water for gravy to serve in sauce boat.

Put paper cuffs around roast before serving.

## *Garni*

| | |
|---|---|
| cream puff cases or | currant preserves or |
| patty shells | currant jelly |

In small cream puff cases or patty shells, place spoonfuls of whole currant preserves or currant jelly, arrange around roast.

*Ulysses Simpson Grant*

*Julia Dent Grant*

# Ulysses S. GRANT

WHEN ULYSSES S. GRANT took the oath of office in March 1869 the city of Washington was mobbed with visitors who had come to see their soldier hero assume the highest office in the land. The weather was cold and a blizzard threatened, but the people's enthusiasm made it a memorable occasion nonetheless. As soon as the ceremony was over a salute was fired, steam whistles blew, bells pealed, bands played, and the crowd cheered. Only Andrew Johnson was absent from the scene, as the bitterness between the two men was too deep to be bridged even casually. After the ceremony the Grants returned to the White House in the afternoon to greet their throngs of admirers and then went back to their own residence on I Street, a home which Julia Dent Grant was reluctant to leave.

The Inaugural Ball that night was even more disorganized and confused than usual. It was held in the newly finished wing of the Treasury Building, and the company was almost choked by the plaster dust of the construction. The checking facilities failed completely, and only a few of the guests were able to reach the elegant supper included in the celebration. But the President and the new First Lady seemed oblivious to these difficulties and received their guests with smiling faces through all the confusion.

As First Lady one of Mrs. Grant's first tasks was planning for some renovation and redecoration at the White House in the fall. She assumed the duties of the first winter's social season with quiet authority. Thus began the years that Julia was to look back upon as "the happiest of my life."

Mrs. Grant had Cabinet wives and other friends assist her at the weekly afternoon receptions and the honor guard was always invited to lunch in the family dining room beforehand. At times the ladies remained at the table so long that the impatient guests in the East Room would begin to stamp their feet. Then Julia would lead her assistants to the Blue Room from which all daylight had been excluded. The receiving line, headed by Mrs. Grant, greeted all the guests as they streamed past, shaking hands with them and

121

sending them on to the State Dining Room for refreshments. Before the party ended, the President frequently joined the guests to add to their pleasure.

The parading visitors could take note of the new lace curtains and fresh crimson brocatelle draperies at the windows, the glittering chandeliers, the gilt cornices, and the frescoed walls and ceiling.

Julia's reception day was Tuesday until 1875, when she changed it to Saturday. The President received on Thursdays, and all were welcome for the traditional open-house days on New Year's and the Fourth of July. The Grants liked to think that their functions were truly republican in tone— that ladies in silk and ladies in calico, those in diamonds and those in glass, were equally welcome. It was said that "chambermaids elbowed countesses and all enjoyed themselves."

In *The Olivia Letters,* Emily Edson Briggs, a Washington newspaper correspondent who left a record of Washington during the Reconstruction period, observed that a "perfect river of human life" attended these affairs and that guests were usually packed in like sardines.

The state dinners were also rated as successful. One of the first changes Julia had made was in the kitchen staff. The President had installed a quartermaster in the kitchen who viewed the White House table as a sort of supermilitary mess stressing quantity rather than quality. Instead, Julia hired an Italian steward named Melah who had had experience catering in fashionable hotels, and under his direction the White House food became famous. The table seated thirty-six without improvising, and dinners for that number were given almost every week. This is how *The Olivia Letters* describes one of these elegant dinners:

"In the beginning of the feast, fruit, flowers, and sweetmeats grace the table, whilst bread and butter only give a Spartan simplicity to the 'first course,' which is composed of a French vegetable soup, and according to the description by those who have tasted it, no soup, foreign or domestic, has ever been known to equal it.

"The ambrosial soup is followed by a French croquet of meat. Four admirably trained servants remove the plates between each course, and their motions are as perfect as clockwork. These servants are clad in garments of faultless cut, which serve to heighten to the last degree their sable complexion. White kid gloves add the finishing touch to this part of the entertainment. The third

'course' of the dinner is composed of a fillet of beef, flanked on each side by potatoes the size of a walnut, with plenty of mushrooms to keep them company. The next course is dainty in the extreme. It is made up entirely of luscious leg of partridges, and baptized by a French name entirely beyond my comprehension. It will readily be seen that a full description of the twenty-nine courses would be altogether too much for the healthy columns of a newspaper to bear, so we pass to the dessert, not omitting to say that the meridian or noon of the feast is marked by the guests being served bountifully with frozen punch. As a general rule, wine is served about every third course. Six wineglasses of different sizes and a small bouquet of flowers are placed before each guest at the beginning.

"The dessert is inaugurated by the destruction of a rice pudding, it is such a pudding as would make our grandmothers clap their hands with joy. After the rice pudding, canned peaches, pears, and quinces are served. Then follow confectionery, nuts, ice-cream, coffee, and chocolate, and with these warm, soothing drinks the Presidential entertainment comes to an end, and the host and his guests repair to the Red Room, and after fifteen minutes spent in conversation the actors in a state dinner rapidly disappear."

Melah also indulged Julia's liking for Southern food. At formal dinners, the Grants faced each other from either side of the table. Dinner was not allowed to drag. Two hours were permitted at the table and then the guests moved to the Red Room or Blue Room for a few minutes of conversation before retiring.

It took some time to reconcile President Grant to the more formal aspects of White House social life but he finally adapted himself surprisingly well. He learned to wear evening coat and white tie, and he took an interest in the seating arrangements for formal dinners. He personally selected the wines to be served, though his own glass was usually turned down.

It was recorded by Colonel Crook, usher during the administration, that Mrs. Grant was an able housekeeper and that "any morning her stout, comfortable figure might be seen making the rounds of kitchens and pantries and stopping to talk to the servants."

Many of the state dinners consisted of twenty-nine courses with a break after the entrée for Roman punch to fortify the guests. A dinner for thirty-six during this administration might

**Roman punch**  **Hollandaise sauce**  **Fillet de boeuf à la jardinière**

cost as much as $2,000, although the average cost was about $700. For these dinners the State Dining Room was elaborately decorated with garlands of roses and evergreens festooning the ceiling and walls. Potted plants filled every available space on the floor while the table itself was decorated down its great length with epergnes of fruit and garlands of flowers. The centerpiece was often a solid silver ship with a figure depicting Hiawatha sailing on the mirrored lake. This had been a gift to the White House from the Mohawk Indians.

The President usually got up at 7 A.M. and read his daily paper until breakfast. Then he and Mrs. Grant would go down to breakfast arm in arm. Their fare was often broiled Spanish mackerel, steak, bacon and fried apples, buckwheat

cakes, and coffee—a far cry from the cucumbers and coffee the general had had for breakfast during the war years. After the President escorted his wife back to her sitting room they would visit together awhile, and then he set out for his morning walk. He was at his desk by 10 and worked diligently until 3 o'clock in the afternoon.

When dining alone the family usually assembled at 7 o'clock. The Grants were indulgent parents and dinner at the table with the children was apt to be both merry and noisy. The President often rolled bread into little balls to throw at Nellie and Jesse. When someone got hit with a bread ball then they received a kiss for apology. Unfortunately the President would sometimes roll bread balls unconsciously and he was once ob-

**Grant's state china**

served doing it at Lady Thornton's table. The children were in bed by 9. Julia followed before 11, but the President generally stayed up still later.

The social pace grew more furious each year the Grants were in the White House. After the restrictions imposed by the war years and the bitter feelings of the Johnson administration, the people were glad to have the White House doors open to them more often.

The New Year's Day reception in 1872 was considered a brilliant affair. The military and the diplomatic corps attended in all the elegance of their colorful uniforms and native dress. The house was decorated with flowers and the Marine Band played in the corridor. Julia wore a very becoming gown of Venetian red velvet. By this time she had enough experience with official receptions so that the newspaper correspondents could observe that there had never been "so little formality or so much genuine sociability at the White House receptions."

Each summer the Grants returned to their summer cottage at Long Branch, in New Jersey. It was a welcome change from the hectic social life in Washington, and the Grants' son Jesse and his mother always looked sad when it came time to leave and go back to Washington.

The day of the second inauguration in 1873 was one of the coldest on record. With the temperature hovering at 4° above zero and a strong wind blowing, decorations and flags were ripped to shreds and the musicians' breath froze on their instruments. The President's speech could hardly

be heard in the icy gale. But the ball that night was even more uncomfortable. In the big, barn-like temporary building called the "Muslin Palace" the guests danced in their wraps. Hundreds of canaries designed to provide a triumphal chorus huddled in their cages and some even froze to their perches. It was so cold that the food froze solid. By midnight the guests went home to thaw out.

Perhaps the biggest social event of the Grant administration was the wedding of Nellie Grant to the young Englishman, Algernon Charles Frederick Sartoris, in May 1874. The ceremony took place in the East Room in the presence of more than two hundred guests. The room was a bower of flowers and the dais on which Nellie stood was canopied with ferns and vines and surmounted by a wedding bell of snowballs and white roses. Rings with the couple's initials swung at either side of the bell. Afterwards an elaborate dinner was served in the State Dining Room. The fare was as elegant as the occasion demanded, and the menus were printed on white satin with a bridal knot of ribbons. Gifts that had poured in from around the world were on view in the library. It was a fairy-tale wedding for a much-loved and only daughter.

The Grants' last New Year's Day reception was marred by a great snowstorm, but still crowds flocked to the Mansion for their last opportunity to pay their respects to their beloved soldier President.

Mrs. Grant went over the house personally in preparation for the new incoming President and his family. She generously stocked the larder for Mrs. Hayes, and the President ordered a supply of wines for the new tenants.

As a gracious gesture the Grants then gave a State dinner in honor of the Hayes and after the inaugural ceremonies Julia was hostess for the last time at the White House at a luncheon for the new President and Mrs. Hayes.

Immediately after they left the White House the Grants set out on a triumphal round-the-world tour. They were gone over two years and were received as honored guests in every place they visited. They returned to make their home in New York. There the General died in 1885 after a valiant race with death in an effort to finish his memoirs. The money which his literary efforts brought to Mrs. Grant as a widow enabled her to live comfortably until her death, seventeen years later.

# Favorite Recipes

## Fillet de Boeuf à la Jardinière

| | |
|---|---|
| a 5-pound fillet of beef with fat and skin removed | narrow strips of salt pork or bacon, for larding |

### Fillet

Have meat at room temperature. Preheat oven to 500°F. Place fillet, larded with pork or bacon on oiled rack in shallow roasting pan. Place in hot oven and reduce heat to 350°F. Bake without basting about 20 to 30 minutes to the pound, depending on the degree of rareness desired. Turn out on a large hot platter. Serves 8. Drain fat from drippings, and make clear thin gravy to be served in a separate gravy boat.

## Garniture à la Jardinière

| | |
|---|---|
| 1 package frozen cauliflower flowerets | 1 cup fresh or frozen string beans |
| 1 package frozen asparagus tips | 2 cups tiny carrots (canned) or small frenched carrots |
| 1 package frozen Brussels sprouts | butter and sugar for glazing |
| 2 cups fresh or frozen green peas | 2 boiled turnips, diced |
| 1 cup small pearl onions (canned) | For garnishing: parsley sprigs, small red peppers |

Heat all the vegetables. The carrots should be glazed by sautéing in a bit of butter and sugar. The turnips should be tossed in butter. Arrange the hot vegetables in small mounds around the platter of beef, alternating for color. Garnish with parsley and small red peppers. With the vegetables, serve a separate bowl of Hollandaise sauce.

## Hollandaise Sauce

| | |
|---|---|
| 2 egg yolks | dash cayenne pepper |
| ½ cup butter | 1 to 1½ tablespoons |
| ¼ teaspoon salt | lemon juice |

Use a double boiler over water that is hot but not boiling. In top of double boiler, put egg yolks with ⅓ of the butter. Stir mixture constantly. When butter has melted, add another ⅓ of the butter, and as it melts and the mixture thickens, add the remaining ⅓ of the butter. Continue to stir the whole time without interruption. When the mixture is sufficiently thick, remove from heat and stir in seasonings.

## Roman Punch

| | |
|---|---|
| 1 quart lemon sherbet | 1 split of champagne, iced |
| 1 cup choice rum | |

In a chilled bowl, turn out the lemon sherbet. Slowly, mix the rum into it. Now quickly add the champagne which has been chilled, and serve in sherbet glasses. This amount will serve 10. It should be of a mushy texture, to be drunk, not spooned.

**Mrs. U. S. Grant's recipe for veal olives in *Our Own Cook Book*, 1892**

18      OUR OWN COOK BOOK.

or gravy to moisten it, cover with pie-crust, bake in a quick oven for three-fourths of an hour.

### VEAL CUTLETS FRIED.
#### MRS. L. DODGE.

Take half butter and lard in a frying pan, beat 2 eggs, season your cutlets with pepper and salt, dip into the eggs and roll in flour, and fry a nice brown. Cook them on a moderate fire, as veal requires to be better done than beef.

### VEAL OLIVES.
#### MRS. U. S. GRANT.

Slice as large pieces as you can get from a leg of veal; make stuffing of grated bread, butter, a little onion, minced salt, pepper, and spread over the slices. Beat an egg and put over the stuffing; roll each slice up tightly and tie with a thread; stick a few cloves in them, grate bread thickly over them after they are put in the skillet, with butter and onions chopped fine; when done lay them on a dish. Make your gravy and pour over them. Take the threads off and garnish with eggs, boiled hard, and serve. To be cut in slices.

### CORN BEEF HASH.

Take tender boiled corn beef entirely free from fat or gristle, chop fine and mix with it

*Rutherford Birchard Hayes*

*Lucy Ware Webb Hayes*

# Rutherford B. HAYES

WHEN RUTHERFORD B. HAYES, Governor of Ohio, was nominated for President on the Republican ticket, it was not expected that he would win the election. His Democratic opponent was Samuel J. Tilden, who ran ahead of him by half a million popular votes. To the astonishment of all, Hayes won by a single vote in the electoral college—if the votes of Louisiana, South Carolina, and Georgia were really his. In this election, two sets of electors claimed the right to cast those states' votes. Congress finally set up a commission to decide which slate of electors, Republican or Democratic, should be recognized. Only on the very eve of the inauguration did the commission decide to count the votes of the electors representing the Reconstruction governments of the three states and so to make the Republican, Hayes, President.

President-elect and Mrs. Hayes started for Washington before they knew the final decision of the Commission. They were en route to Washington before they received word that Hayes had

been declared officially elected.

That year March 4 fell on Sunday. President Grant, anxious that no further complication should develop, on Saturday, March 3, invited the President-elect and Mrs. Hayes to dinner at the White House. He made of it an elaborate formal occasion with 36 guests and a big bouquet at each lady's plate, with a 10-foot pink azalea plant behind Mrs. Hayes' chair. The Grant Cabinet attended, with members of the Grant and Hayes families and the Chief Justice and his wife. At midnight President-elect Hayes was unobtrusively taken into the Red Room, where, unknown to the other guests, Chief Justice Waite administered the oath of office to him. The signed oath was given to the Secretary of State for safekeeping to be used in any emergency that might arise before the official and public ceremony to be held at the Capitol a day later, on Monday, March 5.

After the inaugural luncheon that day, when the Grants left the White House, the new regime started. Colonel W. H. Crook, Disbursing Officer

126

at the White House for many administrations, wrote, "It was not long after the new President arrived at the White House that everyone felt a new atmosphere." It was the beginning of the reforms of Lucy Webb Hayes, who soon aired the mansion of the fumes of expensive cigar smoke, foreign perfumes, and imported champagne. Virtue became fashionable, and Lucy was hailed as its defender.

The Washington correspondent, Mary Clemmer Ames, described Mrs. Hayes as she looked at the inaugural ceremony: "A fair woman between two little children looks down. She has a singularly gentle and winning face. It looks out from the bands of smooth dark hair with that tender light in the eyes which we have come to associate always with the Madonna. I have never seen such

a face reign in the White House."

The new President and his wife were a well-educated couple, and for the first time the White House was graced by a First Lady who was a college graduate. The Hayes moved in with their five children, ranging in age from their oldest son, Webb, who was to act as his father's secretary, to the baby Scott, who was only 6 years old. Lucy entered the White House as a handsome, matronly woman, kind-hearted, strong-willed, disciplining her family and making her own life and that of her family a model for the whole country. She never swerved from her high ideals and was revered by most of the nation as "the noblest of women."

The President quickly established a daily routine which appears so regular as to be almost dull.

**Scalloped oysters     Roast beef with potato puffs and parsnips     Corned beef with vegetables**

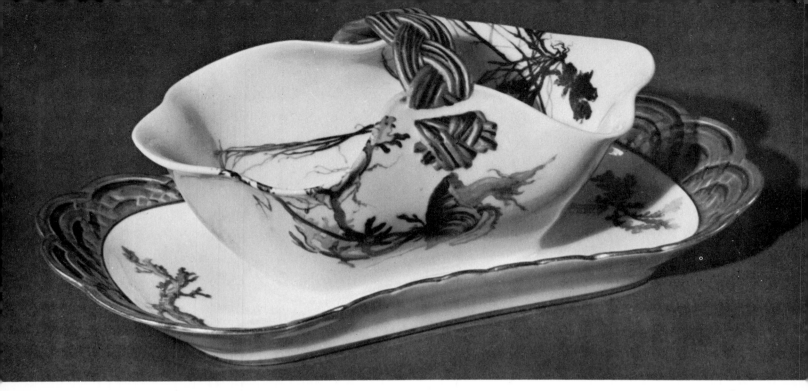

Hayes' state china

On rising he took gymnastic exercises and made it a daily duty to walk a certain distance in the hall after each meal. He restricted himself to a single cup of coffee at breakfast, to one cup of tea at lunch, and did not indulge in tobacco or alcohol. After breakfast he wrote letters until 11 o'clock; then he had Cabinet meetings or official visitors until lunch. After looking over his mail, he went out driving at 3:30 p.m., returning for a short nap before dinner. Every night after dinner the family gathered in the Red Room to sing old ballads, hymns, and Stephen Foster songs. Then

Hayes' state china

to the Blue Room for family prayers. The children were sent off to the library to study their lessons, and until bedtime the President and Mrs. Hayes received guests. This was the time when the Hayes were ready to receive all who might care to come to see them. A report stated that "These quite informal evening gatherings, where all was bright and cheerful and of good report, became the distinctive feature of Mrs. Hayes' regime at the White House."

It was on Sundays that the White House became the true model home of the nation. The President, his wife, and family would walk each Sunday to services at the Foundry Methodist Church. In the evening hymn books were distributed; the Vice President's sister went to the piano, and all who were gathered at the house, both relatives and the official family, joined in singing hymns. Nor was their piety merely a pose. There are many records of Mrs. Hayes' charity to the poor of the city of Washington. On Thanksgiving Day all the secretaries and clerks of the White House and their families came to the mansion to enjoy turkey dinner with the First Family, and at Christmas there were gifts for everyone. Colonel Crook said, "I never knew an employee or servant to be reprimanded during the four years when Mr. and Mrs. Hayes were in the White House."

Naturally there was the usual succession of sumptuous state dinners, and the elegant receptions, customary during every term, were continued. One mammoth banquet for twenty-five hundred people filled the East Room, with the guests seated at a number of small tables; another smaller dinner cost $4,000, a lavish outlay for those days. The first grand banquet given at the White House was an entertainment for Grand Dukes Alexis and Constantin of Russia, who were on an official tour of this country. At the insistence of the Secretary of State, the Hayes bowed to diplomatic custom and permitted wine to be served at the elegant dinner. The worldly brilliance of this affair troubled the Hayes, and shortly thereafter they made public their resolution that as long as they lived at the White House no more wines would be served to dinner guests. This pronouncement earned for Mrs. Hayes the nickname of "Lemonade Lucy." Despite the elegance of all her dinner parties, it is for her ban on alcoholic beverages that Mrs. Hayes is most remembered today. It appears, however, that this was a decision made by the President rather than by Mrs. Hayes.

There was one occasion when it seemed as though some member of the White House staff was playing a trick on the President and Mrs. Hayes. In the course of a dinner one evening, oranges filled with frozen punch were served, and the punch was distinctly flavored with rum. The diplomats at the dinner thought it a great joke and proceeded to tell the story all over town. Ben Perley Poor, the famous journalist of the day, reported that "The President appeared to be wholly ignorant of anything to cause unusual satisfaction." It turned out, however, that the shoe was on the other foot, as the President wrote in his diary, "My orders were to flavor the punch rather strongly with the same flavor that is found in Jamaica rum. This took! There was not a drop of spirits in it."

One of the First Lady's charming habits was to ornament the house with a bevy of young girls, many of them as house guests. For their entertainment Mrs. Hayes once gave an elaborate luncheon for fifty young daughters of prominent Washington families. One of these young house guests was Helen Herron of Cincinnati. This 17-year-old guest returned home so impressed with her experience that she declared she would be satisfied only with a man destined to become President of the United States. Thirty years later, as Helen Herron Taft, the wife of William Howard Taft, she moved into the mansion as its First Lady.

It was, however, the informal evenings at home during the Hayes' tenure that were unique. Little groups of townspeople and tourists were

delighted in the evening to find the merry First Lady and her guests in the parlors where the President joined them when he was not kept away by official duties.

The biggest social event of the Hayes administration was the celebration of the twenty-fifth wedding anniversary of the President and his wife on December 30, 1877. That Sunday afternoon in the Blue Room, the Hayes renewed their marriage vows in the presence of as many of the original wedding guests as were available to come. The minister who performed the original ceremony was on hand, and Mrs. Hayes, dressed in her white satin wedding dress of the fifties, was attended by

**Hayes' state china**

the same bridesmaid. It was a sentimental occasion in the best Victorian tradition.

The next night, New Year's Eve, a public reception was given to celebrate the silver wedding anniversary. At 9 o'clock, to the music of the Wedding March, the President and his wife descended the stairs with their house guests and formed a reception line in the East Room to receive the congratulations of their friends. This time the First Lady wore "white silk with draperies of white brocade, the heart-shaped neck filled with tulle and the half-sleeves ending with lace. . . . Her only ornament was a silver comb fastening back her heavy bands of glossy, black hair."

It was a busy weekend, as the customary New

Year's Day reception for the public took place the next day.

A graphic description of one of these formal receptions probably is adequate for them all. One account runs: "The vestibule and parlors were draped with the nation's colors. The President and Mrs. Hayes stood in the Blue Parlor, the latter dressed becomingly in a suit of garnet silk and velvet. The occasion was more like a brilliant private party than a miscellaneous reception. The East Parlor, into which the guests passed after saluting the President and his wife, was a scene of lively sociability. At ten the President and Mrs. Hayes retired from the parlors, the Marine Band stationed in the vestibule played 'Home Sweet Home,' and the crowd of carriages in waiting bore multitudes of guests away from a more than ordinary attractive Tuesday evening reception."

The Hayes took great pains with their arrangements for all their social events at the White House. For state dinners elaborate and ornamented seating charts were prepared. The menu for the meal was in the center of the chart, with the names of the guests indicated around the edge of the menu. The Hayes introduced the White House crest, an American eagle engraved in gold at the top of formal invitations.

The Hayes table was possibly the most elaborate of any administration. The one large purchase which the First Lady made for the Executive Mansion was an elaborate dinner service, each piece especially designed by the artist, Theodore R. Davis, to depict the flora and fauna of America. There were twelve different designs for the plates used at each course. The artist's designs were placed on china made by Haviland. The service consisted of almost a thousand pieces, and its exuberance of design makes it unique as White House china.

The Hayes first threw open the White House grounds for the annual Easter egg rolls that continue to this day. The children of the city of Washington, from early days of the city, had been accustomed to gather on the Capitol grounds on Easter Monday. Members of Congress had served notice that this practice was killing the grass and the grounds had been closed to the children. The Hayes not only invited the children to come to the White House, they even allowed their two youngest children, Fanny and Scott, to join in the fun.

President Hayes did not wish to run for re-election, but he was delighted when James A. Garfield, the Republican candidate and a personal friend, won the election. The Hayes graciously invited the incoming President's aged mother to be their guest at the White House as soon as she arrived in Washington.

After Garfield's inauguration, the Hayes returned to their home at Spiegel Grove in Fremont, Ohio. Here they lived the rest of their days surrounded by mementoes of their happy days in Washington. It was a happy, busy life, surrounded by their family and friends.

## *Favorite Recipes*

### *Roast Beef*
### *(with Potato Puffs and Parsnips)*

For a beef roast, the sirloin and tenderloin cuts are considered best. They are more expensive, although they are no better than the best cuts of a rib roast, that is, 6th, 7th, and 8th ribs. The latter are served to better advantage by requesting the butcher to remove the bones and roll the meat. Always have him include the bones, as they are valuable for the soup pot. As the rolled roasts are cut evenly, off and across the top in carving, they present an equally good appearance for a second serving. They may even be put on the table a third time, serving it the last time à la jardinière.

To roast or bake beef: Allow 9 minutes to the pound for baking a rolled rib roast; for roasting it, allow 10 minutes to the pound. Sirloin roasts require 8 minutes to the pound for baking, 9 minutes for roasting.

For baking, have the oven very hot (450°F). Before putting in the meat, sprinkle over pepper and salt, and dredge with flour. Pour a little boiling water into the pan before baking, and baste frequently with this liquid.

Roasting, too, requires a hot oven (450°F). Put a little clarified dripping into the dripping pan, baste the meat with this when you begin roasting, and every 15 minutes afterward. Twenty minutes before the meat is done, sprinkle with pepper and salt, dredge with flour, baste with a little butter or dripping. Keep the oven hot, and turn the meat occasionally. It should be brown on the outside.

## Sauce for Roast Beef

There is no better sauce for a good, juicy roast of beef than the simple juice of the meat. Sauce may also be made by adding hot water, flour smoothly beaten up in water, pepper and salt to the contents of the pan, after the beef is cooked.

Be sure to remove all the grease either by pouring it off, or by removing it with a spoon. Stir over slow fire to be sure there are no lumps in the sauce.

For those who wish horseradish sauce:

## Horseradish Sauce

| | |
|---|---|
| 1 teaspoon mustard | 3 tablespoons cream |
| 1 tablespoon vinegar | horseradish, to taste |
| salt | a little sugar |

Mix the first 4 ingredients and add as much horseradish as needed to make it the desired thickness. A little sugar may be added to taste.

## Mashed Potato Puffs

| | |
|---|---|
| 2 cups cold mashed potatoes | ¼ teaspoon pepper |
| 2 tablespoons butter, melted | 2 eggs, separated |
| ¼ teaspoon salt | 6 tablespoons cream |
| | bread crumbs |
| | butter |

Mix the cold mashed potatoes, melted butter, some salt and pepper to a fine, light, and creamy condition; then add eggs well beaten separately, and the cream. Beat it all well and lightly together. Shape the mixture into suitably sized portions and roll in breadcrumbs. Place in a greased pan with butter over each puff, and brown in the oven (400° to 450°F) turning once. Serve hot around the roast.

## Parsnips

parsnips, peeled     butter or drippings

Parboil the parsnips; then, after cutting them lengthwise, sauté them to a light brown in a little hot butter or drippings.

## Corned Beef with Vegetables

| | |
|---|---|
| 5 to 6 pounds corned beef | large cabbage cut into quarters |
| cold water | 1 or 2 small red peppers |
| 6 medium carrots or parsnips | little pieces of butter |
| 1 pound small white onions | little pickles, for garnish |

**Corned beef with vegetables**

Put the corned beef into the pot with enough cold water to cover it. When it comes to a boil, turn down the heat so that it will continue to boil moderately. Too fast boiling renders meat tough, but the water should never be allowed to stop boiling until the meat is done. Skim often. Let it boil at least 4 to 5 hours, depending on the size and quality of the meat. It must be thoroughly done.

In England, where this dish is an especial favorite, carrots are always boiled and served with the corned beef. The carrot flavor improves the meat, and the meat improves the carrots. However, do not put carrots or parsnips into the pot until there is only time for them to become thoroughly cooked (about ¾ of an hour) before serving. Put in the onions so that they, too, will be thoroughly cooked only just before serving.

In America, cabbage is often boiled with the corned beef. If cabbage is used, add at the same time 1 or 2 little red peppers. When about to serve, press out all the water from the cabbage, adding little dabs of butter. Serve the meat placed in the center of the vegetables. Pickles may be used as a garnish, with or without vegetables.

### Scalloped Oysters

| | |
|---|---|
| 3 dozen oysters | 2 ounces butter |
| 1 cup of bread or | pepper and salt |
| cracker crumbs | ½ cup of oyster juice |

In a well-greased and buttered pudding dish or casserole, make layers of these ingredients, with bread or cracker crumbs on top. Dab each layer with butter. Bake in a hot oven (400°F) about 15 minutes. Brown under the broiler for a few minutes with the oven door open. Serve hot.

Scalloped oysters may be served cooked in their own shells, or in ovenproof porcelain shells or silver scallop shells, where they present a better appearance than when cooked and served all in one dish, as above.

If cooked in oyster or clam shells, 1 large, or 2 small oysters are placed in each shell, with a few drops of the oyster juice. This is then sprinkled with pepper and salt, and cracker or bread crumbs, dotted with little pieces of butter. When all are ready, they are put into the oven (400°F) for about 15 minutes, or until they are plump and hot. Brown the tops under the broiler for a few minutes with the oven door open. Serve hot.

If they are cooked in silver scallop shells which are larger, several oysters are put into each shell. They are peppered and salted, strewn with cracker crumbs and small dabs of butter, then more layers until the shell is full, or until there are enough oysters in each shell to serve one person. Moisten them with the oyster juice, and strew little dabs of butter over the top. They are merely kept in the oven until they are thoroughly hot, then they are browned under the broiler for a few minutes with the oven door kept open. Serve one shell for each person at table, placing shell on a small plate.

Lucretia Rudolph Garfield

James Abram Garfield

# James A. GARFIELD

WHEN THE Garfield family moved into the White House in 1881 they were already thoroughly familiar with Washington social life. They had lived in the city as part of its official circle since 1863 when General James A. Garfield, of the Ohio Volunteer Infantry, was elected to sit in the House of Representatives. From that time on, the family lived in Washington during the winter and spent their summers at the family farm in Mentor, Ohio. Two of the five Garfield children were born in Washington. In the capital they became a part of an intellectual and social group who shared similar interests and tastes and were active members of the celebrated Literary Society of Washington. James Garfield and Lucretia Rudolph Garfield had known each other since their college days. Both preferred cultural stimulation and intellectual companionship to the usual social whirl that makes up such a large part of the Washington picture.

General Garfield's immediate family gave him the security of a happy home life; the great blessings during his political career were the love of his wife and the companionship of his children. As the cares of the nursery decreased for Lucretia, she became more and more the companion of her husband. They read, dined, made social calls, and traveled together until, by the time they reached the White House, they were nearly inseparable.

Besides being a devoted wife, mother, and daughter-in-law, Mrs. Garfield had been compelled in the early years to take on many domestic chores for her family which were not always as appealing to her as literary and cultural affairs. Long years before she became the First Lady, while she was deep in the mundane task of kneading bread for her household, she had developed a philosophy of life, which became an integral part of her. This she took along with her later and applied to the demands of her new position. Making great batches of bread appeared to be an inescapable duty, so she determined that she would overcome her dislike for this chore by taking a very special interest in it. In this connection she wrote:

"The whole of life became brighter. The very

133

sunshine seemed to be flowing down through my spirit into the white loaves, and now I believe my table is furnished with better bread than ever before; and this truth, as old as creation, seems just now to have become fully mine—that I need not be the shrinking slave of toil, but its regal master."

When Garfield was elected President in 1880 he actually could claim three official elective positions in Washington: He had been elected United States Senator from Ohio while he was still a member of the House of Representatives, and now he was to hold the highest office in the land.

The Garfields' move into the White House on March 4, 1881, was made without trepidation and also without any especially happy anticipations. They were too familiar with Washington ways to show any excitement.

It is easy for us to follow in the President's journal the beginning of the social activity of the administration. On March 10 there was a reception for the Diplomatic Corps. Garfield's comment was that "it was very pleasant. C. [meaning Lucretia, whom he called Crete] grows up to every new emergency with fine tact and faultless taste."

Next was a reception for officers of the Army and Navy. The President's journal records, "The array was brilliant. The Cabinet develops fine social qualities."

The record continues. On March 17 there was a review of the Irish societies celebrating Saint Patrick's Day. They marched around the front circle and through the porte-cochere. There was a reception for Supreme Court judges and Members of Congress and their families. "It was a very pleasant occasion, not too crowded for comfort."

Apart from the constant political visitors at meals, the Garfields gave no formal dinner until April 2 when the President entertained his old college president. The journal makes note of the occasion: "We gave a dinner to Dr. Hopkins of Williams College; present was his wife, Judge Nott and the Dr.'s daughter, Senator Hoar and Dawes and their wives, and Dr. Hawkes. A very

pleasant party and a good dinner *sine vino*. I drew the party into a discussion of the female element in the Catholic worship and its lack in the Protestant Churches."

The Garfields also began to dine outside the White House. Regarding one such occasion, the journal says, "It was a pleasant release from the monotony of the White House to get out for an evening."

Meanwhile, receptions continued as part of the routine at the White House. Mrs. Garfield received guests twice a week, and the President often assisted her for part of the time at these parties.

The President soon found a need for some means of diversion and exercise as a refuge from the flood of officeseekers and political visitors. He enjoyed playing billiards with his friends, and began to take carriage rides with various people. One day he drove with his wife past their old home. In his journal he wrote, "The dear old nest is deserted now. It made me homesick to leave it —or rather to see it." He also resumed his horseback riding, and the journal tells us of occasional escapes into the country around Washington.

Mrs. Garfield found the Executive Mansion sadly in need of refurnishing, so the President busied himself in getting books in an endeavor to discover as much as he could on the subject. "April 9 C. and I drove out . . . to the Library of Congress, to . . . ask Mr. Spofford (Librarian of Congress) to look into the history of the White House and its contents, of which very little seems to be known."

A visitor to the White House has left us a description of an evening he spent there: "There was one evening at the White House . . . that none of those present can have forgotten; for there were not many bright hours in the midst of the dismal shadowing of the drama hastening to the tragic close. Mrs. Garfield, whose chilly sensation was supposed to be trivial, was seated before the fire, and she was pale but animated, surrounded by a group among whom were seated several very dear to her. . . . The President was detained for half an hour beyond the time when he was expected and came in with a quick step and hearty manner, and there soon was a flush of pleasure upon his face that had been touched with the lines of fatigue, as he saw how agreeable the company were. . . . He was well-dressed, of splendid figure, his dome-like head erect, adequately supported by immense shoulders, and he looked the President indeed, and an embodiment of power.

He was feeling that the dark days were behind him, that he was equal to his high fortune, that the world was wide and fair before him. It was a supreme hour—and only an hour."

Mrs. Garfield's "chilly sensation" turned out to be a very serious attack of malaria. For days she lay seriously ill, with her family alternating between hope and fear. To her husband this illness was especially heartrending, as his whole life's happiness was bound up in his companionship with his wife. On May 24 he wrote to a friend, "You can imagine how small and empty all the world has looked to me in comparison with her life." The journal records on May 31: "At last on the 28th day of her illness, the doctor says with emphasis it is ended. She needs now only care and strength . . . a deep strong current of happy peace flows through every heart in the household."

Once again the Garfield family could enjoy social activities. The journal tells us of outings on the Potomac by the children and a three-day trip by the family, with the exception of Mrs. Garfield, to Fortress Monroe and Hampton Institute. In the middle of June, the whole family journeyed to Elberon, New Jersey, to see if the sea air might benefit the convalescent. The President recorded, "The work and worry of Washington seem very far away, and I rest in the large silence of the sea air. I have always felt that the ocean was my friend, and the sight of it brings rest and peace."

On June 27, the President returned to Washington cheered by his wife's improvement, and the prospect of a journey to his alma mater, Williams College, to deliver the Commencement Address on July 3. It was planned that Mrs. Garfield and their daughter would join them in New York for a tour of the New England mountains and a voyage along the coast. The whole family was anticipating a pleasant summer. But it was not to be.

On July 2 as the President arrived at the train station to start his journey he was shot and mortally wounded by an insane officeseeker. He returned to the White House borne gently on a mattress, and lingered in mortal agony for over two months before he died from the effects of the wound. Mrs. Garfield and Molly came from Elberon as fast as they could be brought on a special train, as it was at first thought the President would live only a few hours.

With the eyes of the nation and the prayers of the people focused on the White House, the family lived through the long and terrible ordeal.

**Garfield family china**

The courage and determination of the wounded President were only equaled by the bravery and dignity of his wife. A contemporary description pictures her as "frail, fatigued, desperate, but firm and quiet." In the presence of her husband her smile was always confident and her attitude optimistic. She herself prepared special dishes to tempt the invalid. The attempt to interest the patient in food is also recorded by Colonel Crook, the Disbursing Officer of the White House. He says that the consulting doctors thought the appetite of the ill man might be tempted if he could have some squirrel soup, of which he was very fond. For this purpose, Crook was given a permit to shoot squirrels on the grounds of the Soldiers' Home. Unfortunately, the President never got well enough for the Colonel even to go after the squirrels.

Despite a special air-conditioning system installed for the comfort of the patient, he longed for the seashore. He was taken to Elberon on a special train early in September, and there he died on September 19.

Lucretia Garfield, who was only 49 years old when she became a widow, lived to raise and educate her talented children and enjoy her grandchildren. She died at the age of 85 years in California in 1918.

## Favorite Recipes

### Bread

*Do not constantly make bread in the same shapes: each morning, try to have some variations. Plain light bread dough may be made into loaves, rolls, twist, turnovers, light biscuit, etc., and these changes of shape make a pleasant and appetizing variety in the appearance of the table.*

*It is a nice plan after making out eight rolls [of dough] to roll them with greased hands till each one will reach across the pan (four and one-half inches), making eight slices of bread which pull off beautifully when well done, and thus save the task of slicing with a knife. It requires an hour to bake this bread properly.*

### Brown Bread

*One quart of light bread sponge, one-half teacup of molasses. Stir into the above, with a large spoon, unbolted wheat meal, until it is a stiff dough. Grease a deep pan, put the mixture in; when light, put the pan over a kettle of hot water (the bread well covered), and steam for half an hour. Then put in the oven and bake until done. Especially good for dyspeptics.*

*a tablespoonful of white sugar.*

*Make up a soft dough with cold water in summer and milk-warm in winter. This must be kneaded for thirty minutes, and then set to rise, in a cool place in summer, and a warm one in winter; must never be kept more than milk warm.*

*Two hours after breakfast, make the dough into the desired shapes, handling it lightly,* without kneading it, *first rubbing lard over the hands, and taking special care to grease the bread on top. Then set it to rise again.*

*Thirty minutes are sufficient for baking it, unless it be in the form of a loaf or rolls, in which case, it must be baked fifteen minutes longer. Excellent muffins may be made by the above recipe, adding two eggs well beaten, so that from the same batch of dough both plain bread and muffins may be made. Iron moulds are best for baking.*

*For those who prefer warm bread for dinner, it is a good plan to reserve a portion of the breakfast dough, setting it away in a cool place till two hours before dinner, then make into turnovers or twist, set it to rise and bake it for dinner, as for breakfast. Very nice on a cold day, and greatly preferable to warmed-over bread.*

### Potato Bread

*1 quart flour, 4 eggs, 4 good sized Irish potatoes, boiled, mashed and strained through a colander, 2 ounces of butter, as much yeast as is needed to make it rise. To be made up with water, not so stiff as light dough. Bake in a loaf or rolls.*

### Breakfast Bread

*1 quart flour, lard the size of a walnut, 1 small Irish potato, boiled and mashed fine, 1 heaping teaspoonful of salt, half a teacup of good yeast, into which put*

**The Garfield home**

**Garfield family china**

## Mrs. Garfield's White Loaf Bread

| | |
|---|---|
| 1 cup scalded milk | over 1 tablespoon |
| 1 cup hot water | sugar |
| 1½ tablespoons lard or | 6½ cups bread flour |
| unsalted butter | 1 tablespoon sugar |
| 1 yeast cake crumbled | 2½ teaspoons salt |

Crumble yeast cake over sugar, and let it stand to liquefy. Put lard or butter in large mixing bowl, add hot water, 1 tablespoon sugar, salt, and scalded milk. Cool to lukewarm (85°F). Add yeast mixture and mix well. Sift in half of the flour, beating well.

Now add remainder of the flour, mixing by hand. When dough begins to leave sides of the bowl, turn out on lightly floured pastry cloth or board. Cover with a cloth, and let it stand for 10 to 15 minutes.

Knead by folding dough toward you and pressing with heel of hand, giving a slight turn. Repeat until dough becomes smooth, elastic, and satiny. Air blisters will appear, and the dough will no longer stick to the board. Knead lightly for about 10 minutes, then shape into large ball.

Grease the large bowl well with lard, and turn ball of dough over in it to cover the surface with grease. Cover with a damp cloth and set to raise in an area free from draft. At a temperature of 75° to 80°, it should rise.

If the room should be cold, place on a rack above warm water. Allow to double in bulk, but do not let it overrise, or you will have a sour, coarse bread. The rising takes about 2 hours.

Now punch the dough down with a floured fist. Work edges to the center, turn bottom to the top. Turn out on board and divide into 4 equal portions. Shape by turning edges under, and leave on board covered with a cloth for another 10 minutes.

Take 2 5x9-inch heavy bread pans. Shape the twin loaves by folding edges under, and shape into a rectangle. Place 2 shapes of dough into each pan.

Preheat oven to 450°F. Again cover loaves with damp cloth, and let rise in warm place until not quite double in bulk. Bake for 10 minutes, then reduce heat to 350°F, and bake for 30 minutes longer. When it is done, bread should shrink from sides of pan. Before removing from oven, brush crust lightly with melted butter. Close oven door, and in a few minutes remove from oven. Let stand a few minutes and turn out on a rack in a warm place away from drafts.

*Chester Alan Arthur*

*Ellen Lewis Herndon Arthur*

# Chester A. ARTHUR

During the long days when President Garfield lay at death's door, his Vice President, Chester A. Arthur, stayed in Washington, to be available if necessary. It was a difficult position in which the Presidential successor was placed, but in the words of his contemporaries he "conducted himself with dignity and decorum." As the time dragged into months his position became actually embarrassing.

President Arthur finally took the oath of office late at night on September 19, 1881, and then went directly to Elberon, New Jersey, to pay his respects to the late President and his family. On arriving back in Washington the new President went directly to the home of his friend Senator Jones on Capitol Hill where he had stayed for most of that long and trying summer. The White House was not ready for occupancy so Senator Jones' house was converted into a temporary Executive Mansion with offices on the first floor and living quarters above.

After it was vacated by the Garfield family the White House was found to be sadly in need of renovation. Its use as a hospital for the late President had prevented normal maintenance and had subjected the house to unusual wear. President Arthur wished it put into proper condition before he moved in, and as he was personally interested in his household surroundings and found attention to them relaxing he gave the work the closest supervision. After dinner he would ride over from his temporary quarters to inspect what was being done and to give directions for continuing work. In addition to the usual refinishing of walls and the replacement of worn carpets, curtains, and upholstery, additional furniture was ordered for the downstairs rooms. Upstairs special attention was given to redecorating the President's study, and new wood-burning fireplaces with new brass fireplace equipment were placed in every room. For the first time an elevator and additional plumbing were installed for the convenience of the first family. It was at this time that President Arthur ordered the accumulation of many administrations to be cleared from the storerooms and sold at public auction. Twenty-four wagonloads of items were sold at one huge public auction.

During those autumn months before he moved into the White House and while he was living on Capitol Hill, President Arthur was glad to dine out. Generally he was reluctant to bring pleasant evenings to a close. A member of the family of the Secretary of State James G. Blaine complained, "Etiquette requiring everyone to stay till he leaves, it becomes an interesting problem how to end a dinner before twelve o'clock." It was a relief to everyone including the President when the house was ready in December and the President and his family could move in.

The President's family consisted of his young daughter and a teenage son. His beautiful and competent wife, Ellen Herndon Arthur, had died early in the year of his election. He persuaded his younger sister, Mary Arthur McElroy, to come from Albany for the winter months to act as hostess of the Executive Mansion. She brought with her her two young daughters and a French governess who looked after the girls and their 10-year-old cousin, Nell Arthur.

People who had known Chester Arthur in New York expected that the new President would not only improve the quality of the social activity of the White House, but would also take an active part in it, planning many details of the state entertainments himself.

Mrs. McElroy immediately proved herself to be a tactful and gracious hostess, and White House hospitality became unusually pleasant. She made her formal receptions less stilted and succeeded in establishing a personal relationship with her guests. She often invited ladies of Washington society to receive with her on formal occasions and at the New Year's Day reception was assisted by forty of them. President Arthur did not accord his sister the precedence reserved for the President's wife. Perhaps he could not bear to place anyone else in the place which rightfully belonged to his beloved Ellen. At social affairs he was wont to give his arm to the wife of the Speaker of the House of Representatives as the ranking lady present.

With his sister's able assistance the President attempted to maintain a strict barrier between official and private life at the White House. He was especially anxious that his children should be spared the injurious effects of publicity, flattery, and temporary luxury. By his orders Nell was raised in comparative seclusion and with strict simplicity. Most of her time was spent with her cousins, her governess, and her aunt. The President spent as much time as he could with her, and she often accompanied him on his late afternoon drives. Her brother Alan was in college at Princeton but made frequent trips to Washington.

Soon after he was settled in the White House the President established a routine for his days. He rose at 9 o'clock, ate a "Continental breakfast" while dressing, and went directly to his office. Mondays he tried to keep free from callers, but on other days he received members of Congress between 10 and 12. On Tuesdays and Fridays he met with his Cabinet at noon. He had a light lunch at 1, worked on his mail and received visitors on appointment until 4 or 5, when he took a drive or went riding. Family dinner was at 7.

This program was often interrupted by special occasions—official ceremonies, short trips out of the city, state dinners, receptions, and social events outside of the White House which the President often attended. To compensate for this time, he would resume work in the late evening and sometimes continue until 2 or 3 in the morning. He enjoyed spending his evenings with his personal friends and when they came to the White House the evening would end with a delectable

Mary Arthur McElroy

midnight supper in the private dining room, which he had redecorated to his own taste.

President Arthur had brought to Washington a French chef who had previously been employed by New York gourmets. In addition the kitchen was staffed by a "faithful and devoted" family cook who came to the White House with the Arthurs and returned to New York with them at the end of the administration. Chester Arthur was an epicure. He knew and liked good food and drink, and he insisted on it for himself and his guests. Household orders from his New York home included fine wines, good cigars, and gourmet foods, and these same were served at the White House.

There were no official entertainments at the Executive Mansion that first winter out of respect for the late President, but in March Arthur gave his first state dinner for ex-President and Mrs. Grant, and others soon followed. Mrs. James G. Blaine wrote to one of her children: "I dined at the President's Wednesday. The dinner was extremely elegant, hardly a trace of the old White House taint being perceptible anywhere, the flowers, the damask, the silver, the attendants, all showing the latest style and an abandon in expense and taste. But this is all there is of it."

President Arthur had soon established his reputation for hospitality. One of his contemporaries described him as "a very prince of hospitality and nothing could betray him into discourtesy."

President Arthur spent much of his time at a retreat he had established in the President's old summer residence on the grounds of the Soldiers' Home in Washington. Here he sent many of his possessions from his New York home and the most choice of the cast-offs from the White House. It was so comfortable and secluded that he often stayed on in the house with his sister and the children until Christmas week. With the move back into town for the New Year's Day reception the social season would begin for another year.

During the summer of 1882 additional redecoration was done at the White House, including the large screen of Tiffany glass placed in the main corridor which for the next twenty-five years was the most noticeable decoration of the house.

The first New Year's Day reception for the administration took place on January 1, 1883.

That day the crowds were so big that the President could not follow his preferred custom of moving from group to group in the East Room but had to join Mrs. McElroy and the ladies in a reception line while the guests filed past. The winter was unusually gay with a succession of official and private receptions, several notable weddings, and innumerable dinners and balls. The President continued to dine at the homes of certain Senators and others in public office.

In the midst of the gay round a welcome addition was a concert in the White House given by Adelina Patti on Washington's Birthday.

By that spring the strain of continual activity, both social and political, was beginning to tell upon the President. He appeared to have been threatened with a serious illness, so he embarked on a fishing trip to Florida which was followed by a more extensive journey to Yellowstone National Park. On his return in September he was improved in health and his zest for public life had been restored.

President Arthur had hoped to win the nomination of his party for the next Presidential election but was defeated at the convention. It was a bitter blow to him, but he accepted it with good sportsmanship and his last winter in Washington was almost as gay as the previous ones had been.

On February 22, 1885, the completed Washington Monument was formally presented to the United States at a ceremony which took place at the base of the shaft. President Arthur's speech that day was a short and pertinent tribute to George Washington.

The President's last day at the White House was a long and busy one. It was almost dawn of March 4 when he retired after holding a long Cabinet meeting, making farewell calls, signing bills, and supervising arrangements to move out of the mansion. All his belongings were packed for their return to his New York home when he left for the Capitol. He had ordered a suitable luncheon to be ready after the inaugural ceremonies in honor of President Grover Cleveland and his sister Rose.

The Washington friends of Chester Arthur and Mrs. McElroy prevailed upon them to stay on in Washington for several weeks, during which they were royally entertained. When the ex-President finally left the city it was never to return. He tried to resume his legal activities in New York, but ill health forced him into retirement. He died in 1886 of the effects of Bright's disease and a heart condition, the first symptoms of which had been noted during his Presidency.

## Favorite Recipes

**Mutton chops**

### Mutton Chops

**chops from a loin of
mutton
salt and pepper**

Get the desired number of chops from a loin of mutton. They are to be used without the bone, so cut off the bone close to the meat, trimming off all skin and fat. Beat the chops to make them tender; season with salt and pepper to taste.

Have the griddle very hot, rub it with salt, and lay on the chops. Turn them often, being careful of blaze from the suet. When chops are thoroughly done, place on a hot platter, with generous dabs of butter on each.

*Another way of dressing mutton chops:*

| | |
|---|---|
| salt and pepper | 2 cups grated bread |
| melted butter | crumbs |

Trim the chops, cutting off the bone close to the meat, and trimming off all skin and fat. Season with salt and pepper to taste.

Lay them in melted butter, in a large dish. When they have imbibed a sufficient quantity of the melted butter, remove them, cover with grated bread crumbs. Place them under broiler, and be careful that the bread crumbs do not burn. When sufficiently brown, turn, and brown on other side. Serve with mushroom catchup.

Baked salmon

## Mushroom Catchup

| 10 pounds mushrooms | 1 teaspoon ground |
| ½ cup salt | cloves |
| 1 large onion, chopped | 1 teaspoon horseradish |
| 1 teaspoon ground | pinch of cayenne |
| allspice | 1 cup vinegar |

Wipe mushrooms with a damp cloth. Chop them fine and mix well with salt. Let them stand overnight. Next day, wash them, and to the pulp and juice add the chopped onion, spices, and vinegar. Heat until boiling, and simmer until thick for about ½ hour, stirring occasionally. If desired, strain. If too thick, add vinegar.

Seal in hot sterilized jars. Makes about 5 pints.

## Baked Salmon

| Desired size salmon | ¼ teaspoon pepper |
| or salmon trout, | 3 cups of bread, |
| split by the | cubed |
| fishman | butter, for basting |
| 1 teaspoon salt | |

Wash and dry the fish. Sprinkle the inside with salt and pepper. Stuff with 3 cups seasoned cubed bread. Have ready a small grating in a baking pan; lay the fish on this, with bits of butter over it. Set in hot oven (450°) for 10 minutes, then reduce heat to 425°F, and bake 30 to 35 minutes longer, until tender.

Baste frequently and generously with butter. When the fish is nicely browned, butter a sheet of white paper and lay it over the fish, to prevent its getting too dry. Place on a hot dish.

## Gravy

| 1 teaspoon milk | 1 Irish potato, boiled |
| 1 teaspoon vinegar | and mashed |
| pepper and salt | |

## Garnish

| cracker crumbs, | parsley |
| browned in butter | lemon |

Using the gravy in the pan, add 1 teaspoon milk, 1 teaspoon vinegar, pepper and salt, and a mashed Irish potato smoothly mixed in. Boil up once or twice and serve with the fish. Over all, sift browned cracker crumbs. Garnish with sprigs of parsley and thin slices of lemon.

Stephen Grover Cleveland

Frances Folsom Cleveland

# Grover
# CLEVELAND

As soon as Grover Cleveland arrived in the White House, he settled at once into a comfortable routine of life. As compared with the formality of the Arthur administration, with its lavish entertainments, it was a simple ménage. Miss Rose Cleveland, sister of the President, acted as First Lady, assisted by another sister, Mrs. Hoyt. The President's mulatto servant, William Sinclair, who had come with him from the Governor's Mansion in Albany, was made White House steward. The French chef, M. Fortin, of the Arthur administration was still at the White House, but despite the excellence of the cuisine, President Cleveland never really liked French cooking. He once wrote, "I must go to dinner. I wish it was to eat a pickled herring, Swiss cheese and a chop at Louis' instead of the French stuff I shall find." So great was the President's desire for plainer cooking that he wrote to Governor Hill at Albany, asking him if he could have one Eliza by name from the staff of the Governor's Mansion. To which Governor Hill replied, "I do not know whether she desires or is willing to leave,

but I shall say to her that she can do as she pleases about it."

One of the Washington newspaper correspondents recorded that the "woman he brought from Albany with him knows exactly what he likes. She cooks for him (for breakfast) oatmeal, beefsteak, eggs or a chop with coffee to wash it down."

Grover Cleveland found the White House in good condition after the thorough redecoration it had undergone during the Arthur administration.

The social affairs of the administration gave the new President little concern. His sister Rose, attractive and petite, had an air of distinction which made her an impressive hostess. Like her brother, she was a person of stern purpose and strong will. Her tastes were literary and she leaned to social reform. She had graduated from Houghton Seminary, and had taught first at that school and later in a collegiate institute at Lafayette, Indiana. Visitors to the White House found her an excellent conversationalist, and although she had little natural liking for politicians, she was demo-

146

cratic in her attitudes, and universally kind to all visitors to the White House.

Newspaper correspondent Frank Carpenter said of Rose Cleveland that she: "presides over the White House, bosses the servants and occasionally holds an afternoon reception when the public is privileged to go and see her. . . . At state dinners she sits in the great dining room like a queen, but she has to smile unconcernedly when a backwoods Congressman, dressed in his long frock coat, eats with his knife or drinks the thin lemon water out of the finger bowls."

Miss Cleveland lectured widely and was the author of several books on reforming the education of women. One of her books appeared in 1885 and received excellent publicity and good reviews. Within a year twelve editions were published. She admitted about herself that, behind her formal smile, she relieved the monotony of shaking hands for an hour in the receiving line at the White House by conjugating Greek verbs.

This administration's first reception was given on March 21 to allow the Diplomatic Corps and the Members of Congress to meet the new Cabinet. The newspapers pronounced the party a success and Miss Cleveland charming.

The President set an example of industry for all members of his staff with his personal work habits. He rose early and was in his office before 9 in the morning. At 10 he received business visitors for two or three hours. Those whose calls were personal or of a social nature were requested by public notice to come to the White House only at 1:30 P.M. on Mondays, Wednesdays, and Fridays, when the President shook hands with long lines of visitors in the East Room. Luncheon was

**White cake with white frosting**      **Turban of chicken, Cleveland style**      **White cake with chocolate frosting**

at 2 o'clock. The Cabinet met on Tuesday and Thursday afternoons. In the evenings the President and his secretary worked long hours in the library, often until 2 o'clock in the morning. Cleveland liked to take a late afternoon drive; early in the morning he often walked in the ellipse and down to the Washington Monument.

Socially, Washington expected little from the Cleveland administration, and rightly so. The President cared little for dinners or receptions, accepted few invitations, and entertained only when it was absolutely necessary. To counteract some of the unpleasant publicity surrounding his campaign, Cleveland wished to show the people of the United States that the White House would be managed with decorum. His sister helped him

provide a dignified atmosphere in the Executive Mansion, but the thing that did the most to win over the people was his marriage to Frances Folsom on July 2, 1886.

Pretty Miss Folsom was 22 years old. She had been Cleveland's legal ward since her father's death when she was a child of only 11. Oscar Folsom, Frances's father, had been Cleveland's law partner, and when he died he left his daughter and the business affairs of his estate to the care of his friend and business associate.

The President had taken great pains to keep his interest in the young girl a secret. It was decided that the wedding ceremony could best be protected from the prying press if it was to take

**The White House kitchen, 1890**

place in the White House. So on June 2, 1886, at 7 in the evening, the beautiful young bride walked down the stairs on the arm of her husband-to-be, and they were married in the Blue Room, which had been transformed into a bower of flowers. The simple ceremony, attended by the President's Cabinet and a few personal friends, was followed by an informal reception and supper in the State Dining Room. The press had a field day with the wedding and the brief honeymoon which followed at Deer Creek Park in the mountains of Maryland.

Probably because the journalists would not accord them the courtesy of even a minimum of privacy, the President and his bride purchased a private home in what was then suburban Washington, a comfortable, old-fashioned place with a wonderful view. Here the Clevelands managed to live an ordinary life except during the social season, when official entertaining made it necessary for them to live at the White House.

The new bride of the White House immediately became the darling of the American people. She was very pretty, tall and graceful, and had charmingly unaffected manners. After the wedding, both the President and the White House underwent a change for the better. Few young women of her age would have been equal to the exacting demands of the position of First Lady. Frances Folsom Cleveland carried her zest for life and her interest in people into the routine of official dinners and duties. Her official social program opened with the New Year's Day reception in 1887.

*Carp's Washington* describes this New Year's Day reception as: "gorgeous, gay and giddy. The Executive Mansion never looked cleaner or grander, and since it was open to any who might wish to come, the crowd has never before been bigger. The dear people come by the thousands. Of all classes, ages and sizes, of all colors, sexes and conditions, they formed long lines reaching from the White House door around the paved walk all the way to the War Department."

The White House bride also served as hostess at levees, luncheons, and teas.

President Cleveland was in the habit of giving each of his dinner guests a souvenir. Each lady received a ribbon about three feet long and three inches wide, on one end of which was stamped a picture of the White House, and on the other the national colors, with the coat of arms of the United States in gold. To this was added the name of the guest and the date of the dinner in gold letters.

The gentlemen received a smaller piece on which appeared only the coat of arms, the name of the guest, and the date of the reception.

The attendance at receptions during the last social season of the Cleveland administration averaged about 9,000 people. The line waiting to be received often stretched from the White House entrance to the Treasury Building.

It was a blow to the Clevelands when the President failed in his bid for reelection, due in some part to an infamous campaign of rumors spread about the domestic felicity of the Clevelands. When Mrs. Cleveland left the White House, however, she said to the servants, "I want you to take good care of the house. . . . We are coming back just four years from today."

And back they came, just four years later. The Clevelands now had a little daughter, Ruth, born in New York in 1891. The public interest in the baby and their lack of privacy in the White House forced the Clevelands to rent "Woodley," a fine old estate in northwest Washington, and here during their second administration they again led a private family life.

The second administration began brilliantly with a visit to the World's Fair in Chicago and the entertainment of the Princess Eulalia of Spain in the White House. The state dinner was served in the East Room to accommodate the number of guests invited.

It was during this second administration that President Cleveland was operated on for cancer of the roof of his mouth. The operation was done in complete secrecy on shipboard while the yacht was at sea. It was a success and did not become known by the country until twenty-five years later.

The Cleveland family was enlarged by a second daughter born in the White House and a third, born at their summer home in Massachusetts before the administration ended.

The Clevelands' second administration ended with a private dinner for President-elect McKinley at the White House. As Mrs. McKinley was an invalid, she and her husband were the only guests invited. However, because Mrs. McKinley was ill that evening President-elect McKinley was the single guest.

The Clevelands then retired to a comfortable home in Princeton, New Jersey. Their happiness in these years of retirement was greatly enhanced by the birth of two sons. Mr. Cleveland died in Princeton in 1908. His charming and gracious widow lived on until 1947.

## Favorite Recipes

### Turban of Chicken, Cleveland Style

*Take two fowls, singe, draw and wipe them well, bone and cut them into quarters, then put them into a sautépan with one ounce of butter, salt and pepper and half a glassful of Madeira wine; boil slowly for ten minutes. Take one breakfast cupful of chicken forcemeat and add to it one chopped truffle, three chopped mushrooms and half an ounce of cooked minced tongue and stir well. Put the forcemeat on a dish, lay the pieces of chicken on top, crown-shaped, and decorate with twelve whole mushrooms and two thinly sliced truffles. Add half a pint of Spanish sauce, a teaspoonful of chopped chives and a small pat of fresh butter to the chicken gravy. Pour this immediately over the fowls, put the dish in the oven and cook slowly for ten minutes; squeeze over the juice of half a lemon and serve with six heart-shaped croutons of fried bread.*

Turban of chicken, Cleveland style

| | |
|---|---|
| 6 breasts of chicken | 1 teaspoon tomato |
| ½ pound boiled tongue |    paste |
| 3 egg whites, not | ¾ cup strong chicken |
|    beaten |    stock |
| 1½ cups light cream | ½ cup Madeira wine |
| 2 large truffles | ¼ cup dry white wine |
| ½ pound white mush- | 1 teaspoon red |
|    rooms of even |    currant jelly |
|    size | 1 teaspoon lemon |
| ¼ cup brandy |    juice |
|    salt | 6 slices bread cut into |
|    freshly ground white |    heart shapes (use |
|    pepper |    cookie cutter) |
| 1 chicken liver | 1 ounce butter, for |
| 1 teaspoon potato |    sautéing |
|    flour | |

Carefully remove skin and bone from 6 chicken breasts. Cut each in half. Take 3 of these half-breasts, and cut each half-breast into 3 thin slices horizontally. Put slices of raw chicken between 2 pieces of waxed paper, and beat with a cleaver until very thin.

Butter a ring mold, and line it with the thin slices of chicken. Put the rest of the chicken through a fine-plated meat chopper, together with the tongue, half of the raw mushrooms, and 1 truffle, reserving the rest of the mushrooms and the other truffle.

Put the chopped mixture into a mixer bowl with unbeaten egg whites, mix well, and slowly add the light cream. Season with salt and pepper; fill into mold. Cover over with raw pieces of chicken, and cover the whole mold with a piece of buttered wax paper.

Preheat oven to 350°F, and stand the tightly closed mold in a shallow pan over hot water. While it is cooking, heat ½ ounce of butter in a small heavy pan, and in it brown the chicken liver quickly on each side. Flame with the brandy, and remove. Stir in another tablespoon butter, potato flour, and tomato paste. Stir until smooth. When smooth, mix in the chicken stock, Madeira, and white wine, season with salt and pepper and stir gently over fire until it comes to a boil.

Now add the chicken liver and simmer gently for ½ hour. Strain, spoon a little of this gravy over the chicken mold when it has been turned over onto a hot round platter. Flute the remainder of the whole mushrooms, sauté them briskly in a little butter, lemon juice, and seasoning. Arrange the mushrooms on top of the mold. Garnish the round dish with heart-shaped croutons of bread fried in butter until they are a golden color. Set little slices of truffle between the mushrooms, for decoration.

State china of the Benjamin Harrison administration, used by Cleveland during his second administration.

## White Cake

| | |
|---|---|
| 1 cup butter | 1 cup cornstarch |
| 3 cups sugar | 3 cups flour |
| 1 cup milk | 3 teaspoons vanilla |
| 12 egg whites, beaten | extract |
| 3 teaspoons baking powder | |

Cream 1 cup butter with 3 cups of sugar. To this add 1 cup of milk, and then the beaten whites of 12 eggs. Put 3 teaspoons of baking powder into 1 cup of cornstarch and add 3 cups of flour.

Now gradually beat in flour mixture, and flavor with 3 teaspoons vanilla. Beat all together thoroughly.

Put the mixture in three 9-inch round cake pans that have been buttered after being lined with letter paper also well buttered. Preheat oven to 350°F and bake in this moderate oven 25 to 30 minutes. Take out of oven, allow to cool in pans.

**White cake with white frosting**

## White Frosting

| | |
|---|---|
| 2 egg whites | almond extract |
| 1 cup confectioners' sugar | crystallized violets, roses, and leaves |
| ½ teaspoon vanilla or | for decoration |

Beat the egg whites until stiff, then add the sugar gradually. Continue beating until the mixture is smooth and light. Add flavoring and mix well. Use varicolored crystallized fruits and leaves for decoration.

If desired the cake can be covered with whipped cream.

## Chocolate Frosting

| | |
|---|---|
| ½ pound sweet chocolate; half of this is to be dissolved, the other half coarsely shaved for trim | 1 tablespoon rum |
| | 1 tablespoon water |
| | 2 tablespoons sweet butter |
| | 1 tablespoon confectioners' sugar |

Cut half of the chocolate into small pieces, put them into a heavy pan with water and rum. Stir continuously over slow fire until it is dissolved and smooth, and then add the butter bit by bit. Remove from heat and stir until it begins to cool. Completely cover the cake with the frosting, and just before it sets, sprinkle all over the top with the coarsely shaved chocolate. Sprinkle a little confectioners' sugar over the chocolate top.

Benjamin Harrison

Caroline Lavinia Scott Harrison

# Benjamin HARRISON

WHEN PRESIDENT HARRISON arrived at the White House after the inauguration ceremony on March 4, 1889, he found that the outgoing President's wife, Mrs. Cleveland, had prepared a luncheon for his family and that everything was in readiness for the occupancy of the Executive Mansion by the new First Family. A number of personal friends were there for that first meal, and they, with the members of the family, made a merry party.

The Harrisons were not unfamiliar with Washington, as the new President had served six years as United States Senator from Indiana. He and his charming wife had at that time discovered many of the pleasures of living in Washington. Caroline Scott Harrison helped in the hospitals in the city of Washington, was active in church work, and became well informed about political life and official Washington social life. After the "front porch" campaign run from their Indianapolis home, she and her husband moved on to Washington, well aware of the intricacies of living in the White House. They were both people of

good education, accustomed to the best of society and wholly at ease wherever they chanced to be, so the social life of the White House moved along smoothly from the very first.

It was a large and closely knit family group that arrived at the Executive Mansion to take up residence that March 4. In addition to the President and his wife, the official family was composed of Mrs. Harrison's aged father, the Reverend Dr. Scott, the McKees, the Harrisons' married daughter and her family, and Mrs. Harrison's niece, the widowed Mary Scott Dimmick, who would act as secretary for the First Lady. Mrs. James R. McKee assisted her mother with the social duties of the White House while the McKees' two small children, Mary and Benjamin Harrison McKee, were the constant joy not only of their grandparents but of the whole country.

"Baby" McKee, as little Benjamin was quickly christened by the papers, became one of the most celebrated children to live in the White House up to that time, because of the intense interest the press took in reporting on his activities.

Frank G. Carpenter in *Carp's Washington* reported to his readers:

"Toys have been pouring into the White House for Benny McKee and his baby sister Mary Lodge. His pony and cart and his favorite French mechanical dog have lately been put aside for a miniature tennis set with which he plays with a pretty tasseled silk tennis cap on his head, often with his grandfather a fascinated watcher. . . .

"When the Harrisons first moved into the White House, this child had not yet learned to walk well. He still often crawled about like a crab. Many a visitor in the President's study has felt a warm little arm around his leg in the midst of his interview. Once during a conference, when Benny's presence was not noticed, a roll of important papers disappeared. A frantic search was made by the President's secretary, who could not hold back a cry when he pulled the window draperies aside and found Baby McKee stirring the contents of a big spittoon with the precious roll."

The Harrisons' married son, Russell, and his family were also frequent visitors to the White House, and on one of these occasions their little daughter Marthena came down with scarlet fever and the White House had to be quarantined.

It was quite a problem to fit all these people into the small area of the White House which remained the private quarters of the President and his family. The First Lady was so disturbed by the existing conditions that she began to explore all the possible solutions to improve the space problem, ranging from a separate home for the President's private use, leaving the Executive Mansion for entertaining and official business, to the addition of wings to the original house. She finally settled on an appropriation from Congress of $35,000 to renovate the existing structure and to make improvements within that limitation. It was a discouraging task, but Carrie accepted the challenge and at least she was able to get rid of the rodents and insects which had infested the house.

It was at this time that Mrs. Harrison began to be interested in the history of the furnishings of the house. *Carp's Washington* reported to the country on the work being done by Mrs. Harrison:

"The present Mistress of the White House is about the best housekeeper that the Pennsylvania Avenue mansion has yet known. Early in her occupancy she made a survey of the sanitary arrangements of the White House, which has long been damp and unhealthy, and the plumbing re-

pairs were soon done.

"At the request of Mrs. Harrison, the President has ordered an inventory of the furniture of the Executive Mansion. Even the old bits stored away in the attic are to be listed."

While this work was proceeding, the First Lady became interested in the china which had been used by previous administrations, and she gathered it all into the beginnings of a White House China Collection. It is even said that she found the handsome gold plateau (a mirrored centerpiece with metal frame and feet) purchased during the Monroe administration, hidden away in storage, and she is given credit for putting it into use again.

Mrs. Harrison had decided artistic talent, which she expressed, like so many ladies of the day, in the ladylike pastime of china painting. She started a class in china painting at the White House, brought in an excellent artist to instruct the class, and invited members of her official family and personal friends to join. Examples of her own excellent work were donated by her for the

**Fish chowder**

many charitable causes which claimed her assistance. *Carp's Washington* reports that one of her most delightful creations was a porcelain bathtub, which she painted with pink roses for "Baby" McKee, and that when the little boy leaned out of the tub to look at the pretty flowers the water would spill on the floor.

As a result of Mrs. Harrison's interest in china decoration, she personally designed a new state service for use in the White House. The design on the border incorporated the goldenrod flower and the Indian corn, both of which were indigenous to America and accordingly, she felt, appropriate symbols for official decoration.

The Harrison administration seems to have been an especially gay one, and there was a continuous round of entertainments for friends, relatives, and dignitaries. The young people at the White House provided the occasion for a number of private festivities in addition to the usual formal receptions and the customary state dinners. Mrs. Harrison found she was always busy, and she was happy to have the assistance of her daughter. A contemporary account gives an interesting glimpse of domestic arrangements:

"She [Mrs. Harrison] has none of the pretense or affectation of Washington hostesses who ape the embassies' foreign customs and cooking. The President likes the plain dishes of Dolly Johnson, the colored cook he engaged from Kentucky, better than the complicated French menus of her predecessor, Madame Pelouard. In her way Dolly Johnson, too, is an artist. With a Virginia girl named Mary to help her, she can produce a state dinner with as succulent meats and as delicate pastries as delight the patrons of Delmonico's. Both Dolly and Mary wear kerchiefs and aprons, but no caps, for livery is not tolerated in the White House.

"The stories that Mrs. Harrison spends half her time in the kitchen actually taking part in the preparation of food are absurd, but she knows every detail of the household and her servants adore her. No dusty corner in the big mansion escapes her eyes, and each item of the day's menu is discussed with the steward who does the ordering and who supervises the domestic staff."

In addition to the gay festivities which were

so much a part of this administration, the record also shows the happy family life that went on at the time:

"President Harrison and his family usually have prayers before breakfast, which is served at about 9 o'clock. Baby McKee's high chair is pulled close to his grandfather, whose affection for his small namesake is the talk of the nation."

Perhaps the family fun of the Harrison administration is most clearly illustrated by the fact that the first Christmas tree ever to be decorated in the White House was put up for the first Christmas the Harrisons spent there. They were a family which especially enjoyed Christmas and all its traditions, so they celebrated it with enthusiasm, from old Dr. Scott down to the youngest grandchild. The tree was put up in the oval room on the second floor, and it seemed that all the staff of the White House and all the older members of the family, including the President, worked on its elaborate trimmings. Colonel Crook pronounced it "truly the most beautiful I have ever seen before or since."

During the summer of 1892, in the midst of the political campaign, the First Lady became seriously ill with cancer. That October she died in the White House, and her funeral was held in the East Room. Her death was followed by that of her father, and in November the President lost the election to Grover Cleveland.

No New Year's Day reception was held that year because the family was in mourning, but by late January official entertaining was resumed with Mary Harrison McKee acting as the hostess. She did an excellent job for the two months remaining in the administration, but the family was glad to be able to go back to Indianapolis in March and leave behind the joys and sorrows of their four years in Washington.

**Mrs. Harrison's recipe for sausage rolls in *Statesmen's Dishes and How To Cook Them*, 1890**

Sausage Rolls
Make a light biscuit dough—(made with milk) & let it raise over night In the morning roll it out thin & cut into shape with a biscuit cutter In the center of each place a roll of sausage the size of a good sized Hickory nut & roll it up in the dough—After letting

them stand in the pan for a few minutes. take & serve hot
These rolls are also good cold. & when children we used to have them to take to school for our luncheon in bad weather

Caroline Scott Harrison

# *Favorite Recipes*

## *Fish Chowder*

| | |
|---|---|
| 1 medium-sized shad or whitefish | minced fine |
| 2 cups finely diced potatoes | 1 No. 2 can tomatoes |
| ¼ pound bacon or salt pork | 1 teaspoon salt |
| 1 medium-sized onion, | ⅛ teaspoon pepper |
| | 1 pint milk |
| | cracker crumbs |

Cut into small pieces the fish, the potatoes, the onion, and the bacon or salt pork. Fry the bacon and onions a light brown. Put a layer of potatoes in the saucepan, over that a layer of the fish, then a sprinkling of onions and bacon, then a layer of tomatoes. Sprinkle with pepper and salt, alternating the layers, until it is all in. Add enough water to cover, place over a low fire, and let simmer for 25 minutes. Boil 1 pint of milk, thickening it with cracker crumbs; let it stand a moment, and then add to the chowder.

Now stir for the first time, let boil an instant, season to taste. Serve hot.

## *Sausage Rolls*

| | |
|---|---|
| 2 cups sifted flour | ¼ cup shortening |
| 2½ teaspoons baking powder | ⅔ cup milk |
| 1 teaspoon salt | sausage, cut into pieces |

**Sausage rolls**

**Fig pudding**

Make a biscuit dough by combining all the ingredients, except the sausage. Roll the dough out thin, and cut into shape with a biscuit cutter. In the center of each, place a roll of sausage the size of a good-sized hickory nut, and roll it up in the dough. Preheat the oven to 450°, and bake in this hot oven for 10 to 15 minutes.

## *Fig Pudding*

| | |
|---|---|
| 1 cup boiling water | 1 cup molasses |
| 1 cup cut-up figs | 1½ cups flour |
| 2 tablespoons shortening | 1 teaspoon salt |
| 1 whole egg, well beaten | 1 teaspoon soda |

Pour 1 cup boiling water over 1 cup cut-up figs and 2 tablespoons shortening. Beat 1 egg and stir in 1 cup molasses.

Blend in the cut-up figs. Sift together the flour, salt, and soda, and stir into the mixture. Pour into well-greased 1-quart mold. Steam 2 hours. Serve with creamy sauce.

## *Creamy Sauce*

| | |
|---|---|
| 1 egg, whole, beaten | 1 teaspoon vanilla |
| ⅓ cup melted butter | 1 cup heavy cream, whipped stiff |
| 1½ cups sifted confectioners' sugar | |

Beat egg with fork. Blend in the melted butter, sifted confectioners sugar, vanilla. At the end, fold in 1 cup heavy cream, whipped stiff. Serve cold with pudding.

*William McKinley*

*Ida Saxton McKinley*

# William McKINLEY

THE INAUGURATION of President William McKinley, on March 4, 1897, took place under clear skies and mild temperatures. The newsmen called it "McKinley weather" and felt it was a good omen for the new administration. In the reserved section watching the ceremony were the mother of the new President, holding a sheaf of roses, and his invalid wife, Ida Saxton McKinley, whose ashen color aroused anxiety in many in the large audience. After the ceremony the President returned to the White House and with a brief adieu to the outgoing President Cleveland joined his wife to greet the guests who had assembled to welcome him to his new home.

The inaugural luncheon was expertly planned and prepared and smoothly served as President McKinley had wisely decided to continue as steward William Sinclair, who had served during the Cleveland administration.

After the luncheon the President viewed the inaugural parade, received guests all afternoon at the mansion, and that evening he and his wife attended the inaugural ball at the Pension Office.

Although Mrs. McKinley had to leave the ball at an early hour she got through the day's strenuous festivities without a mishap.

The McKinleys arrived at the White House after many years of public service in one political position after another. They were fully familiar with Washington protocol from the years they had spent there when Major McKinley was a member of the House of Representatives. Then they lived in the Ebbitt Hotel in the city, and the Major's devotion to his invalid wife soon became a Washington legend. He set up his office in the hotel so that he could be constantly at her call. Because of Mrs. McKinley's illness, they rarely entertained.

When he became Governor of Ohio the McKinleys again lived in a hotel, as that state was without an executive mansion. It was said that the windows of the Governor's office in the Ohio Capitol were directly across from the windows of their hotel suite so that the Governor could reassure himself about his wife's condition merely by looking out of his window. Every afternoon

Fried  potatoes        Bacon  and  eggs                    Johnny  cakes                    Cherry  pie

at 3, as a greeting, he waved his handkerchief out of the window to her, to be answered by the return greeting of a flutter of white from the hotel window.

The new President's devotion to his ailing wife and his great personal dignity made him an ideal representation of the decorum which was so highly prized at the turn of the century. The people felt that they had a President they could understand and appreciate.

President McKinley returned their interest with affection, and almost immediately the White House seemed to take on a more relaxed atmosphere. The public was again allowed to stroll through the White House grounds, the Mansion became accessible to everyone, and the President moved about his home and the city as he pleased.

People poured through the house daily, and the White House grounds became a regular city park where casual visitors and tourists could eat lunch, snap pictures, or just sit and gawk as official callers came and went to and from the mansion.

At this time, the house itself was in extremely bad condition. Its paint was cracked, wallpaper was peeling in the state reception rooms, the furniture sagged, rugs were worn, and curtains were faded. Floors were creaky and banisters were shaky. When large public receptions were held the staff had to bolster up the floors on the first floor with beams and bricks in the cellar.

All this mattered little to the McKinleys. The President was busy about the nation's business, and Mrs. McKinley spent most of her time in her own room, surrounded by her personal possessions. A maid was close at hand, ready for any emergency, and the President could reach her in an instant, if it became necessary.

Ike Hoover, for many years chief usher, tells us that the White House ran itself during the McKinley administration. Certainly it ran without any appreciable supervision by the President or his wife. Colonel Bingham, the Presidential aide, at one time reported: "I took a look at the radiators . . . and found waste paper, remains of lunches, cigars, cigarettes, and other trash at least a foot deep between the radiators and the window sills."

Though most of the responsibility for social activities rested on the President himself, he seemed to enjoy the stimulation of official entertaining. He had hired a plain cook at forty dollars a month for their family meals, but for the formal dinners he brought a French chef from New York.

The State Dining Room of the mansion was inadequate for large dinners, so tables were set up in the halls to accommodate the overflow of official guests, with protocol strictly followed in seating and serving. Formal dinners were especially trying to Ida, but she was determined not to sacrifice any of her prerogatives as First Lady, and insisted on being present despite the fact that she was subject to epileptic seizures without any warning. To protect both his wife and his guests from embarrassment, the President arranged for his wife to be seated beside him so that he could watch for signs of an approaching attack and take care of the emergency.

In addition to the formal dinners, there were numerous convivial dinners with the members of the Cabinet and personal friends. Many of these were stag affairs. When ladies were present, the gentlemen were apt to retire to the smoking room to discuss horses, family affairs, and personal problems. These smaller dinners could be held in the dining room, and the relaxed, informal atmosphere reflected the congeniality of the McKinley inner circle.

The social schedule included the inevitable New Year's Day reception and large formal receptions. A crowd of 1,000 taxed the facilities of the Mansion, but three times that number were not uncommon. The staff was severely put to the test to provide accommodations and refreshments for a gathering of that size. Gate crashers compounded the problem, for the doors were open to everyone. The President refused to take measures to correct this, as he saw the political value of being available to the common people.

There were normally three noon receptions a week for the public, at which the President himself, standing near the door, shook hands and greeted all visitors. If Ida felt well she would sit in a blue velvet chair beside the President, nodding to the guests as they passed her. The chair was cushioned to prevent her from falling, and she held a bouquet of flowers to ward off shaking hands. If a guest unknowingly extended a hand, Mrs. Hobart, the wife of the Vice President, would inquire politely, "Won't you shake hands with me instead?"

It was not that Mrs. McKinley disliked these formal affairs; it was simply that she could not stand the physical strain. Both her pride at being with her husband and her sincere pleasure in the deference accorded her position were evident.

As for the President, he delighted in the people who came simply to shake his hand. He often said that he got more from his friendly callers than they got from him. "Everyone in the line has a smile and a cheery word. They bring no problems with them, only good will. I feel better after that contact."

The President's chief relaxations, aside from the time spent with his wife in her room, were frequent walks, horseback rides and drives, and a good cigar. His supply of cigars never ran out. Summer evenings often found him sitting in a rocker on the south portico looking out across the lawn towards the Washington Monument enjoying the cool of the evening.

President McKinley was never anything but a moderate social drinker, yet full courses of wine were provided for the guests at the White House during his administration. Andrew Carnegie once sent him a barrel of Scotch whisky, and we may be sure that it was long enjoyed and shared with friends.

Both the President and Mrs. McKinley enjoyed the White House conservatories. Ida often visited them with her nieces and her friends, and delighted in picking the red roses, which were her favorite flowers, or plucking a carnation to take back for the President's lapel. It was said to be a habit of this President's, when he had to decline to do a favor for a visitor, to remove the carnation from his own buttonhole and pin it to the caller's lapel with the request that he give it to his wife with the President's best wishes.

Despite Mrs. McKinley's poor health, the McKinleys enjoyed traveling, and the President rarely made a trip without Ida. After the President's reelection to the Presidency, they took a gala swing around the country, with forty-three guests in attendance.

His wife was traveling with him when he went to Buffalo in September 1901 to attend the Pan-American Exposition. She was not at his side when he was shot, but as usual his first thought was of her: "My wife—be careful about her—she's sleeping—break the news gently to her."

To the surprise of her physician and all who knew her, Mrs. McKinley bore up surprisingly well under the ordeal of the President's wounding, his illness and death, and the state funeral which followed.

The burial was in the McKinley home town of Canton, Ohio. Mrs. McKinley never came back to the White House. Her personal belongings were packed and sent to her by the President's secretary.

She who had lived only for her husband lived on almost six lonely years without him before she died in Canton and was buried beside him.

# Favorite Recipes

## Bacon and Eggs

A good way to cook bacon is as follows:
1. Pan frying: Lay the bacon strips in a cold frying pan, and cook over a moderate flame until the bacon is the desired light golden color. Turn the strips frequently, and pour off the excess melted bacon fat. Save for drippings. Drain the golden brown bacon strips on absorbent paper, and serve hot.
2. Oven broiling and grilling: Lay the bacon slices on cold broiler rack, 5 to 6 inches below the heat. Broil until bacon is the desired light golden color. Turn, and broil on other side. Drain the golden brown bacon strips on absorbent paper, and serve hot.

Mrs. McKinley's tea china

### Fried Eggs

eggs                                salt and pepper
butter, or bacon fat

Heat the butter or bacon fat in a frying pan, and slip in the eggs whole. Cook as many eggs at one time as will fill the pan without touching one another. Cook slowly. Cover the pan as soon as the eggs have been added, and turn heat very low. Salt and pepper to taste.

### Johnny Cakes

⅓ cup granulated          1 cup sour milk
    sugar                        1 cup flour
1 egg, whole                 1 teaspoon soda
¾ cup corn meal           1 teaspoon salt
⅛ pound of butter,
    melted

Mix thoroughly sugar, egg, and about a third of the melted butter. Use the rest of the butter to grease the griddle. Add sour milk and soda, then corn meal, salt, and flour. Allow to stand in a cool place ½ hour. Heat griddle and test it to see if the butter spits. Rub griddle with a little melted butter. Spoon out the mixture onto the hot griddle in tablespoonfuls. Brown on one side, turn over, and brown on the other. Serve at once, hot, with maple syrup, honey, or jam.

### Fried Potatoes

3 medium-sized            ⅛ teaspoon pepper
    potatoes                   1 tablespoon crushed
3 ounces salt butter         rosemary or thyme
¼ teaspoon salt

Peel the potatoes and put them into a pan so that they are just covered with cold water. Bring slowly to boil. Drain, chill, cut in half lengthwise, then cut into slices. Heat 2½ ounces of the salt butter in a heavy skillet, holding out the rest for later. When the butter is foaming, put in the sliced potatoes. Shake over medium heat until the potatoes are golden brown all over. Now add another small lump of butter, salt, freshly ground white pepper, and a tablespoon of crushed rosemary or thyme. Serve hot.

**Mrs. McKinley's demitasse spoons**

with a fork. Brush with a little melted butter and line with a piece of wax paper. Keep the paper down with 2 cups of raw rice. Preheat oven to 375°F and bake for ½ hour. Remove from oven, take paper and rice out. Allow to cool.

When cool, sprinkle the bottom with bread crumbs and sugar, and fill with the following:

### Cherry Pie
#### Crust

| | |
|---|---|
| 4 cups all-purpose flour | yolks, put through strainer |
| 1 teaspoon salt | grated rind of 2 oranges |
| ¾ pound of sweet butter | ⅔ cup orange juice, iced |
| 4 tablespoons coarse granulated sugar | 1 whole egg, beaten |
| 4 hard boiled egg | |

Put flour and salt into a bowl, add butter and work the flour with tips of fingertips until it resembles coarse corn meal. Add grated orange rind, sugar, strained hardboiled egg yolks, and mix lightly. Add iced orange juice and work up quickly into a firm dough.

Take a little less than half of the dough; roll it out and line a 10-inch pie pan with it. Trim the edges off neatly and prick all over the bottom

### Filling

| | |
|---|---|
| 5 cups pitted sweet cherries | 2 tablespoons granulated sugar |
| 1 cup granulated sugar | 1½ cups cherry juice |
| 1 8-ounce jar red currant jelly | 1 tablespoon cornstarch |
| | ⅓ cup cherry liqueur |

Cook cherry juice, orange juice, cherry liqueur, sugar, and red currant jelly in a pan. Mix cornstarch with a little of this liquid and add to liquid, stirring until it thickens. Chill. Add pitted cherries, and fill the semi-baked pie shell. Brush edge with beaten egg and roll out the rest of the dough. Cover the pie. Trim off neatly, and brush all over with beaten egg. Out of the scraps of pastry left from trimming the edges, make flowers and leaves. Brush again with beaten egg, and sprinkle with granulated sugar. Bake in preheated 375°F oven, until light golden brown, about ¾ hour. Remove. Cool.

**McKinley family china**

# Theodore ROOSEVELT

Ten days after the McKinley funeral the Theodore Roosevelts were ready to move into the White House. It was the most exuberant family group ever to descend on the Executive Mansion. The President expected that his children should participate in his philosophy of "the strenuous life," from his beautiful daughter Alice, age seventeen, to the youngest son Archie, who was seven. All six of the children were as active as their father, and Ike Hoover, the chief usher of the White House, prophesied correctly that life in the Executive Mansion with this lively group in residence would be "the wildest scramble in history."

Each child brought his own pets. Vans of tricycles, bicycles, skates, guns, books, and toys of all sorts began to arrive. The family moved into the house and made it their home.

The new First Lady meanwhile could not help but view the dark, old-fashioned interior of the mansion with dismay. At once she set to work rearranging White House furniture, cleaning out dark corners, and taking down the heavy Victorian hangings which kept out the sunshine. The condition of the mansion was so bad that after only a few weeks in office President Roosevelt secured a large appropriation from Congress for repairing and refurnishing the house. The money would pay to have the main house completely modernized and expanded, but, best of all, an office wing could also be built to house the President's staff. For the first time in history the mansion would serve just as living quarters for the President and his family. To do the work Charles McKim, president of the American Institute of Architects, was made the architect of the project, and work was started in June 1902, with the understanding that it would be completed for the winter social season in November. Most of this period the Roosevelt family spent at the summer White House, which was set up at the family home at Sagamore Hill, Long Island, while temporary quarters were set up in Washington in a rented house on Lafayette Square.

Though the hasty remodeling of 1902 left a great deal to be desired in the way of structural improvements, the White House emerged from the sweeping changes as an elegant home equipped with the most modern conveniences.

The office wing was located at the west end of the mansion by clearing away the old conservatory and using as the connecting link the colonnade that had been built by Thomas Jefferson. A new entrance for tourists and guests was made at the east end. The most welcome change on the main floor was the enlargement of the State Dining Room by incorporating into it space that had formerly been used as a corridor and family stairway. The chimney breasts in the East Room were set back into the walls to give the room greater size and a more formal appearance.

The First Lady worked closely with the architects, supervising the location of bathrooms and the installation of additional closets. Her own excellent taste influenced the choice of wallpaper, paints, fabrics, and furnishings.

The first formal function held in the renovated house was a dinner for the Cabinet on December 18, 1902.

The social life of the Theodore Roosevelt administration is one of the most documented of any, because the President, himself a historian, appointed a member of his staff to keep a detailed and continuing record of all official White House events. He felt that such information would prove valuable as a guide to future administrations.

The President and the First Lady were both agreed in their aim to have a social administration that was as good as money and effort could make it. For the first time in history the First Lady hired a social secretary, Miss Belle Hagner, to assist her in seeing that social events ran smoothly. Though Mrs. Roosevelt herself managed to oversee the general housekeeping of the mansion, a caterer was employed for official functions.

From several articles in the *Christian Herald* we are given a glimpse of Mrs. Roosevelt as First Lady:

"Mrs. Roosevelt fills her position with gracious hospitality that is felt and appreciated throughout the country. It is she who sets the social activities in motion when, soon after Congress convenes in December, she begins receiving calls. Everyone who is in the official circle leaves cards at the White House, and many who are not in it, for both the President and Mrs. Roosevelt have scores of friends among "the cave-dwellers," as the permanent residents of the town are called. . . .

"Mornings are filled with subscription musicales, recitals, boards and committee meetings to say nothing of home duties. There are luncheons and teas and never-ending calls. Then the nights are taken up with dinner parties and other forms of entertainment.

"She (Mrs. Roosevelt) has performed her duties to the letter and with 'good measure.' Even before the social season begins she has been in the habit of holding afternoon receptions for members of the Diplomatic Corps and for the ladies of the Embassies and Legations.

"Mrs. Roosevelt has introduced many pretty customs relative to the women of the Cabinet, one of the most sentimental being the presentation to each one of a beautiful bunch of flowers just before each reception, to be carried during receiving hours. Handshaking is thus obviated to a great extent, and the flowers are a complement to each woman's gown."

Mrs. Roosevelt met with the wives of the Cabinet officials in the Green Parlor at the White House every Tuesday morning at 11 o'clock to exchange views on social obligations.

The First Lady gave a musicale nearly every Friday evening during each winter season—combining a concert and reception preceded by a dinner. Invited guests numbered from two hundred to five hundred. They were usually received in the Green Room by Mrs. Roosevelt attended only by Colonel Bromwell, the Superintendent of Buildings and Grounds, who introduced the guests. The concert was held in the East Room, and the President would come in as the music started and remain until it ended.

Following the concert, refreshments were served while the President and Mrs. Roosevelt mingled informally with the guests.

By the beginning of the twentieth century the White House was the scene of regular annual

**Roosevelt's state china**

affairs of great formality. Theodore Roosevelt's calendar for one winter season included:

December 13, Cabinet Dinner, 8 p.m.

January 1, New Year's Day Reception, 11 a.m. to 1:30 p.m.

January 3, Diplomatic Reception, 9 to 10:30 p.m.

January 10, Diplomatic Dinner, 8 p.m.

January 17, Judicial Reception, 9 to 10:30 p.m.

January 24, Supreme Court Dinner, 8 p.m.

January 31, Congressional Reception, 9 to 10:30 p.m.

February 7, Army and Navy Reception, 9 to 10:30 p.m.

Under the Roosevelt regime, the customary dinner hour was half past 7 for small dinners and 8 o'clock for banquets. There was hardly a night without guests, so dinner was invariably served in the State Dining Room. The private dining room was used only for family meals such as breakfast and the few luncheons which were family meals without guests present. Luncheon was usually an informal meal, and if the guests were family friends the children and their governess were also present.

Descriptions of White House banquets of the period speak of fine linens, elaborate flowers, beautiful crystal, fine china, and silver or gilt tableware. There were usually from eight to twelve courses to a dinner, and the entire meal was served in two hours. When not too many guests were present, the dinner was prepared and served by the regular kitchen staff. When there were large numbers of guests the services of a caterer were required.

During the meal the Marine Band played. When dinner was over the President would rise, and immediately the rest of the guests would also rise. The men retired to the private dining room to smoke, and coffee was served. Mrs. Roosevelt and the ladies meanwhile gathered in one of the reception rooms where the gentlemen later joined them.

A Washington correspondent for the New York *Sun* reported that at this time the supplies for White House dinners were obtained in open market. Such was the excellence of the supplies that it was hardly necessary to order the required provisions in advance. Formerly, fowls, meats, and fish were obtained directly from the source at the farm and the shore. Now the White House stew-

ard advised the tradesmen of the dates of the dinners and the probable menu, and choice supplies were provided for his inspection. The White House steward was usually one of the earliest buyers at the market. He came with his own wagon and driver, and after choosing the choicest meats from a score or more of butchers, fine fish and shellfish from the fish stalls, and choice vegetables from the farmers, the purchases were driven directly to the White House. By 8 o'clock in the morning preparations had already begun for dinner that night.

The steward reports that only the choicest bits of the supplies purchased were actually served at the dinners. A roast of lamb or filet of beef, for instance, served only four or five persons, with only the choicest sections being eaten. Thus, only the breast of the fowl appeared on the table.

The usual kitchen staff consisted of a cook and several helpers, but for the preparation of a state dinner three French chefs were employed.

In 1906 Alice, the gay and popular daughter of President Roosevelt, was married at the White House to Representative Nicholas Longworth of Ohio. It was the largest wedding ever to be held in the Executive Mansion, with over a thousand guests present. Alice had no attendants and was accompanied only by her father. The groom had a best man and eight ushers. "Princess Alice" was showered with lavish and beautiful wedding gifts which came from every corner of the world. Even after her marriage, Alice returned to the White House each day, and her reign over Washington society continued during all of her long and active life.

The younger daughter of President Roosevelt, Ethel, made her debut at the White House during her father's administration. Archie Butt, military aide to the President, who has left a fascinating account of his years in the White House with Presidents Roosevelt and Taft in the form of letters to his family, describes this party in detail. He reports that the party which he staged was a terrific success. All the state parlors on the main floor were cleared for dancing, and supper was served in the rooms on the ground floor.

It was a gay, imaginative, and robust administration, taking its cue from the frenetic activity of the President. Yet it was an administration which ran smoothly under the strong but gentle hand of Mrs. Roosevelt, whose presence succeeded in creating an atmosphere of dignity and calm in the daily chaos which surrounded her.

◄ Roast suckling pig      Indian pudding      Clove cake

# *Favorite Recipes*

## *Roast Suckling Pig*

| | |
|---|---|
| 1 suckling pig, about 3 weeks old, cleaned and prepared by butcher (about 10 to 12 pounds, dressed, is the best size) | 3 teaspoons salt |
| | 1 tablespoon powdered sage |
| | 3 tablespoons butter |
| | 1 medium-sized onion, minced |
| 6 cups or more, dried bread crumbs | 1 tart apple, peeled and grated |

### *Garnish*

| | |
|---|---|
| 3 tablespoons fresh parsley | cranberries |
| | watercress |
| 1 carrot or lemon or apple, to put in mouth | red cinnamon apples or spiced crabapples |

For the stuffing, simmer heart and liver together with seasoning in 2 cups water, until tender. Chop fine. Sauté onion in some of the butter. Grate apple. Mix chopped heart and liver with crumbs, seasoning, apple, and onion, and moisten with stock. Fill pig with stuffing being careful not to overfill, as it will split. Sew opening together.

Insert a small block of wood in mouth to hold it open. Lower the eyelids and fasten shut. (The butcher should have removed eyeballs.) Skewer legs firmly in place, the forelegs forward and the hindlegs in a crouching position. Rub whole pig well with melted butter, dredge with flour, salt, and pepper. Cover ears and tail with foil, to prevent burning.

Place roast on rack in uncovered pan in 450°F oven for 15 minutes. Reduce heat to 325°F and roast until tender, allowing 30 minutes to the pound. Baste every 15 minutes with drippings, Do not use water. For the final 15 minutes, remove foil from ears and tail.

Place roasted pig on a large platter or board. Place cranberries in eyes, a carrot or lemon or apple in the mouth. Drape a garland of cranberries around the neck. Garnish platter or board with bed of watercress and/or parsley and red cinnamon apples or spiced crabapples.

## *Indian Pudding*

| | |
|---|---|
| 6 tablespoons corn meal | 1 teaspoon grated lemon rind |
| 6 cups milk, scalded | 1 teaspoon ginger |
| ½ cup brown sugar | ½ pound raisins |
| ¼ pound butter | 6 eggs, beaten whole |
| 1 teaspoon salt | |

Combine the corn meal with the scalded milk. Add the sugar, butter, and salt. Let the mixture cool. Then add the lemon rind, ginger, raisins, and eggs. Bake in a buttered 3-quart casserole, set in water, for 2 hours in a slow oven (300°F).

### *Decoration*

orange or lemon
wedges, glazed
with honey

Decorate the top with orange or lemon sections that have been glazed with honey. Serve with cream or vanilla ice cream.

## *Clove Cake*

| | |
|---|---|
| ½ cup of butter | ½ teaspoon of cloves, cinnamon, and allspice |
| ½ cup of milk | |
| ½ cup of molasses | |
| 2 cups flour | 1½ teaspoons nutmeg |
| 2 eggs, whole | ½ pound crystallized ginger and butter, for decoration |
| 3 cups seedless raisins | |
| 1 teaspoon soda, in the molasses | |

Mix butter and milk; add eggs, beating well. Add molasses and soda, milk, and flour that has been sifted together with the spices. Beat well. Add raisins. Bake in greased 8-inch tube pan at 350°F for 45 to 55 minutes.

Brush the top with a little butter, and garnish with overlapping slices of crystallized ginger.

Helen Herron Taft

William Howard Taft

# William H. TAFT

PRESIDENT AND Mrs. Theodore Roosevelt invited the incoming President William H. Taft and Mrs. Taft to spend the night of March 3 with them at the White House. The idea had been President Roosevelt's, who was elated over the victory of his personally selected successor. Mrs. Taft's recollection of the evening shows that it was not a very successful one socially. Already President Roosevelt was becoming annoyed at the way his protegé was assuming the prerogatives of the Presidency and at the selection of his Cabinet.

Mrs. Taft's words sum up the feeling of strain that resulted: "Now there is always bound to be a sadness about the end of an administration, no matter how voluntarily the retiring President may leave office, no matter how welcome the new President and his family may be."

March 3 that year proved to be one of the coldest and most disagreeable nights in Washington history. It snowed all night and the wind blew furiously. The Tafts woke next morning to find it still snowing and sleeting with little im-

provement in temperature. Mr. Taft claimed that this was *his* storm: "I always said it would be a cold day when I got to be President."

The outgoing President and the President-elect rode up to the Capitol together, with Mr. Taft diplomatically allowing President Roosevelt to be the one to acknowledge the cheers of the crowd. After the inaugural ceremony, which had to be held in the Senate chamber because of the inclement weather, Theodore Roosevelt went straight to Union Station to take the train home, and Mrs. Taft rode back down Constitution Avenue with her husband, the first time a First Lady had been accorded this honor. Preparations had been made at the White House for an inaugural luncheon at 1 P.M., but weather delayed many of the guests who came and went all afternoon, with luncheon guests still arriving together with guests who had been invited to tea. The inaugural parade moved slowly on the slippery streets, and the President was late getting back to the White House. The new First Lady was further harassed by the fact that her inaugural ballgown was caught

167

somewhere in the giant transportation freeze up along the East Coast. The gown finally arrived just in time to be worn to the ball, which was held in the Pension Building. The honor guests were comfortable in a private supper room provided for their use but the other guests not only had to dance in their coats, but they ate in them, too, and the elaborate food planned for their enjoyment turned out to be cold and unappetizing.

The Tafts moved into a White House that had been completely renovated during the previous administration. The new First Lady found it so completely to her taste that she made very few changes. She did have an extra large bathtub installed for her 300-pound husband, and the Lincoln bed was moved from the President's bedroom and replaced by twin beds.

Mrs. Taft soon made some changes in the staff of the Mansion to insure a smoothly run household. The steward was replaced by a housekeeper who took over the details of running the large house. This position was held by Mrs. Elizabeth Jaffray, a most efficient and tactful addition to the household. Mrs. Taft also had uniformed servants stationed at the front door to receive visitors and give instructions to sightseers. Mrs. Taft commented that "many a time I have seen strangers wander up to the door looking in vain for someone to whom it seemed right and proper to address a question or hand a visiting card" and that she thought "many a timid visitor has had reason to be thankful for the change." In her opinion these people lent an air of formal dignity to the entrance which it had previously lacked.

The social life of the Taft administration was unusually brilliant and gay. The President and his wife liked to entertain and they had dinner guests, luncheon guests, and sometimes even breakfast guests every day. It was not possible to know the exact number of guests the genial and hospitable President would invite to a meal until the guests were actually seated. Mrs. Taft always made out the day's menus in consultation with the housekeeper and head cook, and her orders had been given for emergency provisions to be held in reserve at all times. The actual preparation of the food would then take place within a half hour of the meal so that it could accommodate the unexpected guests.

The first big party at the White House was the formal reception of the diplomatic corps at which the President and Mrs. Taft received foreign ambassadors and ministers accredited to this country. Many of these people were personal friends of the Tafts resulting from their official position in Washington during the previous administration.

In her *Recollections of Full Years* Mrs. Taft reports that she was at home informally about three afternoons a week when her friends came to see her and when she received many other ladies who wrote and asked permission to call. "I always received in the Red Room," she says, "which with fire and candles lighted, is pleasant enough to be almost cozy, large and imposing though it be." These parties generally were held to twenty or more callers so that Mrs. Taft could have an opportunity to enjoy the visitors and show them some personal attention.

In addition to the more intimate gatherings there were the great formal receptions, such as the afternoon reception for congressional wives, to which 400 were invited. In the summertime garden parties extended the number of guests far beyond this number. The social calendar was full of many small parties, dances, and receptions. Mr. Taft wanted each reception crowded with people and every possible seat filled for a formal dinner. The President insisted that refreshments should be served on every occasion so that Mrs. Jaffray records that they prepared food for an average of 2,000 people for the garden parties and large receptions. Instead of this food being provided by caterers, as had been customary in other administrations, Mrs. Taft had it prepared at the White House. She thought that if the food came from the White House kitchens it would taste better and would be more appreciated by the guests. An added inducement for the Tafts, who had no outside income, was that it was cheaper. All this work was done by three cooks. The head cook, a Swedish woman, had been cook for the Pierpont Morgans and was well qualified for her job.

Lillian Rogers Parks, the upstairs maid at the White House, says in her memoirs that Mrs. Taft had a special cook come in before the state dinners to make the terrapin soup and nothing else, and that Mrs. Taft came to the kitchen to taste it, making her one of the few First Ladies to come to the kitchen.

The bill for groceries and meat in one comparatively quiet month in the early days of the administration amounted to $868.93; it averaged about $1,000 a month. State and official receptions called for an outlay of some $2,000.

Helen Herron Taft, critical and appreciative of food and an excellent manager (except when she lived in the White House she did most of the marketing personally), was sometimes foolhardy in her selection. Archie Butt tells of near tragedy at a dinner for the Republican National Committee in 1911: "I must tell Mrs. Taft not to have any more French artichokes at these dinners. Some night she is going to find some dead guests, for I saw not less than six of those nearest me eating not only the sticky, fungous stuff, but some actually trying to chew up the leaves. The only other time I have seen this was at the Ohio dinner when Nick Longworth called my attention to it. Last night I had to stop ———— for I think he would have choked to death trying to masticate the leaves and the fungous part."

Mrs. Jaffray reports that rarely was there a big lunch or dinner without champagne, and Ona Jeffries in *In and Out of the White House* says that the Tafts' champagne punch became famous. Yet it is recorded that the President himself did not touch wines and was an absolute abstainer.

Mrs. Taft recalls that the long terrace leading from the State Dining Room out over the west colonnade proved to be most useful for large dinner parties when dining indoors would have been rather unpleasant. Mr. Taft had one of his Congressional dinners served on the terrace during the first summer they were in the White House. Mrs. Taft also found that the long terrace leading from the East Room was a delightful promenade for guests on warm evenings.

Early in that first summer in the White House Mrs. Taft was successful in establishing Potomac Park as a fashionable place to go at the end of a day for a stroll or a drive while listening

**Spiced cherries**                    **Chicken croquettes**                    **Lobster à la Newburg**

Taft family china

to music. The attendance of the President and Mrs. Taft and their obvious enjoyment of the park and the music soon made the idea a social success.

Unfortunately, soon after this, Mrs. Taft had a mild stroke brought on by the many social activities and the mental and physical strain of life in the White House. It was a long time before she had fully recovered, but in the interim the social activities continued with her supervision and planning and the assistance of her family in carrying out the plans.

One of the gay events of the administration was the coming-out party of the Tafts' daughter Helen, who made her debut in 1909 with a tea for 1,200 and a dance in the East Room for 300. With the versatile and charming Archie Butt, military aide to the President, as the impresario of the occasion, the party was delightful. Butt had an area for the band constructed on the roof

of the East Wing, completely surrounding the big triple window of the East Room. All the window-panes and sashes were taken out. With the music in its own special alcove, the entire floor of the room was available for dancing, and the music was pronounced perfect.

Another especially successful occasion was the garden party to celebrate the silver wedding anniversary of the President and Mrs. Taft. Archie Butt called this party "the most brilliant function ever held" in the White House and the First Lady refers to it as the "greatest event" of their four years in the White House. Her recollection of the party was that four or five thousand people attended and "that a more brilliant throng was never gathered in this country."

It was a night garden party and every tree and bush was strung with lights, and strings of lanterns decked the lawn. The fountain played at its topmost height in every color of the rainbow.

To the south the Washington Monument gleamed against the sky, and at the other end of the lawn the White House was ablaze with lights and open for the guests to refresh themselves at the long tables laid out in the dining room and vestibule.

It must have seemed like a dream come true to Mrs. Taft, who had been a guest in the White House as a 17-year-old girl when President and Mrs. Rutherford B. Hayes celebrated their twenty-fifth wedding anniversary. It seems likely that her ambition to be First Lady dated from that visit.

The last year the Tafts spent in the White House was marred by the bitter political campaign in which Theodore Roosevelt split the Republican Party by running against his old friend and political protegé. As a result the Democratic candidate, Woodrow Wilson, was elected, and Mr. Taft retired to private life as an elder statesman and member of the faculty of Yale University.

In 1921 Mr. Taft realized his life's ambition when he was appointed Chief Justice of the Supreme Court. He and his wife returned to Washington where they spent the remaining years of their lives as honored members of the exclusive Washington official social circle.

# Favorite Recipes

## Lobster à la Newburg

| | |
|---|---|
| 3 1½-pound lobsters | dash of nutmeg |
| salted water, boiling, to cover | ½ cup dry sherry |
| | 1½ cups heavy cream |
| 4 tablespoons butter | 4 egg yolks, beaten |
| ½ teaspoon paprika | 6 slices of toast, |
| dash of cayenne | golden brown |

Allowing ½ lobster for each person, boil lobsters in boiling salted water 20 minutes. Remove meat from shells, saving out meat from claws in one piece. Cut the rest into ½-inch pieces. Set aside lobster coral for chopping for garnish.

Sauté lobsters' meat in butter 3 minutes. Add paprika, cayenne, nutmeg, and sherry. Cook until wine is reduced to 2 tablespoons. Blend cream with egg yolks. Add to lobster and cook over low heat until sauce thickens. Serve hot with lobster claw for decoration, and chopped lobster coral sprinkled on top.

## Spiced Cherries or Dawson Plums

| | |
|---|---|
| 7 pounds fresh fruit— red sour cherries, or dawson plums | 3 cups vinegar |
| | 1 ounce whole cloves |
| | 1 ounce whole cinnamon |
| 4 pounds granulated sugar | |

Place fruit and spices in kettle in alternate layers, and let stand overnight. Boil sugar and vinegar together; pour hot over fruit. Bring to a boil, and boil 1 minute.

For later use, pour into sterilized glass jars and seal.

## Chicken Croquettes

| | |
|---|---|
| 3 cups finely chopped cooked turkey or chicken | 1 pint light cream |
| | 2 whole eggs, slightly beaten |
| dash of pepper | bread crumbs |
| dash of nutmeg | lard or oil or shortening, for frying |
| ¼ cup chopped onion | |
| ⅓ cup butter | |
| ⅓ cup flour | |

Chop cold turkey or chicken very fine. Season with pepper, nutmeg, and onion. Melt butter, add flour, and mix until smooth. Add cream and cook slowly, stirring constantly until sauce is thick. Add salt and chopped fowl. Chill. Shape into croquettes. Dip croquettes into egg, then into bread crumbs. Roll lightly into shape. Fry in boiling fat (380°F) until browned, about 5 minutes. Makes 6 servings.

**Lobster à la Newburg**

*Ellen Louise Axson Wilson*

*Thomas Woodrow Wilson*

*Edith Bolling Galt Wilson*

# Woodrow WILSON

PRESIDENT TAFT was pleased to welcome the incoming President Wilson to Washington and to the White House. He himself escorted Mr. Wilson to the Capitol for the inaugural ceremonies and then drove back to the White House with him and stayed for lunch to introduce the new family to the mansion. It is reported that Mr. Taft, as he left, told them "I'm glad to be going—this is the lonesomest place in the world."

The Wilsons moved into the house without ceremony and settled down to the same kind of happy family life they had known in all their other homes. There was not even an inaugural ball, as the new President, son of a Presbyterian minister, and his wife, who was a minister's daughter, considered such a ball a frivolity not in keeping with the seriousness of the office.

Thus began an administration in which the close-knit family life of the President, his wife, and their three daughters was far more important than their public entertaining.

Ellen Axson Wilson, the new First Lady, was a calm and poised hostess who managed state events with natural, gracious hospitality. She held a series of most successful semiweekly receptions for Washington society.

But far more than the social life, Mrs. Wilson enjoyed the opportunity the position of First Lady gave her to "leave the world a better place than she had found it."

Lillian Roger Parks, in her book *Thirty Years Backstairs at the White House,* says that her mother, the second maid at that time, came home and told her family, "I think we have an angel in the White House. She is talking about helping the poor and improving the housing."

The slums of the nation's capital horrified her. As a member of the board of the Associated Charities in Washington, she was soon actively engaged in social service work in the city. At her instigation a survey was made of alley dwellings and tenement housing; this was called to congressional attention, and Congress was asked for remedial housing legislation.

In addition to her charitable activities the First Lady found time for her art work. Lillian

Rogers Parks reports that Mrs. Wilson spent many happy hours at her easel in the White House and that she sold some of her paintings for worthwhile causes, such as the education of Southern mountaineers and the crippled children of Washington.

Ellen Wilson also turned her artistic talents to making the White House a more beautiful and comfortable place in which to live. She loved to garden, and she planned, supervised, and planted a rose garden on the south lawn between the White House and the President's office. Here she spent many pleasant hours in company with the President, who had a telephone installed there so he could keep in touch with his office.

The upstairs oval sitting room was made comfortable and homelike with fine paintings and statuary, the family piano, and the family's personal library. The Wilsons considered it to be "almost as homelike as any home we had ever lived in."

Mrs. Wilson thought the family dining room a dark and somber room, so she had a small table placed in the south end of the State Dining Room overlooking the south lawn and the Washington Monument, with a view of the river in the distance.

Mrs. Jaffray had remained as housekeeper, and the Swedish cook who had worked for Mrs. Taft also stayed on at the White House, but Mrs. Wilson brought with her from New Jersey her own cook who ruled the kitchen.

The overworked kitchen staff must have welcomed the respite from the busy entertaining of the Taft administration. Other than close personal friends, there was seldom anyone at dinner except for the state occasions.

The Wilsons' three daughters added to the social activities of the administration. Under the guiding hand of Belle Hagner, the competent social secretary who had also been secretary to Mrs. Roosevelt, the girls spent each night in a social whirl going their separate ways so that each could be guest of honor at some party and spread the prestige of the White House to more segments of Washington society.

Two of the girls, Jessie and Eleanor, were married at the White House. Jessie had a magnificent wedding in the East Room. Backstairs, Mrs. Parks reported, "Everyone in the kitchen held their breath to keep from disturbing the cake. . . ." It had been baked in the White House kitchen by Mme. Blanche Roles of New York and stood

almost three feet in diameter, and weighed a hundred and thirty pounds. Jessie's wedding took place in November 1913, and in May 1914, Eleanor married William Gibbs McAdoo, the Secretary of the Treasury, in the Blue Room. It was a much smaller wedding than her sister's, as her mother was already ill.

Ellen Axson Wilson, the first wife of the President, died in the White House in August that same year. The family was desolate. President Wilson was a lost and lonely man. Margaret, the remaining unmarried daughter, was absorbed in her career as a concert singer, and showed no interest in White House entertaining. The social secretary, Belle Hagner, left to get married, and the President, who was accustomed to being surrounded by a group of adoring women, was left with the company of only one, his cousin Miss Helen Bones, who had been his wife's personal secretary.

It is easy to understand that President Wilson was at once attracted to the charming widow, Edith Bolling Galt, when she visited the White House that next spring. Mrs. Galt had been brought to call on Miss Bones by Admiral Cary Grayson, the White House physician, but her friendship with Miss Bones soon served as a convenient screen for the President's courtship

**The library of the Wilson home**

**Roast turkey with cornbread stuffing**

during the summer and fall. The engagement was announced in October, and they were married at Mrs. Galt's home on December 10, 1915. It was a quiet wedding, with both bride and groom unattended. Immediately following the ceremony they went to Hot Springs, Virginia, for their honeymoon.

The social season under the new Mrs. Wilson was a brilliant one, starting off with a diplomatic reception in January 1916. "Mrs. Wilson stood tall and beautiful in a white gown, brocaded with silver and draped with white tulle."

Mrs. Edith Wilson moved into the White House with only a few of her favorite possessions.

The position of secretary was taken over by Edith Benham. Together the First Lady and her secretary reduced the invitation lists for receptions to a reasonable size. Mrs. Wilson also stopped the custom of inviting certain favored guests "behind the lines" at receptions, as it had become a source of discontent in Washington social circles.

Despite the fact that many people thought the President's remarriage so soon after the death of his first wife would defeat him at the polls, he won the election of 1916 by a narrow margin. In just one month after his inauguration he had convened Congress in special session to hear his war message calling for the entrance of the United States into World War I.

With the White House the center of the conduct of the war, the grounds were closed and guarded, and all social functions were discontinued. With the rest of the country Mrs. Wilson soon had her household observing meatless days, heatless days, and gasless Sundays.

The First Lady learned to help her husband at his desk with all the tasks she could share, and when she could not help she sat in the room with him, knitting. She also spent hours at her sewing machine making pajamas for the soldiers; she rolled bandages for the Red Cross and worked at their canteen in Union Station. She had sheep grazing to keep the White House lawn cropped and so save manpower, and their wool was sold for a fabulous amount for the benefit of the Red Cross.

When the war was over, President Wilson went abroad to attend the peace conference. He and Mrs. Wilson found that these trips became triumphal tours as they were welcomed in all the countries of our allies, not only for the assistance of the United States in the war but for the idealistic concept which the President hoped to impose on the peace.

Unfortunately his own country refused to ratify the League of Nations, so President Wilson set out on a tour around the country to gain public support for his plan. Sheer exhaustion brought on by the strain of the war, the peace conference, and the speaking tour brought on a complete collapse, and Woodrow Wilson returned to the White House so seriously ill that his life was despaired of. During his illness the First Lady stepped into authority as she shielded her husband from the cares and worries of his office. This is the period which is sometimes referred to as

"Mrs. Wilson's Regency." She digested papers presented for his attention, screened all visitors, relayed his decisions, and successfully maintained the pretense of his authority for all her actions. It was a labor of love of a woman concerned only with the thought that she must preserve her husband's will to live. The responsibilities that were taken on by a First Lady during this period were without parallel in the history of the country.

**Another corner of the Wilson house library**

The President never regained his health, but he improved enough to be active once again before he left the White House in 1921.

With the approaching end of the administration, life became more relaxed in the White House. The President worked in the mornings, lunched, napped, and took drives with his wife. After dinner they would watch movies on a screen in the East Room, play solitaire, or Mrs. Wilson would read to her husband. They also spent hours planning and anticipating their retirement.

On leaving the White House the Wilsons moved to a comfortable home on S Street in Washington. There Wilson died a few years later without ever being well again. His widow lived on for almost forty years, devoting the rest of her life to the preservation and popularization of the memory of Woodrow Wilson. Until her death in 1961 the former First Lady held a unique and unchallenged position in Washington social life.

# *Favorite Recipes*

### *Roast Turkey*
### *(with Cornbread Stuffing)*

| | |
|---|---|
| 10 to 12-pound turkey | salt, pepper |
| unsalted melted fat | paprika |

After washing the turkey inside and out, dry with a cloth. Rub the inside with salt, and fill the body cavity loosely with the stuffing (see below). Sew up the incision, or secure with skewers.

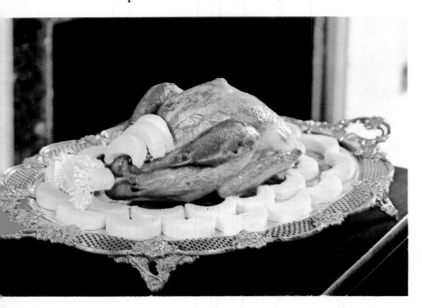

Place the bird, breast up, in a roasting pan. Brush the breast, legs, wings with the melted fat.

Preheat oven to 300°F, and roast the turkey, uncovered, in the oven until tender, allowing 25 minutes to the pound. Baste frequently with pan drippings.

When turkey is half cooked, season to taste with salt, pepper, and paprika.

### *Old Virginia Cornbread Stuffing*

| | |
|---|---|
| turkey giblets and neck | 3 tablespoons finely chopped onion |
| 2 cups boiling water | 3 tablespoons chopped parsley |
| 1 bay leaf | |
| celery stalks and leaves | 6 tablespoons melted butter |
| salt | ¼ teaspoon pepper |
| 5 to 6 cups dry corn-bread crumbs | 1½ cups chopped celery butter |

Cook giblets and neck in 2 cups boiling water with bay leaf, celery stalks and leaves, and salt to taste, until tender. Drain the stock, and reserve. The giblets can be cut up into small pieces and used in the gravy.

Add to the cornbread crumbs, and mix thoroughly, the onions, parsley, melted butter, pepper, and chopped celery. Moisten lightly with the giblet stock. Any excess stuffing can be baked separately in a buttered casserole, dotting the top of the mixture with dabs of butter.

### *Virginia Skillet Cornbread*

| | |
|---|---|
| 1 cup white corn meal | 3 teaspoons baking powder |
| 2 cups boiling water | |
| 1 cup milk | 2 tablespoons butter |
| 1 teaspoon salt | 4 eggs, well beaten |

Pour boiling water over 1 cup white corn meal. Cool. Beat in the milk, salt, baking powder, butter, and eggs.

Pour into 2-quart skillet. Bake in 400° oven for 25 to 30 minutes.

**The Wilson house drawing room**

Warren Gamaliel Harding

Florence Kling De Wolfe Harding

# Warren G. HARDING

PRESIDENT WARREN G. HARDING came into the White House riding on a wave of popularity. His campaign promise to the American people was a return to "normalcy," and Mrs. Harding assured the voters that she and her husband were just "plain folks" from Ohio. All this had a reassuring sound to a country weary from the war years. It almost seemed an answer to feelings of guilt left by the nation's rejection of the political idealism of President Wilson. The new President and his wife were the very picture of health and happiness on Inaugural Day, March 4, 1921. Outgoing President Wilson looked like a shattered wreck compared to the handsome, silver-haired man who was about to take office and who appeared every inch a President. It was a day without any parade and a minimum of ceremony in deference to the physical condition of President Wilson as well as to the personal wishes of President Harding, who was anxious to play down the military reminders of the war.

A magnificent inaugural ball had been planned by Edward Beale McLean, wealthy Wash-

ington newspaper publisher, who was the inaugural chairman. The plan had to be abandoned because members of the Senate objected to the amount of money such a display would cost. Ned McLean and his wife, Evelyn Walsh McLean, who were personal friends of the Hardings, then staged a private ball of their own in their magnificent Washington home in honor of the officials of the new administration. It was estimated that they spent about the same amount as the public ball might have cost. The ball was the first sign of the preferred position which would be enjoyed by the personal friends of the Hardings during the administration then beginning.

Mrs. Harding's first gesture as First Lady was to open the White House gates to the public— gates which had been closed and guarded during the war years and the illness of President Wilson. She did not object to the crowds of sightseers who once again swarmed over the grounds; indeed, she seemed to welcome them, one report saying that she even used to pull up the window shades so the people could look inside. "It's their White

House," she is quoted as saying. "Let them look in if they want to." It was also reported that sometimes she would go running down the steps to greet the tourists going through the State Rooms with a great big "Hello!" to their surprise and delight.

Yet for all her informality and neighborliness the new First Lady was strict in observing the formal etiquette which lent dignity to the official office of the Presidency of the United States. She insisted that the President be served first at table and that he enter an elevator or a vehicle first because she felt it was a mark of respect owed to her husband's office.

Opening the gates of the mansion to the public was just the beginning of one of the gayest social seasons since the Taft administration. The President and his wife loved to entertain, and in addition to the required state receptions and state dinners they surrounded themselves with their personal friends, so that they were rarely alone. They even attended private parties outside of the White House, where the President, rather pathetically, would ask his hostess and fellow guests to forget that he was President so that both he and they could relax.

During the Harding administration the White House was the scene of huge garden parties. Mrs. Calvin Coolidge, wife of the Vice President, found these most delightful occasions as guests strolled in the garden, enjoying the music of the Marine Band and the sparkling fountain splashing on the south lawn. One of the most publicized of these garden parties was the one given for the veterans of the war so recently ended.

Mrs. Harding quickly found that White House parties were really "big business." Engraved cards were often sent to as many as three thousand guests, and arrangements had to be made with the gardeners for the decorations and with the caterers for refreshments.

The formal receptions followed pretty much the routine of the present day. To the music of the Marine Band the President and his wife made their ceremonial entrance. After all the guests had arrived, they descended the main stairs followed by Cabinet members and their wives. The official party then proceeded to the Blue Room, where the President and the First Lady formally received the assembled guests.

The winter of 1921-1922 was especially gay, with the leaders of nine nations assembled in Washington for the Conference on the Limitation of Armaments. These distinguished guests were all entertained at the White House, and the New Year's Day reception of 1922 was particularly brilliant as the foreign delegations attended as honor guests. For that occasion pink rosebushes and ferns banked the staircase, autumn leaves and palms glowed in the East Room, and pink carnations and old-fashioned bouquets graced the Blue Room.

Another event of significance which took place during this administration was the dedication of the Tomb of the Unknown Soldier in Arlington Cemetery on November 11, 1921. President Harding arrived almost late for the ceremony because of a traffic jam, and Mrs. Coolidge wrote that he told her he had "used language which was not for publication." She also wrote of the ceremony that the "two minutes of silence and bowed heads was the most impressive single event of the whole day . . . Never have I experienced such a long two minutes."

This same social season saw one of the worst disasters of Washington history. The roof of the Knickerbocker Theater collapsed under the weight of twenty-nine inches of snow. Ninety-five persons died in the wreckage, and the city was shocked into mourning. In respect for the deceased the White House canceled all social engagements for a week.

By this time the Prohibition Amendment had been enacted, and wine and liquor were eliminated from all formal White House dinners and receptions. But the President kept a ready supply of hard liquor in the private quarters upstairs for the benefit of his personal guests. When the President and his cronies played poker at their all-night stag sessions, Mrs. Harding was permitted to stay with the party and keep the glasses filled. "The Duchess," as she was called by her husband and his friends, was considered just "one of the gang." Lillian Parks reports that President Harding had a standing order in the kitchen for knockwurst and sauerkraut when he had his card-playing friends in to visit. She also reports on the astonishment and disapproval of the White House staff when the President asked for toothpicks to be kept on the table. "That's being too much a man of the people," the butlers were said to comment disapprovingly, but of course the toothpicks were supplied without question. Even a mere suggestion is treated as a command when it

**Eggplant salad, West Coast style**     **Filet mignon**     **Almond cookies**

is expressed by a President or First Lady.

In September of 1922 the First Lady became seriously ill. When her one remaining kidney became infected it was only the skill of her physician, who was in residence at the White House, that saved her life. She was successful in resisting the infection, and she began to recover, but her illness resulted in six months of seclusion. It was at just that time that it first became apparent to the President and his wife that all was not well in his administration.

A presidential trip to the West and Alaska in the spring of 1923 was intended to calm public fears, roused by the suicides of two Harding associates who had been charged with corruption. The President hoped to recapture his popularity by exposing the country to his personal charm. It appeared, too, that he was eager to leave Washington and its worries far behind.

Even before the trip started the President was showing signs of strain, and Mrs. Harding told Colonel Starling of the Secret Service that the President's doctors should be assigned rooms near him throughout the trip. Her presentiment proved sound, and her precautions were wise. President Harding became ill on the trip, and died suddenly, on August 2, 1923, in San Francisco while his wife was reading to him. A blood clot had formed on the brain and death was instantaneous.

The train bearing the late President's body crossed the country through mourning crowds, taking five days to make the trip from California to Washington. On arrival in the capital, the body was laid in state in the East Room. The next day it was taken to the Capitol for official services. Burial was in Marion, Ohio.

Mrs. Harding returned to Washington on August 11 in the private railway car of her friend, Mrs. McLean. She stayed at the White House for one week, getting her possessions packed for the return to Ohio. Then after a brief stay at Mrs. McLean's home, she returned to Marion where she lived in complete seclusion until her death a year and a half later.

## Favorite Recipes

### Filet Mignon

| | |
|---|---|
| 4 pounds fillet | 1 cup beef or chicken |
| sherry wine | stock |
| juice of 2 lemons | 1½ teaspoons sherry |
| salt and pepper | wine |
| bacon strips | 2 tablespoons lemon |
| 3 tablespoons butter | juice |
| 1½ pounds fresh | can of asparagus |
| mushrooms | tips |
| 2 tablespoons flour | sweet potatoes, |
| 2 tablespoons butter | baked and stuffed |

Marinate the filet with sherry wine and lemon juice; then season with salt and pepper. Place several long slices of bacon across the top, and stick toothpicks into the strips to hold them in place. Broil quickly at high heat for 8 minutes; then broil slowly for 3 minutes.

Cover with 3 teaspoons of butter.

Wash the mushrooms thoroughly, and remove the stems and skin. Add flour, butter, and the stock, and cook until tender, adding 1½ teaspoons sherry wine and a little lemon juice. Serve the

Eggplant salad, West Coast style

mushrooms whole, around the filet. Serve also stuffed sweet potatoes and green asparagus tips, garnished with strips of red pepper.

### Eggplant Salad, West Coast Style

| | |
|---|---|
| 1 dozen eggplants, | 1 tablespoon vinegar |
| each about 4 to 5 | juice of 1 medium- |
| inches | sized lemon |
| butter | salt and pepper |
| salt | ½ teaspoon Worcester- |
| paprika | shire sauce |
| 3 tablespoons | 1 teaspoon chili sauce |
| mayonnaise | |

### Garnish

| | |
|---|---|
| lettuce leaves | 2 eggs, hard cooked |
| (washed and | and chopped fine |
| chilled until crisp) | |

Peel the eggplants. Cut them crosswise into slices about ½-inch thick. Season slices with salt and paprika. Place them on a baking sheet. Put a dab of butter on each, and bake in a hot oven (400°F) until tender, about 15 minutes, turning slices once, and putting a dab of butter on the other side, too.

Marinate the baked slices in a marinade made up of mayonnaise, vinegar, lemon juice, salt and pepper to taste, Worcestershire and chili sauces. Serve cold in bowl, garnished with lettuce. Sprinkle the finely chopped hard cooked eggs over the top.

### Almond Cookies

| | |
|---|---|
| 1 cup sifted flour | 2 eggs (used |
| ⅓ cup sugar | separately) |
| ½ cup grated blanched | pinch of salt |
| almonds | blanched almonds |
| ⅓ cup soft butter | for garnish |
| grated rind of 1 | |
| lemon | |

Sift flour and reserve. Mix sugar, grated almonds, butter, lemon rind, 1 whole egg and salt together thoroughly with wooden spoon. Gradually work in the sifted flour.

Form the dough into a ball, wrap in wax paper, and chill for at least 1 hour. Now roll out the dough ¼ inch thick on a lightly floured board, and with cookie cutters cut into cookies of the desired size and shape. Place on greased baking sheet, brush with the other egg, which has been beaten, decorate each with 3 blanched almonds.

Preheat oven to 350°F. Bake in this moderate oven for about 15 minutes or until light brown.

John Calvin Coolidge

Grace Anna Goodhue Coolidge

# Calvin
# COOLIDGE

THE COOLIDGE ADMINISTRATION provided both social and political life in Washington with a refreshing breath of fresh air, dry and crisp, like the air of the mountains of Mr. Coolidge's native state of Vermont. The death of President Harding brought to the White House his Vice President, Calvin Coolidge, a taciturn Yankee and his pretty, friendly, and vivacious wife, Grace Goodhue Coolidge.

Mr. Coolidge had been both Lieutenant Governor and Governor of the Commonwealth of Massachusetts, yet he and his wife were almost unknown in Washington when they arrived in that city for the inauguration of President Harding. Massachusetts had no governor's mansion so Grace Coolidge had not had an opportunity to shine socially. In Washington, however, she soon became the most popular member of President Harding's official family. With typical New England frugality Mr. Coolidge had decided that the salary of a Vice President was not enough to permit him and Mrs. Coolidge to rent or buy a house in Washington, so they lived in a suite of rooms they rented in the Willard Hotel. Once in residence in the city, Mrs. Coolidge's sweet face, attractive clothes, bright smile, and friendly wave of greeting brought her to the attention of the city. Her instinctive interest in people and her great sympathy for and liking of them made her a most sought-after guest for official affairs. The same could not be said for her husband. He accompanied her everywhere—a small, silent man with a poker face who became a legend because of his lack of social small talk and his complete indifference to the social conventions in Washington life.

The gay life of Washington in no wise altered Mr. Coolidge's chosen pattern of existence. His individuality, however caught the imagination of the public. They were amused by his idiosyncrasies, called him "Silent Cal," and delighted in his dry humor.

The drama of his inauguration in the middle of the night when he was sworn in as President of the United States by the light of a kerosene lamp in the parlor of his father's New England farmhouse immediately caught the fancy of the people. The oath of office was administered by his father who was a notary public, and thereupon the new President went off to sleep for the rest of the night.

On their return to Washington the Coolidges quietly moved into the White House and assumed the role of President and First Lady without any change in their basic living habits. It was a quiet family life in traditional Puritan style. Despite her warm friendliness Mrs. Coolidge never relaxed her standards of modesty or lost her realization that her most important roles were those of wife to Calvin Coolidge and mother to their two sons, and the country admired her for it.

The American people loved Grace Coolidge's warmth and tact and her general ease with people including all the varieties that are brought into contact with a First Lady. As early as the first reception for the judiciary, Chief Justice William H. Taft was reporting that Mrs. Coolidge "looked very pretty and was most gracious. Coolidge is Coolidge and he does the pump-handle work without much grace and without a great deal of enthusiasm." This was to be the pattern for all the social events which followed.

Things moved smoothly even though the White House staff was reported to be doing a lot of complaining about the idiosyncrasies of the new President. There were eighteen domestic servants on the White House staff at the time, plus the personal valet and maid for the Coolidges and extra help for special occasions. The servants had their specific duties and performed them under the supervision of the chief usher, Ike Hoover, and the housekeeper, Mrs. Elizabeth Jaffray, with the First Lady providing only suggestions as to the family's personal wishes. The President himself took an active personal interest in the management of the Executive Mansion. Frequently he would visit the kitchen to peer into what was cooking or inspect the pantry to see what was on the shelves. He personally initialed all the bills and he soon developed an active dislike of Mrs. Jaffray for what he considered her extravagance. As was customary, the menus for the day were sent up to the First Lady with her breakfast tray, and it was not long before a second copy was requested for the personal inspection of the President.

To the end of her career at the White House Mrs. Jaffray used to set out in the morning in her carriage and personally buy provisions for the day at the public market. Once the President complained about the extravagance of six hams being purchased to serve sixty people. Despite the explanation that Virginia hams were small and that one ham was expected to serve ten people, he was not convinced. "Six hams look like an awful lot to me," he reiterated. After he had become Ex-President Coolidge was at one time asked what had been his greatest disappointment in the White House. He replied without hesitation that it was his inability to find out what happened to the leftovers.

To please the President certain favorite recipes were added to the White House menu. Each morning for breakfast he had to have a special hot cereal made from unground wheat and rye. He had to have his corn muffins made according to a certain New England recipe. Baked beans were added to the menus. Since he complained about the White House pies Mrs. Coolidge sent for a recipe which she knew would please him. Even so, by 1926 Mrs. Jaffray had left the White House, probably with relief. She was replaced by Miss Ellen Riley whose efficiency and economy pleased the President.

Despite the emphasis on economy Mrs. Coolidge was able to maintain an atmosphere of gracious hospitality for which the administration was noted. That first winter she gave four state dinners and four musicales. These musicales were presented in the East Room with as many guests as the room would accommodate seated on small gilt chairs, and the President and Mrs. Coolidge sitting in the front row in armchairs. The public receptions were large, sometimes numbering over three thousand guests.

The President often entertained at stag breakfasts which began at much too early an hour to please most of the guests. Mrs. Coolidge gave small receptions for women's groups from all over the country and was usually photographed with them in front of the curving stairway of the South Portico.

Ishbel Ross, who has so delightfully chronicled the Coolidges and the Coolidge administration in her book, *Grace Coolidge and Her Era*, reports that of all the parties given by Mrs. Coolidge "her afternoon teas in the Red Room were the functions which conveyed the most warmth." These were parties for twenty or thirty guests held on Mondays and Fridays during the social season. Mrs. Coolidge would first greet her guests, then she would take her seat by the fire, and enjoy

Custard pie ▲

Corn muffins ▲

Pineapple salad ▶

talking to them individually and in intimate groups. The warmth created by the beauty of the room, the gleaming lights, and the glowing personality of the hostess made each of these parties a memorable occasion for those who attended.

Christmas was celebrated in true New England fashion during the administration. The tree was set up and decorated in the Blue Room. Highlight of the celebration was carol singing on the north portico by the choristers from the First Congregational Church, which the Coolidges attended in Washington. Mrs. Coolidge and their son John joined in the carols and the public was allowed to come on the grounds to hear the music.

On New Year's Day 1924, the Coolidges shook hands with over thirty-five hundred visitors who came to offer the President and his wife the wishes of the season. The annual New Year's Day reception had been held only once since the beginning of World War I and the colorful social event was enjoyed by both the guests and their hostess.

The summer following, the Coolidges' younger son, Calvin, died from a bloodstream infection which began with a blister on his heel from playing tennis in his tennis shoes without socks. The whole nation joined in the sympathy extended to the sorrowing family. It was a most untimely and unlikely death and much of the pleasure the Coolidges felt in being in the White House was lost at young Calvin's death, never to be regained. It was even feared for a while that President Coolidge would withdraw his name as the next Republican nominee for President.

Despite the fact that he did little campaigning, Coolidge was elected President in his own right that November by a heavy majority. The inauguration ceremony was planned without the usual pomp and ceremony in deference to the fact that the President and First Lady were still in mourning. The luncheon usually served to official guests was omitted and the President and Vice President and their wives ate a hasty sandwich before hurrying to review the Inaugural Parade. Fortunately for the Cabinet members and the leaders of Congress who came to watch the parade from the Presidential grandstand, Colonel William Starling, the military aide, on his own initiative provided plenty of food for those in attendance. There was a reception for Governors of the states in the afternoon, followed by a small family party in the evening, and by 9:45 p.m. the President was in bed.

Soon after the election, the President was advised that the roof of the White House was unsafe and that something had to be done about it. Appropriations for the work were finally granted so that the work could begin in 1927. In March the Coolidges moved to the home of Mrs. Eleanor Patterson on Dupont Circle, and made that their temporary White House. It was there that they entertained Charles Lindbergh, just back from his solo flight across the Atlantic. It was through the Coolidges that Lindbergh met the family of Dwight Morrow, who were personal friends of the Coolidges. He later married Anne Morrow, a daughter of the family.

The Coolidges had vacationed in a variety of summer homes in different parts of the country, and that year they went to Game Lodge in the Black Hills of South Dakota. It was from the Black Hills summer White House, on the anniversary of the day in August when he first assumed the Presidency, that President Coolidge issued his famous "I do not choose to run" statement. This much-discussed phrase stopped a boom to work for his reelection before it ever started.

The Coolidges returned in the fall to a much improved White House. More rooms had been added on the third floor, especially the storage space which was so urgently needed, linen closets, a sewing room, a pressing room, and a cedar room. The real innovation was a sun room, with glass on three sides, built above the South Portico. Mrs. Coolidge called it her "Sky Parlor" and equipped it with comfortable porch furniture and a radio. It was a welcome retreat where the First Family could enjoy the out-of-doors in privacy.

Mrs. Coolidge had hoped to furnish the White House with period furniture and, to comply with her wishes, Congress passed a resolution permitting the acceptance of such gifts. Few were offered, but Mrs. Coolidge had the satisfaction before she left the White House of furnishing the Green Room with good pieces. She also herself crocheted a spread for the Lincoln bed which she had placed in that historic room which served as her bedroom.

When the Coolidges left Washington, they drove from the inaugural ceremony at which Herbert Hoover assumed office to Union Station to take a train to Massachusetts. They left just as they had come, without any ostentation or ceremony. With a feeling of relief they returned to their simple home in Northhampton and settled down once again as private American citizens.

# *Favorite Recipes*

Pineapple salad

## *Pineapple Salad*

2 medium-sized     candied cherries
    pineapples     2 packages cream
1 pint fresh straw-     cheese
    berries

Peel one fresh pineapple, and cut it in half lengthwise, right through the stalk. Peel the other pineapple, and cut it into thin slices or chunks, arranging them overlapping, on the bed of the first pineapple. Decorate with cream cheese pressed through a pastry bag with the star tube, and garnish with fresh strawberries and candied cherries.

### *Sauce*

2 eggs, whole     rum or sherry, to
2 cups confectioners' sugar     taste (optional)
1 cup heavy cream

Stir eggs and sugar together until very light and frothy. Gradually stir in the cream. Add rum or sherry if desired. Serve in a sauce boat.

## *Corn Muffins*

1 egg, whole     1 teaspoon sugar
1½ cups buttermilk     3 teaspoons baking
½ teaspoon soda       powder
½ cup sifted flour     1 teaspoon salt
1½ cups corn meal     ¼ cup soft shortening

Beat the egg with a rotary beater, gradually beating in the buttermilk, the dry ingredients, and the soft shortening. Beat until smooth.

Generously butter 12 corn stick pans (which may be bought in any good kitchen or restaurant supply store). Heat the pans in the oven while mixing the batter. Pour the batter into the hot pans, filling them almost full.

Preheat the oven to 450°F, and bake in this hot oven for 10 to 15 minutes. Serve hot.

## *Custard Pie*

pastry for pie crust     ¾ teaspoon vanilla
3 eggs, whole     For garnish: 1 pint
½ cup sugar       cream whipped
⅓ teaspoon salt       with sugar
¼ teaspoon nutmeg       strawberry jelly
2 cups milk

Make pastry for a single-crust pie and fit it loosely into an 8-inch pie plate, building up a high edge to hold the filling.

Beat eggs with rotary beater, then beat in other ingredients. Pour into pastry-lined pie pan. Preheat oven to 450°F. Bake in this oven for 15 minutes, then reduce the heat to 350° and bake until a silver knife inserted into the side of the filling comes out clean, 30 to 35 minutes.

When cool, garnish the entire outer rim with sweetened whipped cream. Put through a pastry bag with star tube. Decorate center with alternating whipped cream and strawberry jelly.

**Coolidge's state china**

Herbert Clark Hoover

Lou Henry Hoover

# Herbert HOOVER

WHEN CALVIN COOLIDGE issued his "I do not choose to run" statement, the selection of Herbert Hoover as the Republican candidate was a foregone conclusion. He had behind him a long career of public service and the public image of him was that of a Quaker who gave up his own lucrative business interests to feed the hungry war refugees of Europe. Then, although himself a Republican, he felt an obligation to accept from Democratic President Wilson the task of World War I Food Administrator. Later, he served as Secretary of Commerce in the Cabinets of both President Harding and President Coolidge. He was a man who worked untiringly for the public good and his reputation was so well established that although he had been a member of the Cabinet, the scandals of the Harding administration never even hinted at his involvement.

Mr. Hoover had as his wife a woman who was as high-minded, public-spirited, and cosmopolitan as he. She, too, had graduated in geology from Stanford University in California and young Herbert Hoover came home from Australia be-

tween mining assignments to marry her and take her with him to China, his next post of duty. It was the first of many countries in which they were to live in the years that followed. Mrs. Hoover made comfortable homes for her family in places as distant as Mandalay, Tokyo, and Leningrad and as close as London, or Washington. She learned to live happily under any conditions and to make her family feel at home wherever they happened to be staying. In her travels Mrs. Hoover learned to speak Chinese fluently and she was able to speak four other modern languages with ease and read two more.

Wherever they went and in whatever home they lived guests were welcome. When Mr. Hoover was Secretary of Commerce it was said that they entertained around the clock in their pleasant home on S Street and that the family rarely sat down to a meal alone—even for breakfast.

It was in those years that Lou Henry Hoover accepted the office of National President of Girl Scouts of the United States of America and before she retired the membership of girls had jumped

186

from a hundred thousand to almost a million, and almost two million dollars had been raised for their treasury.

The new President was very wealthy and hospitality at the White House during his administration was lavish. Miss Ava Long was brought in to be housekeeper for the Mansion. It was said that "they set the best table that was ever set at the White House."

The first social season of the Hoover administration was marred by a disagreement over social precedence involving Dolly Gann, sister and official hostess of Vice President Curtis, and Alice Roosevelt Longworth, wife of the Speaker of the House. The problem was solved when the White House added to its official calendar a dinner in honor of the Vice President at which Mrs. Gann was accorded the prestige of being the ranking honor woman guest and, in addition, a separate reception for the Senate over which the Vice President presides. These two additional functions helped to lessen the crowds at other social functions already on the calendar.

Mrs. Hoover worked out new and more democratic procedures for her White House receptions. Cabinet members were encouraged to circulate with the guests throughout the state rooms instead of all of them congregating in the Blue Room. All invited guests were permitted to use the Blue Room which was no longer reserved for high-ranking guests.

Mrs. Hoover made two other social innovations which were long overdue. She gave her personal support to a move to abolish the custom that required Cabinet wives to return endless calls and to be "at home" to the public on set days every week. She had disliked these onerous duties when she herself was a "Cabinet wife" so she was happy to be able to spare her official family.

Her most daring innovation was to abolish the New Year's Day reception which had been a custom of the Chief Executive from George Washington's administration. Through the years the crowd had grown from the modest one hundred and thirty-five who came to the mansion to say "Happy New Year" to President John Adams and his wife, Abigail, in 1801, to a mob of thousands of persons in the Hoover administration. When Mrs. Hoover looked out of the window at 7 a.m. on the morning of January 1, 1930, the line of guests was already circling the White House grounds. Some had been there since midnight just to get in to shake the hands of the President and his wife on New Year's Day.

The following New Year's Day she announced in advance that the President and his wife would not be at home to receive on New Year's Day and, to emphasize their determination, they left the house for the day. Because of the difficulty of security supervision with the great masses of people who attended, the custom has never been revived.

Lillian Rogers Parks reports that after each social event, Mrs. Hoover would hold a conference with her secretaries and her housekeeper to discuss it and plan how the next affair might be improved.

The Hoovers stayed close to the White House for most of the time. The President ruled out a "Summer White House" because of the work he faced. Instead, the First Family would retreat on weekends to a camp in the Virginia mountains about one hundred miles from the capital. Here the President and his guests could go fishing, hike in the mountains, and enjoy the out-of-doors. Mrs. Hoover was equally delighted with the opportunity these visits to the mountains gave her to enjoy her love of camping. She designed much of the substantial and ingenious furniture used in the summer lodge. Her interest in scouting continued all through her days as First Lady, and national leaders of the Girl Scouts were privileged to hold their conferences at the White House and at the summer lodge.

Mrs. Hoover also continued Mrs. Coolidge's interest in the redecoration and restoration of the White House. She studied old paintings and engravings to learn what the interior of the mansion had been like through the years. At her instigation a research was made through the scanty and ill-

**State china used during Hoover's administration**

**Maryland caramel tomatoes**     **Apricot mousse**     **Presidential corn beef hash**     **Asparagus soufflé**

kept records and a history of White House furnishings was compiled for future identification. In the course of her investigation four of the chairs used at the signing of the Emancipation Proclamation were discovered in a storeroom and brought down to the President's study. Also at this time there were located the bust of President Van Buren and the desk used by President Lincoln at the Soldier's Home.

Perhaps Mrs. Hoover's most unusual accomplishment was to have some of the furniture which was purchased for the White House by President James Monroe copied for the White House of her day, including the desk on which James Monroe signed his message to Congress which contained the Monroe Doctrine.

The Hoover administration was noted for

the charming musicales which were held in the East Room. Mrs. Hoover had fifty armchairs made with handsome carved gilt frames to replace the small gilt chairs on which guests usually perched in crowded discomfort.

The family's private quarters had a friendly lived-in look with comfortable chairs and white bookcases full of the family's books. The rooms were filled with interesting and beautiful objects collected during the Hoovers' travels all over the world. In the upstairs hall Mrs. Hoover put down her South American rugs, she had sofas and chairs arranged in conversational groupings, and in due time she even had a moving picture machine installed in the area.

Lillian Parks' account of the administration reveals that the Hoovers rarely had a meal together without additional guests. The President liked to have stag breakfasts and lunches to discuss politics, and in good weather these might be held under the magnolia tree on the lawn where special dining furniture was set up. There were usually fourteen or eighteen guests to dinner. Before each morning the President had a workout with his medicine ball to keep him in trim physical condition. After breakfast, Mrs. Hoover usually walked with the President over to the Executive Offices. This was often the only time of the whole day that they were able to be together alone.

The first Christmas at the White House the Hoovers' grandchildren were living at the mansion while their father, Herbert Hoover, Jr., recovered from tuberculosis in a hospital in North Carolina. Mrs. Hoover had a Christmas dinner for fifty that year, using a large horseshoe table with a smaller table in the center for the children. The tables were decorated with little bells for the ladies and brass candlesticks for the men. After dinner the President and his four-year old granddaughter led a march of all the guests through the darkened parlors with the ladies ringing the bells and the gentlemen carrying the lighted candles. The march ended on the second floor where, as a great surprise, a motion picture was shown to the guests.

The Christmas tree that year was decorated with real cookies.

It was during the Hoover administration that the country was caught in the throes of the Great Depression. Throughout, the President continued to fight a losing battle against the poverty which threatened to engulf the country. Despite the fact that the crash was brought on by conditions completely beyond the control of President Hoover, he received personal blame from the country, and was defeated in his bid for reelection in 1932.

Mrs. Hoover was especially distressed that the American people had rejected her husband. She waited until the very last minute to get packed for her move from the White House. On the morning of the inauguration the White House staff was still working frantically to get the Hoovers moved out before the Roosevelts began to move in.

Ex-President Herbert Hoover lived long enough for the people of the United States to begin to appreciate and understand his long years of public service. When he died in New York in 1964 he was universally acclaimed for his humanitarian work and honored with the title of "Elder Statesman" by both political parties of his country.

## *Favorite Recipes*

### *Presidential Corn Beef Hash*

| | |
|---|---|
| 2 cups minced corn beef (can be bought canned and broken up with a fork) | 2 tablespoons chopped onion |
| | 2 tablespoons chopped green pepper |
| 4 medium-sized boiled potatoes | salt and pepper, to taste |
| ½ cup hot water | 9 bacon strips |
| 3 tablespoons butter | new potatoes |
| 2 tablespoons chopped parsley | parsley, chopped, for garnish |

Mix all ingredients (except bacon strips and new potatoes) thoroughly, add salt and pepper to taste. Shape into loaf form with bacon strips over the top.

Bake in greased pan in moderate oven (350°) 35 to 40 minutes. Meanwhile, boil the new potatoes, use them as garnish sprinkled with chopped parsley.

Pour tomato sauce over the corn beef hash.

### *Tomato Sauce*

| | |
|---|---|
| 2 tablespoons butter | salt and pepper, to taste |
| 3 chopped tomatoes | |
| 2 teaspoons tomato paste | 1 teaspoon flour |
| | 1 teaspoon sugar |
| 1 clove garlic | 1½ cups water |
| 1 finely chopped onion | |

Heat butter in pan; add onion, garlic, chopped tomatoes, salt, pepper, and sugar. Cook briskly for 10 minutes, stirring occasionally. Add tomato paste, flour, and water. Stir until it comes to a boil. Simmer ½ hour, and strain around the corn beef hash on a hot platter.

**Presidential corn beef hash**

**Maryland caramel tomatoes**

## Maryland Caramel Tomatoes

| | |
|---|---|
| 8 ripe tomatoes of equal size | white pepper |
| | 1½ cups brown sugar |
| 1 tablespoon salt | ¼ cup butter |

Skin the tomatoes. Carefully cut off the tops. Place them in a buttered baking dish suitable to serve them in. Sprinkle with salt, pepper, and brown sugar. Dab each of them with butter.

Preheat oven to 400°F, and bake for ½ hour. Then remove to the top of the stove, and over a low flame, reduce the juice until it is a thick syrup. Then once again bake them in a hot oven (400°F) for ½ hour. Serve hot.

## Asparagus Soufflé

| | |
|---|---|
| ⅓ cup butter | salt, pepper, to taste |
| 3 tablespoons flour | 4 stiffly beaten egg |
| 1 cup milk, or 1 cup half milk and half cream | whites |
| | 1½ cups asparagus tips, for the soufflé |
| 4 egg yolks, well beaten | 2 cups asparagus tips, for garnish |

**Asparagus soufflé**

Melt butter, blend in flour, stirring constantly. When mixture is smooth, gradually add milk or cream mixture, stirring until the mixture thickens. Remove from fire and allow to cool before stirring in the beaten yolks, season with salt and pepper.

Last, fold in the stiffly beaten egg whites.

Arrange 1½ cups of asparagus tips in a generously buttered soufflé dish, and pour the mixture over the asparagus tips. Bake in a moderate (350°) oven for 35 to 40 minutes.

Take the asparagus tips to be used for garnish out of the can, and just before serving, trim the soufflé with the asparagus tips.

## Apricot Mousse

| | |
|---|---|
| 1 cup apricot pulp | 3 drops of almond extract |
| 3 unbeaten egg whites | |
| 4 tablespoons sugar | grated rind of 1 orange |
| 2 tablespoons lemon juice | |

Put all ingredients in a 2-quart bowl, or in an electric mixer. Beat until the mixture will hold up in fluffy peaks.

Chill thoroughly in refrigerator—several hours, if possible. Serve decorated with meringue made as follows:

## Meringue

| | |
|---|---|
| 4 egg whites, beaten stiff | granulated sugar few grains salt |
| 1 cup sifted, | cinnamon or nutmeg |

Beat egg whites until stiff. Gradually sift in 1 cup granulated sugar with few grains of salt, beating continuously. Put into pastry bag, shape into mushroom-shaped meringue on top of custard. Dust lightly with cinnamon or nutmeg.

**Apricot mousse**

*Franklin Delano Roosevelt*

*Anna Eleanor Roosevelt*

# Franklin D. ROOSEVELT

B EFORE THE FRANKLIN ROOSEVELTS moved into
the White House in 1933, Eleanor Roosevelt
paid the usual visit to the Mansion to decide
how the various rooms of the house were to be
used and to plan with the Chief Usher, Ike
Hoover, the arrangements for Inauguration Day.

Mrs. Roosevelt comments that because of the
economic state of the country Inauguration Day
of 1933 was not a "light-hearted occasion" for
either the out-going or the in-coming President, or
for the American people as a whole. The sudden
death of Senator Thomas J. Walsh just before
the inauguration had caused the cancellation of
most of the ceremonies planned for the day at
the White House, but there was buffet lunch for
the family and a few friends and a reception in
the afternoon. The President did not attend the
Inaugural Ball that evening but Mrs. Roosevelt
went with the younger members of the family.

The White House at once became a busy
center of activity to meet the financial crisis which
faced the country. To the First Lady was left the
task of establishing her own secretarial staff and

of organizing the household. There were many
things about living in the White House that
proved a nuisance to a family as energetic, gregarious, and independent as were all these members
of the Roosevelt family. Mrs. Roosevelt mentions,
for example, that the children, who had been in
the habit of raiding the icebox when they were
hungry, were upset to find that at the White
House the icebox was kept locked at night.

Mrs. Roosevelt's personal staff consisted of
Miss Malvina Thompson who acted as her personal secretary and Mrs. Edith Helm who was her
social secretary. Mrs. Helm had lived in Washington for many years and had been Mrs. Wilson's
secretary at the White House so she was fully
familiar with all the intricacies of social protocol
in which Mrs. Roosevelt herself took little interest.

The Roosevelts soon established a pattern of
living which continued through most of their
twelve years at the Mansion. Mrs. Roosevelt usually
got up at 8 o'clock and had breakfast in the West
Hall. The President had his breakfast tray in bed.
Mrs. Roosevelt then had a conference with the

housekeeper, the chief usher, and the social secretary, in turn. The housekeeper was Mrs. Henry Nesbitt who made out the menus, bought the food, and gave the orders to the household staff for the day.

Mrs. Roosevelt reports that while her husband was not too difficult to please about food, he went out for meals so seldom that meals at the White House prepared by the same cook became monotonous to him. For that reason, after 1941, the cook from Hyde Park was installed in a small kitchen on the third floor and she cooked two meals a day for the President to give him some variety.

Although Mrs. Roosevelt felt that her husband was not especially interested in food, there were those who considered him somewhat of a connoisseur, in contrast to Mrs. Roosevelt who had little interest in food. The amusing story is told that Franklin Roosevelt once wrote his wife a note claiming that he "bit two foreign powers this morning" because he had been served nothing but sweetbreads since his recent complaint that he had been given chicken to eat six times in a single week.

According to Lillian Rogers Parks, the President would occasionally go on an economy binge to make up for the food he felt was being wasted in the White House. She says he liked to carve the meats himself so that he could be sure that all of it served its proper purpose. Mrs. Roosevelt would have another turkey carved at the same time to speed the service as it took the President considerable time to carve in his effort to be sure that none of the bird was wasted.

Mrs. Roosevelt found that year by year, as his health deteriorated, the President took less and less interest in his food. She said she would always be grateful for the many gifts of game, cheese, fish, turkeys, and the like because he seemed to eat these with more enjoyment.

Mrs. Nesbitt, however, says that ". . . Mrs. Roosevelt was interested, not only in American cookery, but its history, and she wanted to get American women interested and proud of our traditions. She invited Mrs. Sheila Hibbens, the authority on American menus, to come to the White House and spend several days conferring with me."

Mrs. Roosevelt in her book, *This I Remember,* refers to the interesting fact that, while formal dinners and state parties are paid for out of government funds, meals for any family or personal friends were paid for by the President personally on a pro rata share of the cost.

Each day the First Lady and the chief usher would confer on the people expected to arrive at the Mansion that day. It was his responsibility to make arrangements to have these people admitted to the White House grounds.

The conference with Mrs. Helm consisted in plans for public functions, scheduled receptions, and other ceremonial duties. Mrs. Roosevelt admitted that though at first when she was First Lady she did not take a personal interest in these social affairs, she had come to realize that they had meaning and value. She learned that to many people the White House has great significance and that the First Lady is a symbol. The White House, too, is a symbol—a symbol of the government, and any personal association with the White House, no matter how fleeting, is an inspiration and challenge to those who come to visit the historic mansion.

Through Mrs. Roosevelt's eyes we are privileged to glimpse one of the traditional ceremonies which accompanies White House entertaining. She tells of the color guard that comes up to the President's study just before the President goes down to a big reception, to take from the room the flag of the United States and the President's own standard. They march into the room, face the flags and salute; the flags are taken out of their standards on either side of the fireplace; the guard marches down the stairs with them and places them at the door of the room where the President receives. This ceremony so pleased the Roosevelts that they often invited the people who dined with them before these receptions to come upstairs and watch it with them.

Bess Furman, then White House correspondent for the Associated Press, who came to know Mrs. Roosevelt intimately, says in her book, *White House Profile,* that all the details of ordinary life were so well organized at the White House that despite all Mrs. Roosevelt's varied activities she usually found time to have tea with her husband and share with him the events of her own busy day. And she would make keen reports of what she had observed on her trips about the country to put in the basket by his bedside for his personal information.

Mrs. Roosevelt set a new record for a First Lady's activities outside of the White House, especially in the field of social welfare, but she was always at the White House when it was important

Martha Washington crab soup ▲

Kedgeree ▲

Boiled salmon with egg sauce ▲

Pecan pie ▶

for her to be there. Each social season from late fall to early spring, she stood beside her husband in the Blue Room shaking hands with the long lines attending the official receptions. For the official state dinners she sat across from him in the State Dining Room.

Mrs. Nesbitt in her book, *White House Diary*, describes the State Dining Room as it looked on these occasions: ". . . The table was set for formal, with service plates, napkins, and wineglasses, and all the silver, save for dessert, water glasses, the little colonial salt cellars of cut glass in the diamond design—and never any pepper shakers. For official affairs the nut dishes were decorative gold china; there were little silver ones for the family meals. The centerpiece for the family was always a bowl of flowers. A big silver ship in full sail was for teas. But for the formal affairs we used

**Library of the Roosevelt home, Hyde Park**

the Monroe gold service. There was always a lot of to-do about this service, which was purchased by President Monroe in France, but to tell the truth it was brass, and plated, with the gold worn off. There was a big centerpiece and candelabra. . . . There were probably twelve bowls of flowers on the horseshoe table. We had flowers from our own hothouses until the war . . . Yellow roses were Mrs. Roosevelt's favorites, and we always tried to get them for her. . . ."

To these long-established domestic entertain-

ments were added the formal dinners and luncheons in honor of the ever-increasing numbers of heads of foreign governments, the highlight of these visits being the one made by King George and Queen Elizabeth of England in June 1939. The President and Mrs. Roosevelt decided it would be a good idea to give the British royal visitors American food to eat and to entertain them with American folk arts so that they could learn something about this country while they were here. This was the reason for the famous menu at the picnic at Hyde Park at which "hot dogs" were served. At the same time the guests were offered smoked turkey and other delicious native food from different parts of the country, such as hams cured in different ways, baked beans, and strawberry shortcake for dessert. At the picnic the entertainment consisted of songs and stories by two American Indians.

The approach of World War II became evident in White House social life with the "frigid nods and stiff bows" at a "brilliant but tension-shot" reception held to open the 1939 social season. There were eight hundred guests in attendance including representatives from fifty-three nations, many of whom were on less than cordial terms with each other.

A sign of the times is in a note that on Christmas Day 1941 President Roosevelt entertained the Right Honorable Winston Churchill at dinner, in addition to various British wartime military leaders. Churchill arrived two weeks after Pearl Harbor and stayed for twenty-four days. It was at this meeting that the overall strategy of the Allies in World War II was planned.

With the outbreak of the war all of the usual events of the social season were canceled and the security precautions at the White House were immediately tightened. It was just as well. All of the President's time was taken with his wartime duties and Mrs. Roosevelt's time was devoted to the welfare of the men and women fighting the war.

The White House went on an austerity plan. Mrs. Roosevelt explained to the White House staff that part of her "defense effort" was to cut down on the servants' food. She advised them that they would have "one egg instead of two, one slice of bacon, toast, and coffee for breakfast. And the large midday meal will consist of whatever is available on the market." From Lillian Rogers Parks we learn that to save the housekeeper the nuisance of ration stamps, all the servants were supposed to bring their own sugar.

The White House was closed to tourists, but Mrs. Roosevelt received wounded veterans from hospitals in the area, showing them the house, and ending with tea in the State Dining Room. She also made many trips during this period, visiting Great Britain to inspect their war activities in person. At her husband's suggestion she toured the bases in the Pacific in 1943, and in 1944 she visited the lonely Caribbean and South American bases. On each trip she carried messages from her husband to the fighting men and returned to give him first-hand information from the war theater. In war as in peace Mrs. Roosevelt used her eyes and her legs to assist her husband with his immeasurable responsibilities.

For the President's fourth inauguration in 1945 he insisted that all thirteen of his grandchildren should come to the White House for the occasion. Perhaps he had a premonition even then that he was failing in health. After his trip to Yalta he became less and less willing to see people for any length of time. For the first time in his Presidency he addressed the Congress from a seated position. He decided that he needed a rest at Warm Springs, the polio treatment center in Georgia which he used to visit periodically. It was on this trip on April 12, 1945, that he suffered the cerebral hemorrhage which resulted in his death a few hours later.

The body was brought back to Washington by train and at every station and crossroad the people waited to watch it pass so that they could pay their last tribute to their wartime President. After funeral services in the East Room Franklin Delano Roosevelt was buried, as he had wished to be, in the rose garden at his home in Hyde Park, New York.

It was an end of an era when the Roosevelts left the White House. They had lived in the mansion for over twelve years, a longer period of time than any other Presidential family.

**Roosevelt's state china**

# Favorite Recipes

## Boiled Salmon with Egg Sauce

| | |
|---|---|
| 3 to 4 pound fresh salmon | hard cooked eggs, parsley, for garnish |
| 1 cup vinegar | |
| 2 tablespoons salt | |

To cook the salmon; place the fish in boiling water to cover (salmon may be wrapped in muslin first), add the vinegar and the salt. Cook salmon until tender (about 30 to 40 minutes), not allowing the water to boil too vigorously lest the tender fish flesh break.

## Egg Sauce

| | |
|---|---|
| 2 cups milk or cream | ½ teaspoon salt |
| 2 tablespoons butter | ⅛ teaspoon pepper |
| 2 tablespoons flour | 2 hard cooked eggs |

To make the sauce: melt the butter and stir in the flour and seasoning. Remove from fire. Gradually pour in the milk or cream which has first been warmed, stirring constantly, and cook over low heat until thickened. Now mash the hard cooked eggs with a fork, and add to sauce. Pour sauce over fish. Decorate with hard cooked eggs cut in half and garnished with parsley.

## Martha Washington Crab Soup

| | |
|---|---|
| 1½ pounds crab meat in chunks | 1 tablespoon Worcestershire sauce |
| 1 quart milk or light cream | ½ cup sherry |
| 2 tablespoons butter | salt, pepper, to taste |
| 2 hard cooked eggs | paprika for garnish |
| 1 tablespoon flour grated lemon peel | |

**Pecan pie**

In the top of a double boiler, blend the butter and flour. Add the eggs which have been mashed, then the lemon peel; then, gradually add the milk. Stir until it thickens. Add the crab meat; let it simmer for 5 minutes. Then add the seasoning. Just before serving, stir in the sherry and let it get hot again (do not allow to boil). Sprinkle with paprika.

### Kedgeree

| | |
|---|---|
| 1 cup boiled flaked whitefish | ½ teaspoon salt pepper |
| 1 cup boiled rice | ¼ cup cream |
| 2 or 3 hard-boiled eggs, minced | 1 teaspoon grated onions (optional) |
| 2 tablespoons butter | parsley, for garnish |

Mix fish and rice. Moisten with cream or fish stock, and sauté lightly in melted butter (it must

be fluffy). Add salt, pepper and minced hard boiled eggs. Heat in top of double boiler. Serve hot, trimmed with parsley sprigs.

### Pecan Pie Crust

| | |
|---|---|
| 1½ cups flour | 1 teaspoon baking |
| ½ cup shortening | powder |
| ½ teaspoon salt | ¼ cup ice water |

Measure 1½ cups flour; resift with salt and baking powder. Divide shortening into two equal parts. Cut half into the flour mixture until it looks like corn meal. Cut the remaining half of the shortening coarsely until the size of large green peas. Over the mixture sprinkle 3 tablespoons of ice water. Blend lightly.

If the dough holds together, add no more liquid; if not, add additional water. Line pie pan with pie crust.

### Pecan Pie Filling

| | |
|---|---|
| 3 or 4 eggs | ¼ teaspoon salt |
| 1 cup brown sugar | whole pecans for |
| ⅓ cup butter | garnish |
| 1 cup light corn syrup | 1 pint cream, |
| 1 teaspoon vanilla | whipped, for |
| 1 cup chopped pecans | garnish |

Cream ⅓ cup butter with 1 cup brown sugar. Beat in one egg at a time, stir in 1 cup light corn syrup, 1 cup coarsely chopped pecans, 1 teaspoon vanilla, and ¼ teaspoon salt.

Fill the pie shell with the mixture. Preheat the oven to 375°F, and bake the pie in this moderate oven for about 35 to 40 minutes.

When the pie is set and has cooled off, decorate the top with pecan halves. Garnish with whipped cream around the entire edge. The whipped cream may be further trimmed with tiny leaves baked from left-over small pieces of pie crust dough.

*Harry S. Truman*

*Elizabeth Virginia Wallace Truman*

# Harry S. TRUMAN

THE SUDDEN death of President Franklin D. Roosevelt brought into the White House the new President, Harry S. Truman, his wife Bess, and their attractive college-age daughter, Margaret. The country soon found that the Truman family was vastly different from the Roosevelt family, which had dominated the Washington scene for twelve years. The President himself was a hard-working, outspoken, impulsive midwestern politician, in contrast to the suave sophisticate, Franklin Delano Roosevelt. Mrs. Truman's great interest in life was her husband and family—not for her were the extensive public activities Mrs. Roosevelt had brought into the position of First Lady. Both the new President and his wife centered all their love and attention on their only child Margaret, and she wholeheartedly returned their affection. Their close-knit family relationship prompted the White House staff to nickname them the "Three Musketeers."

Bess Wallace Truman came to the position of First Lady with a strong distaste for the job and for the continuous publicity that surrounded it. She was a reserved woman, basically rather shy, and her feelings about being in the public eye were probably influenced by her small-town, Southern background, which, according to Victorian tradition, permitted a lady's name to appear in the papers only three times in her whole life, once to announce her birth, a second time to announce her marriage, and a third time to announce her death.

Despite her intense dislike of having to be in the spotlight, Bess Truman went about the duties of being First Lady with a dignity which soon commanded the public's respect. She made a sincere effort to keep out of the newspapers. The press conferences that had been begun by Eleanor Roosevelt were discontinued by Mrs. Truman, who took no public part in the political events of the administration.

Instead she met numbers of groups visiting the White House, she christened ships and planes, opened bazaars, attended luncheons, and was hostess at receptions and state dinners at the White House. She shook so many hands that she had to

receive physical therapy to rest her own hand after a public reception. Her manner on these occasions was so reserved and formal that to many she seemed to be cold and forbidding.

But to her family she was a delightful, warm-hearted person with a sense of humor which made her companionship a pleasure. Her years of working by the side of her husband while he was Senator had made her quite familiar with major governmental problems, and she delighted to discuss them in serious, considered conversation with her husband and close friends. President Truman said, in tribute to her personal assistance in the White House, "She is my chief adviser always."

Bess Truman was an excellent housekeeper. Lillian Rogers Parks says, "For the first time, to my knowledge, a First Lady took the bookkeeping part of the White House in hand and ran it herself. She took a look at the food bill and cut out breakfast for the daily sleep-out employees.

Every day she sat at a desk and tried to run the White House as though it were a business, which indeed it is." She was always aware of the menus and saw to it that good food carefully prepared was served. She believed in having refreshments prepared in the White House for all social functions, even for guests who came to tea by the thousands.

The Trumans liked to eat together as a family whenever it was possible, including breakfast. After breakfast they separated, each to do his respective job—the President to his Executive offices, Mrs. Truman to attend to the duties of First Lady, and Margaret to attend college. After Margaret's graduation in 1946 she spent a great deal of her time in New York, where she first studied for the concert stage, and after that sang on concert tours around the country. Her parents gave her career their sincere personal support. Despite an occasional bad review of her voice, the critics expressed appreciation of her friendly personality and her fresh, glowing appearance. Much to Margaret's embarrassment, the President's paternal pride in her career would not permit him to accept gracefully any criticism at all of her sing-

ing ability, and he once caused a great many headlines when he publicly severely reprimanded a critic for a bad review of Margaret's Washington concert.

Mrs. Truman's closest personal friends were a group of girls with whom she had grown up in Independence, Missouri. These ladies played bridge together for a good many years, and Mrs. Truman looked forward to resuming her place in the club every summer when she returned to Independence. She invited her bridge club to come to Washington to visit in the White House as a group. Lillian Parks lets us know that Mrs. Truman made more fuss when her old bridge club from Independence arrived than when she entertained the social leaders of Washington. The group swam in the President's pool, were carried about town on elegant sightseeing tours, and were guests of honor at a luncheon party given them by the First Lady.

**Truman's state service**

When President Truman decided to run for the Presidency in the election of 1948 he was considered to have very little chance of winning the election. Political forecasters and political polls were unanimous in prophesying that the Republican candidate, Thomas E. Dewey, would be the next President. Harry Truman very shrewdly took his campaign to the people themselves in whistle-stop tours that covered most of the country. Standing on the rear platform of his train, he would make his appeal for votes and then introduce to the crowds his wife as "The Boss"

and his attractive daughter as "The Boss's boss." What he said to his audiences pleased them. They liked the casual friendliness of the little family, and enjoyed the gallant fight they, as a unit, were making to win the election. To the surprise of the nation, the country woke, the morning after the election, to find that Truman had won one of the most exciting elections in our times and would remain as President for the next four years. The President was elated; for the First Lady it meant another four years of the life she disliked.

By this time White House entertaining entailed longer invitation lists than at any previous administration as Washington assumed the position of a world capital after the end of World War II. Now it became necessary to have two state dinners to entertain the ranking members of the Diplomatic Corps, as space was no longer sufficient to accommodate them all at one time. Reception lines in the East Room were four rows deep inside the room and sometimes extended down the stairs and into the lower corridor, moving slowly into single file to pass the official receiving line in the Blue Room. In planning these affairs Mrs. Truman had the invaluable assistance of Mrs. Edith Helm, who as social secretary had helped both Mrs. Woodrow Wilson and Mrs. Franklin Roosevelt.

The crowds grew bigger and bigger with resulting wear and tear on the historic house in which the President and his family lived. Shortly before Mr. Truman's reelection, in the midst of a formal reception for officials of the Federal Government the President had heard the chandelier above his head in the Blue Room making an unnatural tinkling.

An investigation of the cause of the vibration showed that the floor of the second-floor oval study was in precarious condition. Thorough studies revealed that structurally the White House was about to collapse. The only part of the original mansion found to be sound was the old outer wall. The President and his family thereupon moved into the Blair House, the nation's guest house across Pennsylvania Avenue from the White House. The complete job of making the White House safe for Presidents of coming generations took three years and cost over five million dollars. At one point of the work the four walls stood as an empty shell with only a roof over the top, while bulldozers worked on the ground level to excavate a two-story basement.

The move to the Blair-Lee House necessitated a curtailment of social activities during the President's second term. The obligatory state dinners were held at one of Washington's hotels. The First Lady continued to report her activities to the press through Mrs. Helm. Her public appearances continued without letup, but she never made a public speech on any of these occasions.

At one point the President was subjected to an assassination attempt by Puerto Rican nationalists who tried to storm Blair House. He escaped injury only through the vigilance of his Secret Service guards, one of whom was killed in the ensuing struggle. The affair gave the First Lady a further reason to dislike the job.

Perhaps the social highlight of the second Truman administration was the visit, in 1951, of Princess Elizabeth, heir to the throne of Great Britain, and her husband, Prince Philip. It was not an easy task to accommodate royalty in the temporary White House, but it was done successfully by Mrs. Truman and her staff, including even a state dinner in their honor.

Living at Blair-Lee House continued to complicate the social affairs of the second term. A whole series of parties had to be given where one used to suffice. Mrs. Truman met the problem with her usual gracious consideration for her guests. She even inaugurated a series of parties for wounded war veterans who were still being treated in the military hospitals in the Washington area.

The move back into the newly renovated mansion took place in 1952, only a few months before the Trumans were to retire to their home in Independence. Now the house was not only structurally safe, but it had also been made more convenient in the family living quarters and in certain sections of the public area. Perhaps the most striking changes were the relocation of the main stairway and the painting of the dark, somber paneling of the State Dining Room a soft celadon green. The public was given a personal tour of the renovation by the President himself, who did a nationwide television tour to show the people what had been done to their Executive Mansion.

It was with great relief that Mrs. Truman learned that her husband would not run again. After the inauguration of President Eisenhower, the Trumans returned to their family home in Independence where the President presided over his presidential papers until his death, and where Mrs. Truman, in her nineties, continues to enjoy the quiet companionship of family and friends, out of the spotlight, but in the affection of the nation.

**Mural in the lobby of the Harry S. Truman Library, Independence, Missouri**

# *Favorite Recipes*

## *Tuna and Noodle Casserole*

| | |
|---|---|
| 1 7-ounce can of tuna fish, drained | boiling salted water |
| ½ package of egg noodles | dabs of butter |
| | hard cooked egg and parsley for garnish |

### *White Cheese Sauce*

| | |
|---|---|
| 2 tablespoons butter | ⅛ teaspoon pepper |
| 1½ cup milk | ¼ pound sharp ched- |
| ¼ teaspoon salt | dar cheese, grated |
| 1½ tablespoons flour | |

Boil the noodles in boiling salted water for 12 minutes, or until tender. Drain well.

Drain the tuna, and flake with a fork.

Make a cheese sauce as follows: Over low heat, melt the butter, and blend in the flour, stirring constantly until smooth. Gradually add the milk, continuing to stir constantly until the boiling point is reached. Now add the grated cheddar cheese, and the seasonings, to taste. Reduce heat and cook for 3 minutes longer, stirring all the while.

Into a well-buttered casserole put alternate layers of the boiled noodles and the tuna, covering it all with the cheese sauce. Dab generously with dabs of butter.

Meat loaf

Bake in a moderate oven (375°F) for 30 minutes.

Garnish with sliced hard boiled egg or eggs, and sprigs of parsley.

## *Meat Loaf*

| | |
|---|---|
| 2 pounds ground beef | For basting: ½ cup |
| 2 egg yolks | melted butter |
| 4 tablespoons parsley, minced fine | 1 cup boiling water |
| 2 tablespoons butter | tomato sauce (can be bought in cans) |
| ¼ cup bread crumbs | |
| 2 tablespoons chili sauce | 1 can frozen peas butter |
| 2 teaspoons salt | For garnish: parsley and |
| ½ teaspoon pepper | radish roses |
| 1 teaspoon onion juice | |

Combine the ingredients and shape in a loaf. Butter a loaf pan, and place meat in pan.

Bake in a moderate oven (350°) for 1 hour, basting it frequently with butter and water combination.

Remove from loaf pan onto heated platter. Garnish with sprigs of parsley and radish roses.

Serve with tomato sauce and green peas, to which a dab of butter is added when served.

## *Ozark Pudding*

| | |
|---|---|
| 1 egg, whole | peeled, cored, and diced |
| ¾ cup of sugar | |
| 1 tablespoon flour | 1 teaspoon vanilla extract |
| 1 teaspoon baking powder | |
| ⅛ teaspoon salt | ½ cup chopped wal- nuts, to garnish |
| 5 small raw apples, | 1 pint heavy cream |

Beat egg and sugar a long time until very smooth and light. Mix flour, baking powder, salt, and stir in the sugar and egg mixture. Add apples, nuts, and vanilla. Bake in a buttered covered dish in a 350°F oven for 35 minutes, or until apples are nearly tender.

Now, remove cover to brown top. Serve pudding cold with whipped cream. Garnish with chopped walnuts.

*Dwight David Eisenhower*

*Mamie Geneva Doud Eisenhower*

# Dwight D. EISENHOWER

MAMIE DOUD EISENHOWER, the wife of President-elect Eisenhower, visited the White House in December before the inauguration for a tour of the mansion. She had been in the state rooms many times, so she did not spend very much time on the main floor. It was the second floor in which she could exercise her love of homemaking, and she immediately envisioned ways to make it comfortable and pleasant for the General and herself, with accommodations for her son and his family when they could be persuaded to join them for a visit.

Mamie was happy with her new home. It was in the best of condition after the renovation during the Truman administration. The spacious rooms gave a sense of serenity and dignity which she found very pleasing. She could move in with the assurance that she and her husband would be together and settled in a home they could call their own for the next four years, with a good possibility of extending the time to eight years.

The Eisenhowers spent the night before the inauguration at the Statler Hotel in Washington.

The day started with the attendance of the President, his wife, and members of their combined families at church—a group of thirty-four people in all. Washington was crowded with gay and friendly throngs who had come to see their soldier-hero take the oath of office. The inaugural ceremony was given an additional touch with a sincere prayer offered by the new President before he delivered his Inaugural Address. Together the new President and his popular wife sat in the reviewing stand for five hours to watch the elaborate parade staged in their honor. Before they finally entered their new home, night had come.

The Eisenhowers very quickly settled into a routine, and the new First Lady soon took the reigns of management of the White House into her own hands. She was well trained for the executive side of the job, as she had run many houses staffed by government employees in her long career as the wife of an army officer. The Eisenhowers had brought with them their own personal servants, and Mrs. Eisenhower also had brought as her personal social secretary a capable young woman, Mary Jane McCaffree, who had been assigned to help her since the beginning of the Presidential campaign.

Mrs. Eisenhower soon found that her job was actually to run two households: the Eisenhowers' own, which included their family and personal guests, and the state establishment for official entertaining.

The new First Lady and the housekeeper, Mrs. Mabel C. Walker, discussed all the details and Mrs. Eisenhower herself ordered all the meals, whether it was a supper for two to be served to the President and herself in front of the TV set or a state dinner for one hundred guests or more.

For state dinners Mamie and Ike sat side by side in big carved chairs at an E-shaped table in the State Dining Room. The menus of these dinners were as elaborate as the protocol. One typical state dinner consisted of the following: first course: bluepoint oysters on the half-shell; second course: clear soup with marrow balls, sherry; third course: lobster thermidor, sauterne; fourth course: roast Long Island duckling, apple sauce, currant jelly, gravy, wild rice, string beans, buttered beets, breadsticks, burgundy; fifth course: orange and roquefort cheese, salad, wafers, champagne; sixth course: Spanish cream, caramel sauce, assorted cupcakes; finally: nuts, candies, and a demitasse.

On the lucky evenings when they were alone, the Eisenhowers liked to have their supper on trays, and perhaps invite some of their old friends in for a movie or a bridge game. Sometimes they ended up singing, while Mamie played the electric organ which had been Mrs. Doud's birthday present to her daughter.

The First Lady quickly adapted to life in the White House. As General Eisenhower explained to an interviewing newspaper woman, "From 1945 on Mrs. Ike and I had been moving in official circles all the time. In Europe there wasn't a royal

**Eisenhower's state china**

family or head of government that she hadn't met and been entertained by. So that part of going into the White House limelight wasn't difficult."

Mrs. Eisenhower's greatest difficulty was the poor health that had plagued her from childhood. A rheumatic heart limited her social activities and made it essential for her to conserve her strength. Most of every morning she spent in bed. Sometimes she had to rest all day before a state dinner or a reception. Then she was able to preside at the function as if she enjoyed every minute of it. Each guest was greeted with warmth and given a personal welcome which made the occasion a memorable one.

Despite her uncertain health, Mrs. Eisenhower was available for receptions, teas, dedication ceremonies, public tours—all part of the task of being First Lady. She received many delegations for her husband in addition to her own receptions for women's organizations. Her sincere interest in people made it possible for her to meet numbers of people graciously. It was estimated that during her first social season in the White House, from January to June of 1953, she shook some 16,000 hands at official functions.

Social events at the White House were drastically curtailed after the President suffered a heart attack and had a major operation in the summer of 1956. To save the energy of both the President and the First Lady all the large receptions usually scheduled for the social season were eliminated, and state dinners became luncheons whenever possible.

Lillian Rogers Parks, from her vantage point as seamstress at the White House, tells us that Mrs. Eisenhower had a French chef for a while at the White House. François Rysavy was one of the most famous cooks and pastrymen in this country. He stayed at the White House three years, then decided that he preferred to return to Hollywood to cook for the movie stars.

The President's favorite relaxation was a game of golf, and he played at every opportunity. He even had a putting green on the White House lawn so that he could practice whenever he had a few free minutes. The Eisenhowers spent so many vacations at the golf course in Augusta, Georgia, that one of the cottages was permanently reserved for their personal use.

Mrs. Eisenhower enjoyed relaxing over a game of canasta, and she played every free afternoon with a group of personal friends from her

**Tomato pudding**                **Quail hash**                **Frosted mint delight**

days as an "Army wife." This group of privileged ladies was jokingly dubbed by the press, "Mamie's Bridge Cabinet." She often spent Saturday afternoons watching a movie at the White House with her grandchildren. One of the modernizations of the Truman renovation had been the installation of a small private theater complete with a projection booth, off the corridor to the East Wing of the White House.

The Eisenhowers were devoted to their grandchildren and every visit they made to the White House was enjoyed by all generations. Special quarters had been set up for the children on the third floor, with a small kitchen available for ease in fixing their food and providing snacks.

During their years in the White House the Eisenhowers were at last to enjoy the pleasures of owning a home of their own. In 1950 before the General was elected President, they had purchased a farm in Gettysburg. Early in the administration they remodeled the 200-year old farmhouse which was on the farm, and it became their weekend retreat. Now Mamie had an opportunity to plan, decorate, and be hostess in her own home. Their

private home was jealously guarded from the press and from the public, so that they could enjoy complete privacy during their weekends at the farm.

During the Eisenhower administration, the presidential retreat in the Catoctin Mountains was renovated and named Camp David after their much-loved oldest grandson. This provided the family with another charming spot for weekends near the Washington area.

One of Mrs. Eisenhower's personal projects as First Lady was the White House china collection. She had the collection identified and catalogued, and its display was renovated with her interest and approval. She also was able to secure some pieces of presidential china for the White House collection to represent the missing administrations. The collection had been in storage during the war years and the Truman renovation, and a great deal of work was necessary to sort, identify, and arrange it for exhibition.

The Eisenhower administration is to be recorded as a social success. For the first time in many years the people had a First Lady who felt that her first duty was to serve as the official hostess of the nation. Mamie Eisenhower accepted the work involved and actually enjoyed the position, an enjoyment that was reflected by her guests. They could sense the preparations that had been made to welcome visitors, and they could appreciate the careful management which made possible the carefree manner of their host and hostess.

At the end of the administration the Eisen-

howers moved into their Gettysburg home for a well-earned retirement. After her husband's death in 1969, Mrs. Eisenhower spent more time with her family and friends, and especially enjoyed the companionship of her grandchildren. She died in 1979 after a short illness, and is buried beside her husband in Abilene, Kansas.

# Favorite Recipes

**Quail hash**

## Quail Hash

| quail | flour |
|-------|-------|
| good chicken stock | sprigs of parsley for |
| salt and pepper | garnish |

Put into saucepan whatever number of quail seems sufficient for the company. Cover well with stock. Cook slowly 15 to 20 minutes, according to their size, or until the meat can be removed from the bones easily. Reserve the stock.

Strip the meat. Dice it, and season to taste.

With small amount of additional stock, make gravy with flour (browned or not as you choose), and pour over diced quail.

Cover and simmer 10 minutes longer. Serve in casserole, garnished with sprigs of parsley.

**Frosted mint delight**

### Tomato Pudding

| 1 10-ounce can tomato | ¼ teaspoon salt |
|-------|-------|
| puree | 1 cup white bread cut |
| ¼ cup boiling water | into 1-inch cubes |
| 6 tablespoons light | ¼ cup melted butter |
| brown sugar | |

Add sugar and salt to tomato puree and water, and boil 5 minutes. Place bread cubes in casserole.

Pour melted butter over them. Add the tomato mixture. Bake covered for 30 minutes at 375°F. Serve with the quail, or other meats.

### Frosted Mint Delight

| 2 1-pound cans | 1 pint of whipping |
|-------|-------|
| crushed pineapple, | cream, reserve |
| reserve 1 cup juice | some for garnish |
| ¾ cup pure mint- | 2 teaspoons confec- |
| flavored apple jelly | tioners' sugar |
| 1 envelope unflavored | |
| gelatin | |

Have crushed pineapple and whipped cream chilled. Melt the mint-flavored jelly and mix the crushed pineapple into it. Dissolve the gelatin in 1 cup of the juice from the pineapple. Mix the gelatin mixture and fold it into the pineapple mixture. Now whip the cream, sweeten it with the sugar, and fold it into the combined mixture. Put into the freezer until firm, but do not freeze solid.

This recipe serves 10 or 12. Serve in parfait glasses, topped with whipped cream. Accompany each plate with a few cookies.

Jacqueline Lee Bouvier Kennedy

John Fitzgerald Kennedy

# John F.
# KENNEDY

WITH THE ELECTION OF President John F. Kennedy in 1960, the White House became home for a couple who were possibly the most sophisticated President and First Lady in the long history of the mansion.

Jacqueline Bouvier Kennedy's background was an old-established family with roots on the East Coast. From the day of her birth she was surrounded by money and the gracious things which money can buy. She grew up with a knowledge and love of the arts which she put to use as soon as she became First Lady.

She had always been interested in houses and their decoration and had a personal love of fine antique furniture and related decorative accessories. On her first visit to the White House in December when Mamie Eisenhower personally gave her a tour of her new home, Mrs. Kennedy was distressed at the department-store reproductions with which the house was then furnished. She flew off to a Christmas vacation at Palm Beach loaded down with books on the White House and its history.

She decided then that her contribution to the position of First Lady would be an effort to return to the White House objects of historical associations with the house and its previous occupants and to supplement these historical pieces with other things of similar design and period which had artistic merit. As soon as her decision was made she began to study every phase of White House history; she was intrigued with pictures of interiors of the White House made during past administrations and read avidly descriptions of purchases, and all available source material on White House furnishings throughout the years. Within three days after the inauguration she was explaining her plans to the head of the Fine Arts Commission to secure his approval and assistance for her plan. She appointed a committee of antiquarians to assist her with the project. As soon as her plans began to be publicized they met with an eager public response. She began to receive gifts of furniture for the mansion and funds to assist in purchasing other pieces. At her instigation Congress passed a bill giving permanent museum status to the White House with the provision that any of the furnishings received for the White House that was not actually to be used there would be placed in the custody of the Smithsonian Institution.

In the meantime she and the White House curator she had appointed were searching the White House storerooms, attic, and cellar, for all treasures from previous administrations which were stored away, perhaps unrecognized. It was a tremendous and successful venture. Mrs. Kennedy was personally active in every step that was taken. She was never too busy to give even the smallest detail consideration. She formed the White House Historical Association to publish *The White House—An Historic Guide* to provide a continuing source of income for the purchase of art objects and furniture for future administrations. She gave her own report to the country of the work that was being done on an hour-long television program over a nationwide network. Her interest and enthusiasm in what was being accomplished and her personal charm made the program a great success and brought the mansion even more into the public consciousness.

The White House Restoration project took up most of the First Lady's time during the first two years of the administration. By then all the major public rooms had been redecorated to her exacting standards and most of the family rooms on the second floor had been completed. She felt that they "could then relax and look for great paintings and objects of historic interest and work on filling the library with appropriate books."

While Mrs. Kennedy placed her family duties and the care of her two small children, Caroline and John Jr., above all other obligations, she also devoted a great deal of her time and energy to the interests of young people and the encouragement of the arts. In 1961, she inaugurated a series of Musical Programs for Youth by Youth. Young people from the Washington area were invited to these afternoon concerts, to hear performances by their contemporaries attending music schools and camps throughout the country.

Leading artists of the theater, the opera, concert, stage, and the dance were invited to perform at the White House and the few public appearances made by Mrs. Kennedy as First Lady were usually at cultural affairs—a play, a symphony, or a ballet. Indeed, she performed none of the usual political tasks such as christening ships, cutting ribbons, attending luncheons, or official open-

ings, on the plea that her young children prevented her participation in this kind of activity.

Jacqueline Kennedy likes to be original and the social life of the White House during the Kennedy administration soon reflected her distinctive personality. She was especially anxious to reduce the formality of official receptions. Her first White House reception was held on a Sunday afternoon. There was no formal receiving line but she and the President mingled with the guests much as they would have done in their own home. Fires were burning cheerfully in the fireplaces, attractive flowers decorated the rooms, and ashtrays were placed about invitingly to indicate that smoking was permissible. This formula worked so well that for parties at which the guest list was less than ninety persons the receiving line was a thing of the past. Instead of dinners and receptions limited to diplomats, Congressmen, judges, etc., the First Lady began to mix guests so that people would have a chance to see someone other than persons in the same official circle as themselves.

Jacqueline Kennedy also initiated original ways to serve official meals at the White House. One luncheon for women of the press was served at small tables in the East Room. When the State Dining Room would not accommodate all the dinner guests, the Blue Room was used for the extra tables. When the President of Pakistan visited this country the dinner in his honor was staged on the terrace at Mount Vernon with the guests conveyed to the party aboard the Presidential yacht. It was an innovation which was most successful, with the pleasant summer evening, the river view from Mt. Vernon, and the historical significance of the setting all contributing to the pleasure of the guests.

Eating at the White House became a "fine art" along with Mrs. Kennedy's other innovations. The kitchen was presided over by a French chef, René Verdon, who had formerly been employed at the Hotel Carlyle in New York City. Before M. Verdon arrived at the White House Mrs. Kennedy had made headlines when she, or someone acting for her, tried unsuccessfully to hire a famous French chef away from the French Embassy in London.

Mrs. Kennedy cut the dinner menu to four courses to save time and to bring the meal more in line with the eating habits of our own day. It resulted in state dinners which were elegant and unhurried with ample time for official toasts.

**Poulet à l'estragon     Beef stroganoff     Soufflé froid au chocolat**

Among the elegant dinners given was one for Nobel Prize winners of the Western Hemisphere. After-dinner entertainment for the guests was the actor, Frederic March, reading unpublished excerpts from the writings of the late Ernest Hemingway, Nobel Prize author. Other entertainments for dinner guests included a concert by the world-famous cellist, Pablo Casals, ballet by leading American ballet companies, Shakespeare performed on stage in the East Room by the Stratford, Connecticut company, a concert featuring American jazz, and many famous artists of the concert stage.

It was at President Kennedy's suggestion that new ambassadors presented their credentials to him at the glittering annual diplomatic reception.

The skirl and wail of the bagpipes shook the East Room chandeliers at the State Dinner given for Prime Minister Sean Lemass of Ireland. The Black Watch Band and Pipes played again that fall for a group of Washington children, including Caroline and little John, who were thrilled by the marching men in kilts and the wailing of the pipes.

In addition to the state dinners and official receptions, the Kennedys entertained about twice as many visiting heads of state as previous administrations. The President himself was often host at stag lunches entertaining members of Congress and he even entertained at an occasional stag dinner. The White House correspondent for Hearst newspapers, Marianne Means, in her book *The Woman in the White House* says that "The President goes over proposed guest lists for functions and usually stops to taste the wine on his way from the office to dress for a dinner." But, she emphasizes, "All other aspects of the White House social life are Mrs. Kennedy's responsibility."

Mrs. Kennedy made a special contribution to her husband's administration on her trips abroad, which was an aspect of her official position that appealed to her personally. She traveled with the President on state visits to Canada, France, Austria, England, Colombia, Venezuela, and Mexico. She was greeted with such enthusiasm and acclaim that the President once introduced himself in Paris as "the man who accompanied Jacqueline Kennedy to Paris." The people responded to her great personal dignity, her genuine interest in the countries she visited, and to her beautiful clothes. Another great asset was her linguistic ability in French and Spanish, which was often put to use on these trips. In Paris she conversed in French with President de Gaulle with as much poise as she showed when she spoke Spanish to a group of farmers in a field in Venezuela. Her delight in foreign travel resulted in an invitation to a semi-official tour of India and Pakistan in 1962, and she made several trips to Italy and to Greece for

her own personal pleasure.

It has been said that as First Lady Mrs. Kennedy's private social life and the official social life were two separate things. Her personal friends were not people of political importance to the administration. These friends the Kennedys often entertained at private parties in the White House. The parties had a somewhat international flavor with guests from the fashionable resorts of Europe and America flying in to be present. It was then that the formal rooms resounded with the talk and laughter of congenial young people, and the best dance bands of the country furnished the music for dancing the "Twist" and the "Cha-Cha."

There was such vitality about both the social and political activities of the Kennedy administration that it made the assassination of the President in Dallas in November 1963 even harder to grasp. The last and perhaps the most memorable of all the official formalities to take place in the White House during the Kennedy administration were the official ceremonies honoring the late President as his body lay in state in the East Room and leaders came from all over the world to pay their final tribute of respect.

## *Favorite Recipes*

### *Beef Stroganoff*

| | |
|---|---|
| 2 pounds sirloin of beef | 2 tablespoons tomato juice or paste |
| 2½ tablespoons flour | 3 tablespoons grated onion |
| 2 tablespoons butter | |
| 2 cups beef stock | 3 tablespoons butter for sauteing |
| ½ cup sour cream | |

Cut beef into thin strips, sprinkle freely with salt and pepper, let stand covered for 2 hours in cool place.

Make a roux by blending flour with butter over gentle heat until mixture bubbles and is smooth. Gradually stir in beef stock and cook until mixture begins to thicken. Boil for 2 minutes, then add sour cream alternately with tomato juice or paste, stirring constantly. Simmer very gently, without boiling, 1 minute.

Brown beef in 3 tablespoons butter with grated onion. When the meat is browned, pour the meat, onion, and butter into the sauce, taste for seasoning, and simmer gently, or cook in double boiler over hot water for 20 minutes.

### *Poulet à l'Estragon*

| | |
|---|---|
| 1 chicken, 3 pounds | ½ cup dry white wine |
| 2 tablespoons flour | ½ cup stock |
| salt | 1 bay leaf |
| pepper | 1 pinch thyme |
| clarified butter for sauteing | 2 stems parsley |
| | 1 small bunch fresh tarragon |
| 2 or 3 shallots | |

Cut chicken into 8 or 10 pieces or leave whole. Combine flour, salt, and pepper. Coat chicken with flour mixture. Brown on all sides in hot clarified butter. Cut shallots very fine and spread over chicken. Simmer for a few minutes. Add wine, stock, and the bouquet of herbs using the stem only of tarragon, saving leaves. Cover and simmer cut up chicken 25 minutes or until tender. Simmer the whole chicken 45 minutes, turning frequently. When chicken is tender, remove and keep hot.

### *Sauce*

An attractive platter for an elegant table

setting can be achieved, as shown in the picture on page 209, by making a glaze or sauce as follows:

| | |
|---|---|
| 1 cup light cream | ¼ cup grated Parmesan cheese |

To the pan juices, add cream and cheese, and any flour not used in coating chicken. Simmer gently until sauce thickens. Strain sauce over chicken. Garnish with tarragon leaves, whole or chopped.

## Boula-Boula (American Soup)

| | |
|---|---|
| 2 cups freshly shelled green peas | 1 cup sherry |
| 2 cups canned green turtle soup | ½ cup whipping cream |
| | 1 tablespoon sweet butter |

Cook the green peas in boiling salted water; strain through a fine sieve or an electric blender to get a puree; reheat it. Add 1 tablespoon sweet butter, salt and white pepper to taste. Blend with the green turtle soup and 1 cup of sherry; heat to just under the boiling point. Put the soup into serving cups; cover each cup with a spoonful of unsweetened whipped cream, then put the cups under the broiler to brown the topping. Serve at once.

## Soufflé Froid au Chocolat

| | |
|---|---|
| 1 envelope unflavored gelatin, softened in | ¾ cup granulated sugar |
| 3 tablespoons cold water | 1 teaspoon vanilla extract |
| 2 squares unsweetened chocolate | ¼ teaspoon salt |
| 1 cup milk | 2 cups heavy cream |
| ½ cup confectioners' sugar | |

Melt chocolate squares over hot (but not boiling) water. Heat milk just enough so that a film shows on the surface, then stir it into the melted chocolate slowly. Add confectioners' sugar. Beat with whip until smooth. Cook, stirring constantly, over low direct heat until mixture simmers. Remove from the heat and mix into it the softened gelatin, the granulated sugar, vanilla extract, and salt. Put it in the refrigerator and chill until slightly thick. Then beat mixture until it is light and airy-looking.

In a separate bowl beat heavy cream until it holds a shape. Then combine the two mixtures.

# DINNER

Quenelles of Sole au Gratin

Roast Sirloin Vert Pré
Peas à la Française
Potatoes Gaufrettes

Galantine of Chicken
Green Salad

Bombe Glacée Fellab
Petits-fours sec

The White House
Tuesday, May 22, 1962

**Menu for a private dinner given by the Kennedys**

Pour soufflé into a 2-quart soufflé dish or serving bowl. Chill 2 or 3 hours in refrigerator until ready to serve.

Double recipe to make a tall soufflé as shown in the picture on page 209. Tie a collar of double wax paper that has been lightly oiled around soufflé dish. Chill soufflé at least 3 hours. Soufflé can be garnished with shaved semi-sweet chocolate, whipped cream and chocolate cornucopias, and chocolate discs.

To make chocolate decorations, spread melted semi-sweet chocolate on wax paper on cookie sheet. Chill until firm. Cut out discs with round cookie cutters. To make cornucopias, cut 2-inch squares of chocolate, and allow chocolate to stand at room temperature to soften slightly, then roll into cornucopia shapes. Chill and fill with whipped cream.

Claudia Alta Taylor Johnson

Lyndon Baines Johnson

# Lyndon B. JOHNSON

THE CRUEL tragedy of President Kennedy's assassination brought to the White House as President and First Lady, Lyndon B. Johnson and his wife, Lady Bird, presenting them with the difficult task of following one of the most glamorous social administrations in the history of the Executive Mansion.

The new First Lady was probably one of the best qualified persons ever to step into such a difficult role.

She had behind her twenty-seven years of experience on the national political scene and a personal knowledge of, and great interest in, the operation of government in Washington. She was the partner, confidante, and helpmate of a man who rose from a job as congressional secretary to Member of Congress, serving twelve years in the Senate—six of these as Majority Leader—and then three years as Vice President.

Lady Bird had been her husband's loyal supporter in each step of his career.

While Lyndon B. Johnson was Vice President of the United States, Lady Bird got her first taste

of being one of America's ambassadors of good will. She traveled to thirty-three foreign countries in less than three years. She said she served as "an extra pair of eyes and ears for Lyndon." She was especially interested in what she calls the "women-doers" of each nation and asked especially to have a chance to meet these women, to learn the problems of each country and how they were trying to solve them.

When Mrs. Johnson became First Lady, the women-doers of our own country became her honored guests at White House luncheons. She brought together women of every profession so that each could benefit by the knowledge acquired by the others, and at the same time national attention could be focused on the fine work they were doing. Lady Bird felt that these women should be admired and imitated as living examples of her personal belief that, "In this space age, passive citizenship is a luxury no one can afford. . . . Our challenge is to seize the burdens of our generation and make them lighter for those who follow us."

The first state dinner at the White House

after Mrs. Johnson became First Lady was for President and Mrs. Antonio Segni of Italy. The guest list of one hundred forty people mixed diplomats and politicians into a congenial group. Invitations called for "Black-tie" instead of the "White-tie" dress usually required for state dinners. President Johnson disliked having to dress in "White tie and tails," and most social functions at the White House during his administration were "Black tie," meaning dinner jackets for the men and long dresses for the ladies. After welcoming the Segnis on the North Portico, the Johnsons took them to their private quarters on the second floor, where an exchange of gifts was made as a symbol of the friendship between the United States and Italy. The President and the First Lady and their guests of honor then assembled at the head of the staircase for the ceremonial entrance down the red-carpeted steps, with the Marine Band playing "Hail to the Chief." Downstairs the Johnsons stood just inside the door of the East Room to receive their other guests.

The dinner menu had been selected by Mrs. Johnson from suggestions made by the then White House chef, René Verdon. It featured crabmeat Maryland, fillet of beef, waffled potatoes, string beans amandine, endive and watercress salad, cheese and coffee mousse. The table was festive with spring flowers and was set with the green and gold china of the Truman and Eisenhower administrations and the blue and gold of the administration of President Franklin D. Roosevelt.

Coffee was served after dinner in the Red and Green Rooms, after which the guests assembled in the East Room, which had been set up as a concert hall. Here they were entertained with a program of Italian opera sung by American performers and the New Christy Minstrels singing American folk music in a genuine hootenanny.

The Johnsons' first state dinner was a prototype of many to follow, as world leaders one after another made visits to Washington to reassure themselves and their countrymen about the new President of the United States.

When Lady Bird Johnson became First Lady, she inherited much beautiful White House china, but no single service large enough for the huge state dinners that have become common in recent administrations. To remedy the situation, Mrs. Johnson brought together Tiffany and Company, the designer Van Day Truex, and the painter André Piette to create a dinner service reflecting the floral beauty of America, a theme closely linked with her own passion for the beautification of our country. Forty different wildflowers appear on various pieces of the new service, and the dessert

**State dining room of the White House with a refreshment table set for an afternoon reception, April 1964**

plates feature the state flowers of the fifty states and the District of Columbia. The service plate is bordered with wildflowers and centered with a spread-winged American eagle and shield taken from the state service of President James Monroe.

The china, the gift of an anonymous donor, serves 216 persons. It was introduced on May 9, 1968, at a ceremony and reception for more than 150 guests, including craftsmen involved in the design and execution of the china, which was produced by Castleton China of New Castle, Pennsylvania.

The first state dinner at which the new White House china was used was on May 27, 1968, honoring Prime Minister and Mrs. John Grey Gorton of Australia. The menu on that occasion included Chesapeake crabmeat, roast duckling Bigarade, wild rice, green beans amandine, Bibb lettuce, assorted cheeses, and chocolate mint Bettina.

The Johnsons took with them to the White House Zephyr Wright, who had been cook for the family since Mr. Johnson was a member of the House of Representatives. She prepared all of the First Family's private meals in the new kitchen on the second floor of the White House. Zephyr Wright cooked primarily to please the President, and she kept a close eye on the low-calorie diet that was a feature of family dining.

René Verdon, the French chef who joined the White House staff during the Kennedy administration, had charge of food for special occasions, assisted by four additional cooks with special skills. Henry Haller became the White House chef after René Verdon's departure. Mrs. Mary Kaltman served as the Housekeeper, with over all responsibility for all aspects of food preparation.

President and Mrs. Johnson's years in the White House were marked by two single personal events, the weddings of their daughters Luci Baines and Lynda Bird. Luci, the younger, was married on August 6, 1966, to Patrick Nugent. The marriage was solemnized at the National Shrine of the Immaculate Conception and was followed by a White House reception. The bride, wearing a gown of white rosepoint Alençon lace, greeted guests with her husband and parents in the Blue Room. Three buffet tables offered a traditional wedding feast of hot and cold dishes. The hot entrees included casserole of sliced chicken, Steamship Rounds of beef, shrimp and lump crabmeat in New Orleans Creole sauce, and sweetbreads and mushrooms in cream; among the cold dishes were supreme of turkey, supreme of duckling à l'Orange, glazed fresh salmon, and glazed lobster en Bellevue.

**Chef Henry Haller came to the White House during the Johnson administration**

**White House wedding of Lynda Bird Johnson and Charles Spittal Robb**

The seven-layer wedding cake was a bridal favorite —a summer fruit cake.

When Lynda Bird Johnson was married to Charles S. Robb, on December 9, 1967, it was the first wedding of a President's daughter in the White House since Eleanor Randolph, Woodrow Wilson's daughter, married William McAdoo in 1914. The ceremony was private and was held in the East Room. The bride chose a traditional gown of Abraham's pearl white silk satin faced in faille, with a front panel outlined in embroidered flowers and seed pearls and matching embroidery outlining the high collar and the cuffs of the long sleeves.

As with Luci's, Lynda Bird's reception featured an elaborate buffet. The hot dishes included lobster barquettes, crabmeat bouchées, stuffed mushrooms, miniature shishkebab, and Quiche Lorraine. Among cold platters were sliced smoked salmon with capers, molds of chicken liver paté, iced shrimp, and assorted cheeses and finger sandwiches. The bride chose an old-fashioned pound cake for the five-layer wedding cake. It was iced in white fondant and decorated with sugar scrolls, loops, and braids, pulled-sugar roses, and white lovebirds, and topped with a sugar basket of real white roses.

Both the girls entertained their bridesmaids at the White House and gave them mementoes of the occasion. Although the menus varied at the two affairs, both concluded with a dessert of Flowerpot Sundaes. These are made by taking small ceramic pots of white, green, and pink, and placing a piece of yellow cake split and spread with apricot jam in the bottom of each. Fill with vanilla ice cream to within $\frac{1}{2}$ inch of the rim, and place on top another piece of cake spread with apricot jam. Cut a paper straw three inches long and insert it in the pot so that two inches extend above the pot. Swirl very stiff meringue on top of the pot until it reaches the top of the straw. At the last minute, place in a very hot oven and brown the meringue. Just before serving, insert an appropriate flower in the straw to complete the Flowerpot Sundaes. Lynda Bird, having a winter wedding, used a sprig of holly and a red rose. Luci, a summer bride, chose a sweetheart rose.

It has been remarked that while the Kennedys kept their private life and personal friends separate from their official life, the Johnsons' friends were the people they worked with—members of Congress, Cabinet officials, White House staff members, and members of the press. Lady Bird and her husband brought the people to the White House. For Mrs. Johnson it was no problem if a group of three thousand people wanted to come to the White House. A tour was arranged, refreshments were ordered, and often the Johnsons themselves made an appearance. The American people were their life. That is why it seemed a perfectly natural thing for the President to open the gates of the White House and invite the public to join him on a walk through the garden. More and more people of every walk of life were invited to the White House, and the Johnson administration was judged by many to be the friendliest administration in the history of the mansion. The Johnsons retired to their ranch in Austin, Texas where Mrs. Johnson lives today. President Johnson died in 1973.

**Johnson's state china**

# *Favorite Recipes*

### *Pedernales River Chili*

| | |
|---|---|
| 4 pounds chili meat | 6 teaspoons chili |
| 8 tablespoons bacon | powder |
| drippings | 1½ cups canned whole |
| 1 large onion, chopped | tomatoes |
| 2 cloves garlic | 2 No. 2½ cans kidney |
| 1 teaspoon ground | beans |
| oregano | 2-6 generous dashes |
| 1 teaspoon comino | liquid hot pepper |
| seed | sauce |
| 1 string dried | salt, to taste |
| mushrooms | 2 cups hot water |

Chili meat is coarsely ground round steak or well-trimmed chuck meat. If specially ground, ask the butcher to use ¾-inch plate for coarse grind.

Place ground meat, onions, garlic, and bacon drippings in large, heavy frying pan or Dutch oven. Cook until light-colored. Add oregano, comino seed, chili powder, tomatoes, kidney beans, hot pepper sauce, dried mushrooms, salt, and hot water. Bring to a boil, lower heat and simmer about 1 hour. Skim off fat during cooking. Serve hot in individual casseroles.

### *Summer Fruit Cake*

| | |
|---|---|
| ½ cup white seedless | 5 egg whites |
| raisins | ¾ cup chopped |
| apple juice | candied |
| 1¾ cups sifted cake flour | pineapple |
| 1 teaspoon double- | 1 cup chopped |
| acting baking | pecans |
| powder | ½ teaspoon almond |
| ¼ teaspoon salt | extract |
| ½ cup butter | ½ teaspoon vanilla |
| ¾ cup sugar | extract |

Cover raisins with apple juice and let soak in refrigerator 2 or 3 days or until raisins are plump. Drain.

Start heating oven to 300°F. Grease an 8x4x3-inch pan; line with heavy paper and grease again.

Sift flour once and measure. Add baking powder and salt, sift together three times.

Cream butter thoroughly; gradually add sugar; cream until light and fluffy. Add egg whites, one at a time, beating thoroughly after each. Add fruits, nuts, and flavoring and mix well.

Add flour, a little at a time, beating after each addition until smooth. Pour into greased pan.

Bake in 300°F. oven 1 hour and 15 minutes or until done. Makes 8 to 10 servings.

Spinach parmesan

### *Spinach Parmesan*

| | |
|---|---|
| 3 pounds fresh | minced fine |
| spinach, carefully | 6 tablespoons heavy |
| washed, or frozen | cream |
| spinach, thawed | 5 tablespoons butter, |
| 6 tablespoons Parme- | melted |
| san cheese, grated | ½ cup cracker crumbs |
| 6 tablespoons onion, | |

Cook spinach until tender, drain thoroughly, and chop coarsely. Add cheese, onion, cream, and 4 tablespoons of the butter. Pour into shallow well-greased ring form. Sprinkle with crumbs mixed with remaining butter. Bake for 10 to 15 minutes.

Garnish spinach ring with puff paste pastry.

### *Lobster Barquettes*

| | |
|---|---|
| 1 tablespoon finely | 1 cup whipped cream |
| chopped shallots | 1 cup Hollandaise |
| 2 tablespoons butter | sauce |
| 2 cups diced cooked | pinch cayenne |
| lobster meat | pepper |
| ½ cup cream sauce | grated Parmesan |
| 24 barquettes (oval | cheese |
| pastry shells) | |

Sauté shallot in butter until clear. Add lobster meat and cream sauce. Mix carefully and fill each barquette about ¾ full.

Start heating broiler as manufacturer directs.

Fold whipped cream into Hollandaise sauce. Add pinch of cayenne pepper. Spread over lobster mixture; dust with grated cheese. Place under broiler until sauce is bubbly and slightly browned —makes 24, a wonderful appetizer.

Richard Milhous Nixon

Patricia Ryan Nixon

# Richard M. NIXON

PATRICIA RYAN NIXON entered the White House with an intimate knowledge of it acquired as wife of the Vice President during the Eisenhower administration.

Mrs. Nixon was born Patricia Ryan, on March 16, 1912, in the mining town of Ely, Nevada, the daughter of Mr. and Mrs. William Ryan. After her father was injured in a mine accident, the family moved to a farm near Artesia, California. Pat's mother died when she was twelve years old, and for the next five years Pat kept house for her father and brothers and helped to harvest the crops in the field. She was just seventeen when her father died.

After Pat graduated from high school, she worked as a bank teller in California to earn the money to continue her education. In 1930 she left the bank to drive some elderly family friends East. She stayed on to work as an X-ray assistant in a hospital in the New York City area until she had enough money to permit her to enter the University of Southern California. She then continued to work her way through college as a switchboard

operator, as a movie extra and as a sales clerk in a department store. Patricia Ryan graduated with a degree in merchandising in 1937 and took a position to teach commercial subjects in the high school in Whittier, California, not too far from her old home in Artesia.

For the next four years Pat taught typing, stenography, bookkeeping, and business law to high school students; she was also faculty adviser for the "Pep Committee," coaching cheer leaders; and she directed school plays. She was soon involved in community activities as well, and her favorite relaxation was a little theater group, which was active in town. When she was given the lead in the play *The Dark Tower* in 1938, the leading man was Richard Milhous Nixon, who had just returned to his home town to practice law.

Two years later, on June 21, 1940, Dick Nixon and Patricia Ryan were married at Mission Inn in Riverside, California. As with many other young couples just starting married life, money was scarce. Their first home was an apartment over a garage in Whittier. Pat continued to teach school until the Nixons moved to Washington, D.C., in January, 1942. Her husband had accepted a position as an attorney in the Office of Economic Management. For the years of World War II, which followed immediately, Pat Nixon was a service wife and followed her husband as he served on active duty in the Navy. When the war was over, Mr. Nixon entered political life as the Republican candidate for California's 12th Congressional District in 1946. This was the beginning of his political career, which has spanned 29 years, and Mrs. Nixon worked at his side on every campaign since that first one. They had two daughters, Patricia, called Tricia, born in 1946 and Julie, born in 1948. Those early years saw Mr. Nixon elected to the House of Representatives, then to the United States Senate and finally to the position of Vice President of the United States.

As wife of the Vice President, Mrs. Nixon shared in his official duties. The Nixons traveled together over much of the world as President Eisenhower's goodwill ambassadors and they enter-tained many official guests in their unpretentious home in Northwest Washington.

The years after the Vice Presidency brought many changes and financial success to the Nixons. Mr. Nixon left California following defeat in a bid for State Governor and he and his family moved to New York City where he practiced law and the family lived in an apartment on Fifth Avenue. Here the girls made their debut and graduated from college.

In November of 1968, Mr. Nixon was elected President of the United States. Before he took office, Julie was married to Dwight David Eisenhower, grandson of President Eisenhower, at Marble Collegiate Church in New York City.

As First Lady, Mrs. Nixon was hostess to the nation. During the first year of the administration, over 50,000 invited guests were entertained at the White House. In addition to presiding at the White House, she traveled to West Africa as the President's official representative and accompanied him to China in 1972 and Russia in 1973.

**Cheese straws**        **Smoked salmon with capers on buttered pumpernickel bread**        **Brie cheese**

The social highlight of the first administration was the June wedding of Tricia, in the Rose Garden of the White House, to Edward Finch Cox of New York. The menu on that occasion was a lavish buffet including smoked salmon, roast beef, shrimps in coconut and the wedding cake was a seven-tier, 350-pound confection about five feet wide at the bottom decorated with love-birds and the initials of the bride and groom.

The autographed copy of the recipe for Beef Wellington, which Mrs. Nixon graciously sent to The First Ladies Cook Book, reflects the Nixons' personal taste for substantial food served in a traditional manner.

President Nixon was returned to the White House with an overwhelming victory in 1972. His second administration soon became so involved with controversy over the Watergate scandal that he resigned the Presidency on August 9, 1974.

*Fillet de Boeuf Wellington*

*Heat oven to 450°. Trim fat from large fillet. Brush well with butter and sprinkle with salt and pepper. Roast about 25 minutes in flat pan with some celery, onion, parsley and one bay leaf. Remove from pan. When fillet is cold spread it with paté de foie gras and wrap it in a pie pastry rolled ⅛ inch thick. Bring pastry over fillet, moisten edges, and press firmly to seal.*

*Beat 2 egg yolks and 4 TBS water — brush over pastry. Put on baking sheet in 450° oven for about 15 minutes or until golden brown.*

*Happy memories!*

*Patricia Nixon*

**Stuffed tomatoes**  **Beef Wellington**  **Hearts of palm and watercress salad**

## *Favorite Recipes*

### *Stuffed Tomatoes*

| | |
|---|---|
| 8 large tomatoes | 2 tablespoons |
| 1½ cups chopped | chopped parsley |
| onions | ¾ cup olive oil |
| ½ pound mushrooms, | 2 eggs, beaten |
| chopped | packaged dry |
| 6 ounces Canadian | bread crumbs |
| bacon | salt |
| 2 tablespoons | pepper |
| chopped chives | |

Wash tomatoes. Remove about ¾ of the centers, being careful not to break the walls. For the stuffing mix together the onions, mushrooms, bacon, chives, and parsley. Start heating oven to 400°F.

Heat ½ cup of the oil in large skillet and sauté mixture for 10 minutes. Remove pan from heat and stir in the beaten eggs, salt and pepper. Fill the tomatoes with the stuffing and place in greased baking dish. Sprinkle with bread crumbs and remaining oil. Bake in a hot oven (400°F.) about 20 to 40 minutes depending on how well-done you like your tomatoes.

### *Walnut Clusters*

| | |
|---|---|
| ½ cup sifted all- | 1 egg |
| purpose flour | 1½ teaspoon vanilla |
| ¼ teaspoon baking | 1½ squares semi-sweet |
| powder | chocolate |
| ¼ teaspoon salt | 2 cups coarsely |
| ¼ cup soft butter | chopped nut |
| ½ cup sugar | meats |

Start heating oven to 350°F. Sift flour, baking powder and salt together, and reserve. Mix butter and sugar together until creamy. Add egg and vanilla; mix well. Melt chocolate in top of double boiler; stir into mixture. Add flour mixture. Fold in nuts.

On greased cookie sheets, drop by teaspoonfuls 1 inch apart. Bake in a 350°F. oven 10 minutes. Cool. If desired, a bit of melted chocolate may be spread on top of each.

### *Vanilla Soufflé*

| | |
|---|---|
| 4 tablespoons butter | ¼ cup (yes, ¼ cup) |
| 2 tablespoons flour | vanilla |
| 1 cup light cream, | ½ teaspoon salt |
| scalded | 6 egg whites, stiffly |
| 5 egg yolks | beaten |
| ¼ cup sugar | |

Start heating oven to 450°F. Butter and sugar a 1½ quart soufflé dish or casserole.

In medium-sized saucepan melt butter; stir in flour and cook until mixture starts to brown. Gradually stir in scalded cream; cook over medium heat stirring constantly for about 5 minutes. Beat egg yolks and sugar together in a large bowl; stir in cream mixture. Add vanilla and salt. Fold in egg whites.

Pour mixture into sugared soufflé dish and bake at 450°F. 10 to 12 minutes. Then lower heat to 350°F. and bake 20 minutes longer. Serve immediately with Vanilla Sauce below. Makes 6 servings.

### *Vanilla Sauce*

| | |
|---|---|
| ¾ cup sugar | 6 egg yolks |
| 1½ to 2 teaspoons | 1 cup milk |
| vanilla | pinch of salt |

Beat sugar, yolks, vanilla and salt together in top of double boiler. Stir in milk. Cook over boiling water, stirring constantly until mixture coats a spoon. Chill.

*Gerald Rudolph Ford*

*Elizabeth Bloomer Ford*

# Gerald R. FORD

**W**HEN BETTY FORD moved into the White House in August 1974, she told reporters that she had never really expected to find herself in residence there. Her role for many years was that of wife of the Minority Leader of the House of Representatives, Congressman from the 5th District of Michigan, and she had looked forward to the day when he would retire to a law practice so they could have more time together.

Instead, in 1973, Gerald Ford had been selected by President Richard Nixon to be the Vice President of the United States when Spiro T. Agnew resigned from the office.

As a congressional wife Betty Ford was well liked by both the people back home in Michigan and by her associates on the Washington political scene. However, her busy life as homemaker and mother had allowed her only limited public exposure before she became second lady of the land. She accepted the new responsibility with dignity and took great pleasure in the obligations which went with the position. Her natural friendliness and poise were assets in meeting the large number

and great variety of people with whom she now came in contact. She was just beginning to supervise the renovation of the official residence for the Vice President and to become accustomed to being wife of the Vice President when the Watergate scandal precipitated the resignation of President Nixon. Gerald Ford took the oath of Office in the East Room of the White House at noon on August 10, and Betty Ford found herself suddenly cast in the role of First Lady.

She was born Elizabeth Anne Bloomer in Chicago, Illinois, and moved with her family to Grand Rapids, Michigan, when she was only three years old. Her father's business provided the family with a comfortable home even during the depression years. Mrs. Ford remembers that discipline in her family was strict but she always had pretty clothes and lots of friends. She was also given dancing lessons which she enjoyed so much that she chose to continue to study for a career in dancing after her graduation from public high school in 1936. Betty attended the Bennington School of Dance in Vermont, where she studied modern dance for two years under some of the best professional dancers of that time. She then went on to more intensive training with the Martha Graham Concert Group in New York and appeared with them on the professional stage. While in New York she also became a John Robert Powers fashion model, working as a professional model when her dance commitments permitted. It was an exciting life and a demanding one. It was also far from her family and friends in Michigan. Her ties with home eventually brought her back to Grand Rapids where she continued to work as a model and became fashion coordinator for a department store in that city. The job gave her the responsibility for organizing fashion shows, planning window displays and even buying in New York for the store. Betty's first marriage when she was 24, to William Warren ended in a divorce five years later on the grounds of incompatibility. Betty resumed her maiden name and turned again to her career. She organized her own dance group in Grand Rapids, as well as volunteering time and her talent to teach creative dance to crippled, handicapped and underprivileged children.

A year later Betty Bloomer began to date the attractive bachelor lawyer, Gerald R. Ford, who had been the star center on the University of Michigan football team. He was running for the office of Representative from the Fifth District of Michigan. The wedding took place on October 15, 1948, and a few weeks later Mr. Ford was elected.

It was the beginning of a career for them both in politics which has been uninterrupted since that date. Betty Ford came to Washington to be close to her husband, and Alexandria, Virginia where they lived became as much home to them as their own state of Michigan. With four children born in the next decade, Betty found herself assuming most of the responsibility for taking care of the family and managing the home because political activities absorbed so much of her husband's time. He was sometimes away from home as many as 200 nights a year campaigning to help keep himself and fellow Republicans in Congress. It was Betty who had to cope with the family activities and the family emergencies. Eventually the tremendous strain began to affect her physically so Mrs. Ford sought the help of both a physician and a psychiatrist in an effort to relieve the pain of a pinched nerve in her neck. The psychiatrist helped her to realize that she should not live just for her family but needed interests of her own, too.

UNITED PRESS INTERNATIONAL

**Queen Elizabeth II of Great Britain with Prince Philip visited the United States in July of the American Bicentennial year. In their honor, President and Mrs. Ford gave a state dinner in the Rose Garden of the White House.**

The ease with which Mrs. Ford stepped in to the role of First Lady and her obvious enjoyment of the challenge of the job demonstrate the soundness of this advice. Her keen mind and self-confidence allowed her to be herself in an honest and forthright fashion speaking out on such controversial issues as the Equal Rights Amendment and abortion, both to the press and to audiences.

Within months of becoming First Lady, Betty Ford underwent major surgery for breast cancer. Her decision to allow the public to know the details of her illness did much to make breast cancer less frightening, and publicity about its detection and treatment probably saved hundreds of lives, including that of Mrs. Nelson D. Rockefeller, wife of the nation's newly confirmed Vice President, who underwent similar surgery two weeks later.

The Fords have a family of four, three boys and a girl. Mike, the oldest boy, was married just before his father became President. Jack and Steve did not change their lifestyle because of the family's move to the White House. Both young men are interested in careers relating to their love of the outdoors. Daughter Susan remained a relaxed and poised young woman. She is continuing her education and is gaining experience as a professional news photographer. The children have campaigned actively and effectively for the election of President Ford. Mrs. Ford has said that she hopes the White House of the Ford administration will be remembered for the family feeling of "unity, harmony and warmth" which the Fords were willing to share with the country.

President and Mrs. Ford have brought to the

**Mrs. Ford likes to feature American arts as cen- ▶ terpieces. This one displays American Indian handicraft.**

White House their own style of gracious hospitality. Their personal attention to their guests and concern for their enjoyment has influenced even the most formal affairs. Mrs. Ford's interest in the performing arts was demonstrated in the entertainment provided for their guests and to support American handicrafts Mrs. Ford used unique items from antique weathervanes to dolls as centerpieces at state dinners and for Christmas decorations. She was made a fellow for life by the National Academy of Design in New York which celebrated its 150th anniversary by honoring Mrs. Ford for her interest in the arts.

The celebration of the Bicentennial in 1976 brought to Washington a continuing parade of world leaders offering their congratulations on the 200th birthday of the nation. Each visiting head of state was entertained with style at the White House. Probably the most elegant state dinner was the one given for Queen Elizabeth of Great Britain and Prince Philip in July. The dinner was served in the Rose Garden where a mammoth tent had been designed to fit over the trees and shrubbery. The menu planned by the First Lady featured the finest of American food chosen especially to emphasize the building of our country and was prepared in the cosmopolitan style which is customary for state dinners by Henry Haller who had been the White House chef to Presidents Johnson and Nixon. The first course was New England lobster served with a remoulade sauce. The main course was roast saddle of Veal with rice croquettes and broccoli Mornay, garden salad was served with

Trappist cheese. Dessert was peach ice-cream bombe with fresh raspberries and petits fours. Wine accompanied each course and dinner was followed by demitasse.

Thrust into the role of President by chance, during their two years in the White House, the Ford's created the warmth and charm of a family home combined with the dignity and elegance expected of the Executive Mansion.

---

**Mrs. Ford took an active interest in planning menus, working closely with White House Chef Henry Haller, who also presided over the kitchen of the Johnson and Nixon administrations (see pg. 214). Here is an especially popular recipe that has been prepared and served under Mr. Haller's direction.**

### Ruby-Red Grapefruit Chicken

| | |
|---|---|
| 2 ruby-red grapefruit | ¼ teaspoon salt |
| ½ cup whole cranberry sauce | 1 fryer, disjointed |
| 1 tablespoon honey | 3 tablespoons butter or |
| ¼ teaspoon cloves | margarine |

Peel and section grapefruit, squeezing all juice from membranes into saucepan. Add cranberry sauce, honey, cloves and salt, mixing well, then bring to a boil. Stir in grapefruit sections. Brown chicken in butter in frypan, then place in shallow baking dish. Baste with grapefruit sauce. Bake in 350-degree oven for about 45 minutes, basting frequently. Serve chicken with remaining grapefruit sauce. Serves 4.

# *Favorite Recipes*

### *Strawberry Mousse*

| | |
|---|---|
| 1½ pints fresh strawberries | 1 tablespoon lemon juice |
| ½ cup sugar | ¾ cup water |
| 1 tablespoon kirschwasser | 2 envelopes unflavored gelatin |
| | 2½ cups whipping cream |

Place 1 pint strawberries, sugar, kirschwasser, lemon juice, and ¼ cup water in an electric-blender container; cover. Blend until smooth.

Sprinkle gelatin over remaining ½ cup water; heat until dissolved; stir into strawberry puree. Chill until mixture begins to thicken.

Whip 1½ cups cream until stiff; fold into thickened strawberry puree. Spoon into a 1½-quart mold. Chill several hours or overnight until firm.

Unmold onto a serving plate. Decorate with remaining 1 cup cream, whipped, and remaining whole strawberries. Makes 10 servings.

### *Chilled Cucumber Soup*

| | |
|---|---|
| 2½ cups chopped pared seeded cucumbers | 4 drops red-pepper seasoning |
| 1 cup chicken broth | 1 tablespoon lemon juice |
| 1 teaspoon salt | 1 cup sour cream |
| Dash of white pepper | ½ cup finely diced cucumber |

Combine chopped cucumbers, chicken broth, salt, pepper, red-pepper seasoning, and lemon juice in an electric-blender container; cover. Blend until smooth.

Add sour cream to mixture; blend well. Chill several hours.

Garnish each serving with finely diced cucumber. Makes 8 servings.

Supreme of seafood neptune

### *Supreme of Seafood Neptune*

| | |
|---|---|
| 1½ cups mayonnaise | 2 cups cooked crabmeat diced |
| ¾ cup chili sauce | 2 cups cooked tiny shrimp |
| 1 tablespoon chopped shallots | 1 cup cooked scallops, diced |
| 2 tablespoons white horseradish, drained | Hearts of palm |
| 1½ teaspoons Worcestershire sauce | Finely minced green pepper |
| 3 drops red-pepper seasoning | Whole shrimp |
| 1 teaspoon salt | Sliced hard-cooked egg |
| Dash of white pepper | Red caviar |
| 1 teaspoon unflavored gelatin | Cherry tomatoes |
| 1 tablespoon boiling water | Parsley |
| | 2 tablespoons oil-and-vinegar dressing |

Combine mayonnaise, chili sauce, shallots, horseradish, Worcestershire sauce, red-pepper seasoning, salt, and pepper; mix until smooth.

Dissolve gelatin in boiling water; stir into sauce mixture; fold in crab meat, shrimp, and scallops. Spoon into a 1¾-quart ring mold. Chill several hours or overnight until firm.

Unmold ring onto a platter. Decorate center with hearts of palm and green pepper. Trim mold with whole shrimps, egg slices topped with caviar, tomatoes, and parsley. Spoon oil-and-vinegar dressing over hearts of palm. Makes 10 first-course servings.

◄**The Lyndon B. Johnson state china with selections from the vermeil flatware collection, gift of several administrations, used in a place setting for President Ford.**

Jimmy (James E.) Carter

Rosalynn Carter

# Jimmy (James E.) Carter

JIMMY (JAMES EARL) CARTER, JR.'s uphill battle for the office of President of the United States found his wife Rosalynn working beside him every step of the way. She has been described by her husband as being "his best friend and chief advisor." During the Democratic primaries Rosalynn Carter campaigned alone in his behalf in 34 different states and before his election in November, 1976, she had visited many more. By campaigning separately the Carters were able to meet twice as many people and discuss issues and problems with twice as many groups, visiting at least 100 cities a week in those last weeks before November 2.

The crowds obviously liked the pretty, young, brown-haired woman who spoke with such confidence of her husband's ability to provide the nation with new dynamic leadership and she never lost faith in his final victory.

The working partnership and mutual devotion of the new President and his wife Rosalynn had its beginning in the small town of Plains, Georgia (pop. 683). Rosalynn Smith was born there on August 18, 1927, the daughter of Mr. and Mrs.

Edgar Smith. Mr. Smith was a mechanic and he drove a school bus. When Rosalynn was only 13 years old her father died, leaving his wife, Allie Murray Smith, with the family of four children to support. Mrs. Smith became a dressmaker and Rosalynn who was the oldest of the children helped with the sewing. Later Mrs. Smith secured a job in the Post Office where she worked until her retirement in 1976.

All during Rosalynn's attendance at Plains High School and later at Georgia Southwestern College (a two year college) she continued to work at part-time jobs to support herself and to help her family. Besides sewing, she worked in a beauty shop and took other part-time jobs. "I have always worked", she said in her campaign biography, "I understand people who work for a living."

One of Rosalynn's best friends in the years in which she was growing up was the sister of James Earl Carter. In a small town like Plains, everyone knew everyone else but Jimmy was a few years older than Rosalynn and she was busy with school and friends her own age. It was not until she was 17 and a freshman in college that Jimmy, home from the U.S. Naval Academy, asked her for a date. The following summer they were married in the little Methodist Church in Plains where Rosalynn worshipped with her family. She was 18 and just graduated from Southwestern College and Jimmy had graduated from the Academy.

The next seven years the Carters traveled in the Navy from Portsmouth, Virginia to Hawaii and to the submarine base in New London, Connecticut. It was during this period that their three sons were born; Jack in 1947, Chip in Hawaii in 1950 and Jeff in Connecticut in 1952. The Carters decided to return to Plains, after Jimmy's father died in 1953. Jimmy became a farmer and started a small business selling fertilizer and seed to other farmers. Rosalynn was soon working full time as the business expanded. Their work made them, in Mrs. Carter's words, "good friends and partners and developed the respect we have for each other."

Their daughter, Amy was born to them in Georgia, in 1967.

Soon after the Carters returned to Georgia, Jimmy Carter became involved in the affairs of his community. He became deacon and Sunday school teacher in the Baptist Church in Plains and Chairman of the County School Board. In 1962 he was

elected State Senator. Rosalynn has been an important member of his political team ever since that first race. It was during the gubernatorial race in 1970 that the Carters decided that they could meet more people if they campaigned separately. He won after an uphill campaign.

The years as First Lady of Georgia were full ones. Rosalynn served on the Governor's Commission to Improve Service for the Mentally and Emotionally Handicapped among others.

When Mrs. Carter was Georgia's First Lady she decided to serve regional foods to official visitors to the Governor's Mansion. She said she learned that people coming to Georgia looked forward to eating a typical southern meal. One dinner at which the German Ambassador was the honored guest illustrates this decision. The first course was minted fruit cup, the second course was quail, broiled peaches, and tomatoes stuffed with chopped collared greens and bacon. (Mrs. Carter said the Ambassador loved the collard greens), and peanut butter chiffon pie for dessert. Mrs. Carter remembers with pleasure having dinner twice in the White House when her husband was governor of Georgia and she has said that she hopes to be able to add some southern food to White House menus.

The Carters' own personal tastes are for basic

**Chicken Supreme**                                    **Eggplant casserole**

foods, combining meat, vegetables, fruit and cereals for a good diet. They like home grown vegetables, casserole dishes, especially those with chicken. They also like fish, "any kind you can broil", and prefer fruit for dessert. Mrs. Carter likes to cook. When she was First Lady of Georgia she enrolled in a cooking class because she missed cooking so much. In addition to regional recipes, her personal collection includes a cosmopolitan variety acquired during her years as a Navy wife as well as those from the cooking class. She grew up in a home where no alcoholic beverages were served but Mrs. Carter uses spirits in many of her recipes.

The whole, close-knit Carter family worked hard to put Jimmy in the White House, even 9-year old Amy Carter contributed her share to the campaign. The oldest son, Jack, is a law graduate, married, and has a small son; the Carters' only grandchild. Chip, the second son, in the family business, and the youngest, Jeff, a student, are also married. All of them were fortunate to be able to devote full time to campaigning for their father. The President's mother, Lillian, was one of the most popular campaigners of the team. Her salty comments and down-to-earth approach to the crowds won many votes for her son.

All of the family share the pleasure of victory.

Rosalynn Carter has already shown interest in mental health and in helping the elderly as the Governor's wife. She says she wants to be on the President's Commission on Mental Health so that she can work to formulate a program for improving services for the mentally deficient. She also wants to survey the resources for the elderly.

She sees the role of First Lady as an active one. "I think the wives of Presidents need to be informed and to speak out on matters important to them. I intend to do that." The equality she achieved and the respect she commanded in campaign strategy meetings promises well for the causes she chooses to sponsor as First Lady.

Mrs. Carter says that, like her husband, religion is the most important thing in her life. Since her marriage she has been a member of the Baptist Church in Plains and she carries her deep conviction into every phase of her life, turning many times each day to prayer for support and inspiration.

Rosalynn Carter loves the small town of Plains and at the conclusion of her husband's administration, settled back into the close community life she has been accustomed to and has kept in touch with throughout her husband's career. Her time is devoted to family activities and to projects, including the writing of a book about her days in the White House.

## *Favorite Recipes*

### *Chicken Supreme*

| | |
|---|---|
| 4 large whole chicken breasts, boned | ¼ teaspoon pepper |
| 1 egg | 6 tablespoons butter |
| ¼ cup milk | 3 tablespoons all-purpose flour |
| ¾ cup dry bread crumbs | 1½ cups chicken broth |
| ½ teaspoon ground cardamon | ½ cup red burgundy wine |
| ½ teaspoon dried chervil | ¼ cup brandy |
| 1 teaspoon salt | |

Cut each chicken breast in half.

Beat egg with milk in a pie plate. Mix bread crumbs and seasonings in another dish.

Dip chicken into egg mixture, then into crumb mixture to coat generously. Brown slowly, part at a time, in butter in a large skillet. Place pieces in a shallow baking dish.

Stir flour into drippings in pan, then stir in chicken broth; cook, stirring constantly, until mixture thickens and boils 1 minute; stir in wine and brandy. Pour over chicken in dish.

Bake at 350° for 45 minutes, or until chicken is tender. Makes 8 servings.

### *Eggplant Casserole*

| | |
|---|---|
| 1 cup chopped onion | ¼ teaspoon dried thyme, crushed |
| 2 cloves garlic, minced | ¼ cup soft bread crumbs |
| 3 tablespoons salad oil | ¼ cup chopped parsley |
| 3 tablespoons butter | 1 large eggplant |
| 2 cups chopped peeled tomatoes | ½ cup shredded mozzarella cheese |
| Salt and pepper | |

Saute onion and garlic in salad oil and butter; stir in tomatoes, 1 teaspoon salt, ⅛ teaspoon pepper, and thyme. Heat to boiling; simmer 15 minutes until thick. Stir in bread crumbs and parsley.

Pare eggplant; cut into 8 even thick slices; dice any trimmings and stir into sauce.

Place eggplant slices in a layer in an oiled shallow broilerproof dish; salt and pepper lightly. Broil 5 minutes, or until lightly browned; remove from broiler; lower oven temperature to 350°.

Turn eggplant; top with tomato sauce and cheese.

Bake at 350° for 30 minutes, or until eggplant is tender. Makes 4 to 6 servings.

## Japanese Fruit Cake

| | |
|---|---|
| 3 cups all-purpose flour | 1 cup milk |
| 1 tablespoon baking powder | 1 teaspoon ground nutmeg |
| ¼ teaspoon salt | 1 teaspoon ground cinnamon |
| 4 eggs, separated | ½ teaspoon ground cloves |
| 1 cup butter | ¾ cup light or dark raisins |
| 2 cups sugar | |
| 1 teaspoon vanilla | |

Grease two 9-inch round layer-cake pans; line with waxed paper; grease paper.

Sift flour, baking powder, and salt into a bowl.

Beat egg whites until stiff in a medium bowl.

Cream butter with sugar until fluffy; beat in egg yolks and vanilla. Stir in flour mixture, alternately with milk, until blended; fold in beaten egg whites. Spoon about ⅔ of the batter into one cake pan.

Stir nutmeg, cinnamon, cloves, and raisins into remaining batter; spoon into second cake pan.

Bake at 375° for 35 minutes, or until a wooden pick inserted into center comes out clean. Cool layers in pans on wire racks 10 minutes; loosen around edges with a knife; turn out onto racks; peel off waxed paper. Cool layers completely.

Make Fruit Filling.

Split each cake layer evenly. Place one raisin layer, cut side up, on a serving plate; top with about 1 cup of the filling. Cover with a plain layer; top with another cup filling. Repeat with remaining layers, using 1 cup filling between and the rest on top of cake. Makes 1 nine-inch four-layer cake.

## Fruit Filling

| | |
|---|---|
| 1 can (20 ozs.) crushed pineapple packed in juice | 1 teaspoon grated lemon rind |
| Water | 2 tablespoons lemon juice |
| 4 tablespoons cornstarch | 2 cups grated unsweetened coconut |
| 2 cups sugar | |

Drain juice from pineapple into a 2-cup measure. (There should be about 1⅓ cups.) Add water to make 2 cups.

Mix cornstarch and sugar in a medium saucepan; stir in the 2 cups pineapple liquid and pineapple. Cook slowly, stirring constantly, until mixture thickens and boils 1 minute; remove from heat. Stir in lemon rind and juice and coconut. Chill thoroughly. Makes 4 cups.

**Japanese fruit cake**

## Peanut Soup

| | |
|---|---|
| ¼ cup finely chopped onion | 1 can (10¾ ozs.) condensed cream of chicken soup |
| 1 tablespoon butter | ¼ cup chopped salted peanuts |
| ½ cup creamy peanut butter | |
| 2¼ cups milk | |

Saute onion in butter until soft but not brown in a large saucepan. Stir in peanut butter and cook slowly, stirring several times, 1 to 2 minutes.

Stir in milk and soup. Heat slowly just until hot. (Do not boil.) Stir in peanuts.

Ladle into a tureen or soup cups. Garnish with peanuts, parsley, and paprika. Makes 8 servings.

## "Plains Special" Cheese Ring

| | |
|---|---|
| 1 pound grated sharp Cheddar cheese | 1 cup mayonnaise |
| 1 cup finely chopped nuts | 1 small onion, grated |
| | Dash of cayenne |
| | Black pepper |

Mix cheese, nuts, mayonnaise, and onion until well blended in a bowl; stir in cayenne and black pepper to taste. Pack into a 5-cup ring mold or any fancy 4-cup mold. Chill overnight until firm.

Unmold onto a serving plate. If using a ring mold, fill center with strawberry preserves. Or serve plain with crackers. Makes 4 cups.

*Ronald Wilson Reagan*

*Nancy Davis Reagan*

# Ronald W. REAGAN

RONALD WILSON REAGAN took the oath of Office of President of the United States on January 20, 1981 with his wife holding the Reagan Bible. Dressed in an eye-catching bright red coat, Nancy Davis Reagan looked petite and fragile standing next to her husband. The admiring gaze and rapt attention with which she listened to the Inaugural Address were already familiar to the American people who had seen her during the campaign on television or in person following every word her husband said with the same devoted concentration. Nancy Reagan leaves no doubt of her sincerity when she says that her life really began with Ronald Reagan. They were both successful Hollywood motion picture stars when they met in 1951, but Nancy had no desire to continue as an actress once she became a wife. As First Lady she sees her main responsibility as providing him with love, comfort and support, and an attractive, liveable home into which he can retreat and relax at the end of his work day.

The day after the inauguration she and her California decorator Ted Graber, a long-time family friend, toured the second and third floors of the White House, checking and listing the furniture and accessories in each room. She then explored the warehouse in which White House furnishings, not in current use, are kept. With pieces selected from storage, and rearrangement of those already in the house, she already had more than a good start on her wish to make the White House a home of which the nation would be proud. It is traditionally the prerogative of the First Lady to redecorate the house to her own taste, and for this purpose each incoming administration from the time of George Washington is given a furnishing allowance by the government. Mrs. Reagan decided to return that fund to the taxpayers and use instead private donations from individuals who wished to share in the project. The response was overwhelming. Donations came from all over the country ranging from substantial amounts to those of $1, $5, and $10. Contributors included school children as well as millionaires. The result of her work has been to provide the family with rooms on the second and third floors which are attractive, elegant, and charming

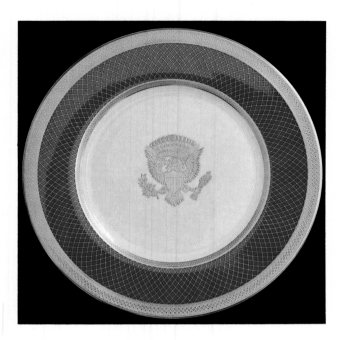

**Reagan's state china**

**Table setting for a state dinner. The numbers are used as an aid to seating guests.**

without sacrificing any of the historical significance of the house. The light colors give a pleasant effect of airiness and comfort which seem to be characteristic of the California style to which the First Family are accustomed. In addition, plumbing and wiring were repaired; floors, and wookwork refinished—all basic necessities for the long-term survival of the Mansion.

Though Mrs. Reagan's first priority is her husband, she came to the White House with several other projects which she has continued to pursue as First Lady. As wife of the Governor of California, she observed, at the Pacific State Hospital for the Mentally Retarded, a project in operation called The Foster Grandparent Program. Some of the elderly who acted as surrogate grandparents were at a stage in their lives when they might have felt lonely or unneeded. The mentally retarded children needed far more love and individual attention than the professional hospital staff was able to give. She was impressed by the improvement shown by the children and the enthusiasm shown by the senior citizens who worked with them. During Governor Reagan's administration, the program became one of those sponsored by ACTION, the volunteer service agency, and it was expanded to include the deaf and juvenile delinquents. This is one of the

**President and Mrs. Reagan dance at their party for the King and Queen of Spain**

projects on which Mrs. Reagan concentrates in the White House. She has met with the heads of ACTION to discuss plans and coordinate nation-wide programs for Foster Grandparents.

Another activity in which she has shown special interest has been developed at Rock Creek Horse Center in the District of Columbia. There, a program to give handicapped children an opportunity to ride horseback has been started. She knows the benefits of riding from personal experience. It is a sport she shares with her husband and her own children. The tremendous pleasure these handicapped children receive when they discover they cannot only stay on the horse but even learn to control one, helps them to face other frightening challenges with a receptive mind.

Mrs. Reagan's emphasis on programs include visits to children's hospitals both in Washington and in other cities across the nation. She thinks it important to get down on her knees to embrace them "so we are all sort of the same size." Despite the press and adult staff who accompany her on such a tour, she concentrates on the children to their obvious delight.

Her most publicized efforts have been aimed at trying to solve the serious problem of the use of drugs and alcohol by the young people in this country. Because she believes that parents and the family are the key to the control of drugs, she has visited some of the parent groups which have sprung up over the country to help their children. Nancy Reagan is an outspoken advocate of parents getting more involved with their children and thinks that providing children with discipline and supervision is the way to show children that they are loved.

This attitude reflects the conventional childhood relationship she had with her parents. Nancy was born in New York, and raised in Chicago, the only daughter of Dr. and Mrs. Loyal Davis. Her mother, Edith Luckett, was a successful and spirited actress who left the stage after her marriage to Dr. Davis, an outstanding neurosurgeon. Nancy's brother, Dr. Richard Davis, is also a neurosurgeon. Nancy grew up in comfortable circumstances, attending excellent schools, going to camp and dancing school. Even at Girl's Latin School she was active in the dramatic club. Soon after she graduated from Smith College, she went to New York to be an actress. After successfully performing in small parts in a number of plays, she had an offer to come to Hollywood for a screen test. There, Nancy performed in eight films in the four years before she married Ronald Reagan. Nancy had no wish to combine career and marriage. She felt marriage and a family were a full-time job. She enjoyed being a wife, homemaker, and mother after the Reagan's two children, Patricia Ann and Ronald Prescott were born. Often President Reagan's two children from his first marriage, Maureen and Michael, were also part of the household. All of the children are now grown and have independent lives of their own, and the Reagans continue to be interested in their childrens' chosen careers.

Nancy Reagan likes to dress elegantly and to entertain elegantly. Shortly before she came to the White House as First Lady, she told a reporter her concept of the role of First Lady. "I want it to be the best of everything." She plans state dinners down to the smallest detail, even having a dress rehearsal to be sure that everything meets her standards. The White House Chef, Henry Haller, made the dessert to be served at the dinner for Prince Charles over five times to be sure the brown sugar feathers on the ice cream looked just like real feathers. Nancy takes a great deal of time with selecting guests, arranging the seating, and choosing the entertainment for state dinners. The result is a well-organized social event at which the guests can relax and enjoy the company, the food, the entertainment, and the surroundings while the staff moves them adroitly through each phase of the evening's festivities. Of necessity, the guest list for a state dinner must in-

clude diplomats and other persons who are connected with the visiting head of state. In addition, Nancy Reagan likes to include personal friends, people from the world of Hollywood, Broadway and sports, members of the Washington establishment, and political supporters. She says, "I like to do a whole mixture of people. That's what makes a party interesting."

One of the most pleasant tasks of Mrs. Reagan's project of redecorating the private quarters of the White House was the selection of a new state dinner service. The new china, which was made by Lenox, is decorated in her favorite color, red. Though the cost of the china ($200,000) was paid by a private donor, Mrs. Reagan was criticized by the press and many people for what seemed to them an unnecessary extravagance in a time of recession and unemployment. The new china was used at the White House for the first time on Feb. 3, 1982 at the official dinner given in honor of the President of the Arab Republic of Egypt and Mrs. Mubarak.

The attempt on President Reagan's life in March, 1981 was a very traumatic experience for Mrs. Reagan. Her husband is the center of her world and his interests are her first priority. She does not apologize for her devotion to her husband in a day when women's liberation is a fashionable theme. In the face of criticism of her life style she said, "All First Ladies are different. You couldn't ask for two more adverse people than Eleanor Roosevelt and Bess Truman. But I am sure Eleanor did what was best for Franklin and Bess did what was best for Harry. Well, I will do what is best for Ronnie and me."

# *Favorite Recipes*

## *Veal Stew with Red Wine*

| | |
|---|---|
| 1½ pounds boneless veal or beef | 12 small onions, peeled |
| 6 slices bacon halved Flour | 1 tablespoon flour |
| | 1½ cups consommé or stock |
| 2 tablespoons bacon fat or shortening | ½ cup dry red wine Salt and pepper |

**Crab-Artichoke Casserole**

**Sweet and Sour Dressing for Fruit Salad**

**Pumpkin Pecan Pie**

Cut veal into 12 chunks. Roll each chunk in bacon. Dredge lightly with flour.

Melt bacon fat in heavy skillet. Add meat and onions. Cook over medium heat, stirring frequently, until meat is browned on all sides. Remove from skillet. Pour off all but 1 tablespoon fat.

Stir in the 1 tablespoon flour. Stir in consommé and wine until smooth. Return veal and onions to skillet. Season to taste with salt and pepper. Cover. Simmer 1½ to 2 hours or until meat is very tender. Makes 4 servings.

## Baja California Chicken

| | |
|---|---|
| 8 boned chicken breasts | ¼ cup tarragon vinegar |
| Seasoned salt | 2 cloves garlic, crushed |
| Pepper | ⅔ cup dry sherry |
| ¼ cup olive oil | |

Sprinkle chicken with seasoned salt and pepper. Heat oil, vinegar, and garlic in large skillet. Sauté chicken, turning frequently, until golden brown. Place chicken in 2-quart baking dish. Pour over sherry.

Bake in 350°F. oven 10 minutes or until chicken is tender. Serve with rice. Makes 8 servings.

## Rancho California Rice

| | |
|---|---|
| 1 cup chopped onion | Salt and pepper |
| ¼ cup butter | 2 cans (8 oz. each) |
| 4 cups cooked rice | whole California |
| 2 cups sour cream | chilis, drained |
| 1 cup cottage cheese | 2 cups grated Cheddar |
| 1 bay leaf, crumbled | cheese |

Sauté onion in butter in large skillet about 5 minutes. Remove from heat. Stir in rice, sour cream, cottage cheese, bay leaf, and salt and pepper to taste. Cut unseeded chilis into strips.

In a greased 2-quart casserole, put a layer of rice mixture, then a layer of chilis, and ⅔ cup cheese. Repeat layering with rice, chilis, ⅔ cup cheese, and remaining rice on top. Bake in a 375°F. oven 25 minutes. Sprinkle with remaining cheese. Bake 10 minutes longer. Makes 8 servings.

## Crab-Artichoke Casserole

| | |
|---|---|
| 3 tablespoons butter | 2 cups canned or |
| 3 tablespoons flour | frozen crabmeat |
| 1½ cups milk | 4 hard-cooked eggs, |
| 1 teaspoon salt | quartered |
| ⅛ teaspoon pepper | 1 can (14 oz.) artichoke |
| ¼ teaspoon | hearts, drained |
| Worcestershire | ⅓ cup grated Parmesan |
| sauce | cheese |

Melt butter in saucepan. Stir in flour until smooth. Gradually add milk and seasonings and cook over low heat, stirring constantly, until mixture is thickened. Remove from heat. Stir in crabmeat. (If using frozen, make certain it is thawed.)

Place eggs and artichoke hearts in bottom of greased 1½-quart casserole. Pour crab-cream sauce over all. Sprinkle with cheese. Bake in a 350°.F oven about 30 minutes. Makes 4-5 servings.

## Sweet and Sour Dressing for Fruit Salad

| | |
|---|---|
| 1 teaspoon celery | ½ teaspoon grated |
| seed | onions |
| 1 tablespoon water | ¾ cup vegetable oil |
| ½ cup sugar | Assorted cut-up |
| 2 tablespoons flour | fruits; melons, |
| 1 teaspoon paprika | orange, bananas, |
| ½ cup cider vinegar | apples, peaches, |
| 1 teaspoon salt | pears, and berries |

Soak celery seed in water in cup. Mix together sugar, flour, and paprika in top of double boiler. Stir in vinegar. Cook over simmering water, stirring frequently, until mixture thickens. Remove from heat. Stir in salt and onion. Cool.

Add oil, a little at a time, beating well with a rotary beater. Drain celery seed through fine strainer. Stir into dressing. Serve with fruit. Yield: 1¼ cups dressing.

## Pumpkin Pecan Pie

| | |
|---|---|
| 1 unbaked 9-inch pie | 1 cup sugar |
| shell | ½ cup dark corn syrup |
| 4 eggs, slightly beaten | 1 teaspoon vanilla |
| 2 cups canned or | ½ teaspoon cinnamon |
| mashed cooked | ¼ teaspoon salt |
| pumpkin | 1 cup chopped pecans |

Flute edge of pie so that it has a high rim to hold filling.

Combine all ingredients except pecans in large bowl. Stir until well blended. Pour into pie shell. Top with pecans. Bake in a 350°F. oven for 45 to 55 minutes or until set. Serve with whipped cream, if desired. Makes 6 to 8 servings.

# General Index